Screening the
Marquis de Sade

Screening the Marquis de Sade

Pleasure, Pain and the Transgressive Body in Film

LINDSAY ANNE HALLAM

McFarland & Company, Inc., Publishers
Jefferson, North Carolina, and London

All photographs are from the Kobal Collection.

LIBRARY OF CONGRESS CATALOGUING-IN-PUBLICATION DATA

Hallam, Lindsay Anne, 1979–
　　Screening the Marquis de Sade : pleasure, pain and the transgressive body in film / Lindsay Anne Hallam.
　　　　p.　　cm.
　　Includes bibliographical references and index.
　　Includes filmography.

　　ISBN 978-0-7864-6296-4
　　softcover : acid free paper ♾

　　　1. Horror films—History and criticism.　2. Thrillers (Motion pictures)—History and criticism.　3. Monsters in motion pictures.　4. Sadism in motion pictures.　5. Suffering in motion pictures.　6. Sade, marquis de, 1740–1814—Influence.　7. Sade, marquis de, 1740–1814—Criticism and interpretation.　I. Title.
PN1995.9.H6H342　2012
791.43'6164—dc23　　　　　　　　　　　　　　2011046296

BRITISH LIBRARY CATALOGUING DATA ARE AVAILABLE

© 2012 Lindsay Anne Hallam. All rights reserved

No part of this book may be reproduced or transmitted in any form or by any means, electronic or mechanical, including photocopying or recording, or by any information storage and retrieval system, without permission in writing from the publisher.

Front cover image © 2012 Shutterstock; front cover design by TG Design

Manufactured in the United States of America

McFarland & Company, Inc., Publishers
　Box 611, Jefferson, North Carolina 28640
　　www.mcfarlandpub.com

Table of Contents

Acknowledgments vii
Preface 1
Introduction: The Philosophy of the Marquis de Sade 5

Part One: The Monster in Horror 17
    1. Vampires 19
    2. Zombies 37
    3. Werewolves 50

Part Two: Monstrous Humans 63
    4. Serial Killers 64
    5. Cannibals 77
    6. The Transhuman 92

Part Three: Victims 111
    7. Women 114
    8. Adolescents 128

Part Four: Sexual Transgressors 147
    9. Sadists 149
    10. Masochists 168

Table of Contents

Conclusion 188
Filmography 191
Chapter Notes 195
Bibliography 205
Index 209

Acknowledgments

I would like to thank Antonio Traverso for his challenging arguments, thoughtful feedback and endless patience.

I am also grateful to Howard Worth and the staff of the Screen Arts Department at Curtin University for providing support, employment and, most importantly, an air-conditioned office that provided much needed relief from a particularly brutal Australian summer.

Thanks to Mikel J. Koven, Xavier Mendik and Rikke Schubart for their help, encouragement and for taking time out to help someone who had no idea what they were doing!

Thank you to the Kobal Collection for allowing me access to their archive and providing permission to reproduce their material.

Special thanks to my family, especially Steve and Anne Hallam, who always supported me, no matter what strange movie I brought into the house. And finally, thanks to Liam Dunn, my partner in film geekdom.

Preface

Cinema's fascination with the depiction of the body, from its agony to its ecstasy, has been relentless since this medium's inception. In fact, the body's experience of pleasure, conflict or trauma has been the basis for the vast majority of film narratives and representations, whether mainstream or alternative. When films take this fascination with the body to explicit extremes through the graphic depiction of sex, violence, or atrocity, as viewers we are both disturbed and confronted with the realization of our own interest in the sight of the body's participation in transgressive acts.

One figure that has been continually marginalized and censored due to the transgression of bodily taboos within his work has been the Marquis de Sade (1740–1814). Sade is a significant figure in this respect, as his works have been at the center of censorship debates ever since they were written. Sade's texts explore, in detail, bodily behavior that is prohibited by law and by social taboo. What is more, Sade celebrates this behavior and accompanies his graphic descriptions with philosophical justification.

During the twentieth century, however, Sade's work began to be studied and examined by other philosophers and thinkers of the time, from psychoanalysts such as Jacques Lacan and Janine Chasseguet-Smirgel to post-structuralists such as Michel Foucault and Gilles Deleuze.[1] It soon became apparent that in Sade's radical thinking were the means to explore the darker aspects of humanity, such as the urge to violate and transgress bodies and taboos. Due to this re-evaluation, Sade has since become a central figure in the critical revision of ideological foundations of the human subject, as he explores precisely the limits of the normative and the transgressive. Whereas before, art works which transgressed bodily norms were rejected and marginalized, scholars found that there was an inherent fascination with pushing these bodily boundaries. Thus, the transgressive body can be defined as a body representation that no longer

Preface

fits into society's normative categories, and instead challenges cultural, biological and sexual norms.

Since Sade proposes a philosophy which also challenges and defies societal norms and laws, representations of the transgressive body are central to his work. That Sade chooses to express this philosophy in the form of stories, novels and plays demonstrates that fiction can be used as a philosophical tool. Thus, it can be argued that other forms of fiction, such as cinema, can also be used in this way — as a tool to challenge and subvert social taboos and bodily norms. Cinema, not unlike literature, is fascinated with depicting the transgressive body in all its states. However, in spite of the correspondence between Sade's body representations and the transgressive bodies depicted in cinema, his philosophy has rarely been systematically applied to film analysis. For just as the bodies and actions described in Sade carry significant meanings, so too does the transgressive body in cinema. Consequently, by applying Sadean philosophy to the analysis of the transgressive body in cinema, this book will examine the boundaries of society's norms regarding sexuality and biology.

The human condition in Sade is essentially a bodily one. Indeed, Sade seems obsessed with breaking conventions and exploring the limits of the body in order to tell us something about the human condition as an embodied condition. By applying Sade's bodily-oriented philosophy to film analysis, this book provides a comprehensive discussion of the cultural significance of the transgressive bodies represented in cinema. By analyzing transgressive representations it becomes apparent that they mean more than themselves. We are, in fact, not so different from these representations: they constitute us both as bodies and as subjects. This book, it is hoped, will contribute to a deeper understanding of the cultural interest in the transgressive representation of the body, which may in turn lead to a better understanding of our nature as human subjects.

Thus, a Sadean reading of the transgressive body onscreen reveals something about the human subject that other frameworks of interpretation of cinema may not — namely, that the symbolic destruction of the social order through bodily transgression is a positive and creative force derived from Sade's concept of nature. According to Sade, the subject is driven primarily by the natural bodily urges that society tries to repress through law and taboo. In Sade's works an alternative hierarchy is created in which those who follow nature's instincts for lust and aggression dominate those still under the sway of society's repression. It is nature, whose instincts and urges are felt and expressed through the body, that is exposed

Preface

as the guiding force of the human subject, a force that works in opposition to external cultural influences. To transgress against these cultural taboos thus strengthens the subject's position within the Sadean natural hierarchy.

While psychoanalysis, feminism, semiotics, and post-structuralism have informed the field of film analysis for many years, using the work of Sade as a way of understanding film is still relatively new within this field. Whereas many analyses use theory to excuse and thus dilute the power of sexual and violent images, the application of Sadean philosophy to film is deliberately transgressive and confrontational, seeking to examine cinematic representations of human relations as unflinchingly as Sade did in his novels.

This book aims to be both academic and also understandable to the more casual reader. I refrain from analyzing adaptations of Sade's work, or films that present Sade's life story (with the exception of Pasolini's *Salò*), and instead use Sade's philosophy to analyze a wider array of films. My purpose in doing so is to develop Sadean philosophy as a form of film theory that can be applied to many films, not just those that deal directly with Sade and his works. Sade is integral to my analysis, as his philosophy provides a method of thinking that uncovers the ways in which cinema challenges bodily norms in order to suggest broader cultural and political transgressions.

Before the film analysis can begin, it is necessary to explain Sade's philosophy in further detail. In the following introductory chapter I will provide a brief explanation of the main Sadean concepts, which will be applied in the film analysis to follow. Investigation into Sade and the transgressive body will then be carried out in four parts. Part One, "The Monster in Horror," will focus on the three main monsters found in the horror genre: vampires, zombies and werewolves. Through the analysis of six horror films, a Sadean reading will uncover that which psychoanalysis, traditionally the main interpretive methodology applied to the analysis of the monster in horror cinema, does not: that the monster's body is a positive representation that demonstrates nature's power. Although Sade's characters are not monstrous in appearance, they have much in common with the monsters found in horror movies in that both the monster and the Sadean libertine are outside of society and therefore represent the "Other." However, a Sadean reading of the monster will show that it is precisely because the monster represents a threat to the established social order that it is a figure of fascination, and that its transgressive power can actually be celebrated rather than marginalized.

Preface

"Monstrous Humans," Part Two, will examine bodies that may look more "normal" than the monster, but who also engage in transgressive behavior: serial killers, cannibals, and the transhuman. These bodies illustrate the repetitive nature of transgression, such that once a limit is transgressed, a cycle of transgression is put into effect. The bodies discussed here transgress to the point that, like the Sadean libertine, they no longer feel that they are a part of humanity. This then allows them to engage in activities that transgress all of the basic taboos of civilized society, leading to increased opportunities for pleasure and dominance.

Yet, despite these opportunities to experience heightened power and pleasure, Part Three, "Victims," examines how the transgressive body can be punished for its transgressions. Here the focus is on the two transgressive bodies that are frequently victimized by society's strict standards: women and adolescents. What becomes apparent through this analysis, however, is that although societal and cultural authorities are capable of the same cruelty and sadism that Sade saw in nature, it is only through further transgression that the victim is able to overcome its subjugation.

Part Four, "Sexual Transgressors," will demonstrate that the transgressive body is a sexual body, as the act of transgression brings with it a highly sexual charge. In the practices of sadism and masochism, seemingly non-sexual acts involving pain and violence are experienced as forms of transgressive pleasure, demonstrating that the sexual and the violent instincts are not separate forces, but are, in fact, connected. This idea is central to Sade's philosophy, as all of his works entail the seeking of sexual satisfaction through the violation of taboos, and the utilization of violence as a vital part of sexuality. Sade is integral to an unflinching examination of all aspects and implications of these sexual transgressions.

Introduction: The Philosophy of the Marquis de Sade

The body is a central notion in Sade's philosophy, as it is the thing through which his ideas are expressed. In fact, in Sade's thought there can be no ideas without the body. Sade's basic principle is that we are all isolated beings, that our bodies are all that we have. Therefore, we need strive only to fulfill our own bodily needs and desires, no matter the cost or imposition on others. Thus, he devotes no thought to the relationship between the body and the society at large; for him, only the selfish pursuit of pleasure is important.

This pursuit of pleasure inevitably involves the sexual function. In Sade, sex is the driving force of all actions. The search for ever greater sexual satisfaction leads to a desire to go beyond the limits imposed on sexual activity, through the transgression of sexual mores in an attempt to push the body to greater heights of ecstasy. By looking beyond normalized heterosexual intercourse, Sade incorporates elements that are usually banished from sexual representation. Some of these elements include: the use of all parts of the body, bisexuality and group sex, blasphemy, images of the abject (namely, death and filth) and other deliberately "scandalous" behaviors. Most controversially, Sade incorporates the infliction of pain and violence on others as a means to obtain sexual gratification.

Such is the power of Sade's representations that his name has come to mean the deliberate hurting of others in order to achieve self-gratification. It must be stressed, however, that the sexual sadism described by Sade is a textual action — that is, only occurring within the realm of fiction. While his own acts of sadism in reality led to his imprisonment, he found that through writing he could continue to explore the darker aspects of sexual desire.[2] It could be argued that writing provided an outlet for him,

Introduction

a cathartic purging of his sexual fantasies, in a way that ensured no harm would come to others; but such an idea is beyond the scope of this book. Sade's writing could also, just as easily, be viewed as a record of sexual dysfunction, proof that his rightful place was inside a jail cell. In fact, Sade's writing did lead to a term of imprisonment.[3] Within the context of this book, however, Sade's work is utilized because it presents a philosophy that explores all aspects of the transgressive body. Its anti-establishment stance, where all societal norms are opposed, conveys a view that, when applied to film theory, uncovers cinema's own capacity to subvert and transgress societal norms and taboos.

Sade's philosophy is developed in his four main novels: *Justine, Juliette, The 120 Days of Sodom* and *Philosophy in the Bedroom*. In his blending of obscene and pornographic images with philosophical discourse, he enables certain themes to emerge which deal with the body and its power to transgress societal taboos. Sade offered an alternative to society's teachings of Virtue and Vice: whereas church and state extolled the rewards of Virtue, Sade explored the freedom that can be found if one follows the path of Vice. In Sade's eyes the role of God and religion has usurped that of nature, as they are tools used to dissuade the people from following nature's urges. What society deems our animal instincts, which must be repressed for the greater good, Sade saw as our true selves; we are defined by our individual urges. This divides people into a strict hierarchy: above are those women and men who live according to their desires, and below are those destined to become mere instruments of the desires of others.

This hierarchy of perpetrator and victim is expressed in his two novels *Justine* and *Juliette*.[4] The two title characters are sisters, Justine being the epitome of virtue while Juliette is the embodiment of vice. Justine is beset by bad luck, with her eternal goodness continuously exploited and her chastity repeatedly violated. Juliette, however, enjoys a charmed life, her sexual promiscuity and criminal nature leading her to wealth and privilege. While Justine denies her carnal desires in order to gain a place in Heaven, Juliette uses her body to attain pleasure and success, and is therefore rewarded. Juliette is the ideal of the Sadean libertine, someone who has situated herself outside of society and acts in opposition to the prevailing morals of the time. The libertine, being bisexual, polymorphously perverse and criminal, consciously decides to embrace all that society represses as a testament to their superiority and power over the masses and the laws that govern them.

Because Sade's libertines feel superior to others, they view themselves

Introduction

as no longer subject to law or standards of behavior. In fact, the libertines instead form their own separate societies. In *Juliette*, for instance, Juliette becomes part of the Sodality of the Friends of Crime, a group who devote themselves to sexual pleasure through crime. Its statute proclaims that the group "considers itself above the law because the law is of mortal and artificial contrivance, whereas the Sodality, natural in its origin and obediences, heeds and respects Nature only."[5] The group does not follow societal law, it instead follows nature. Nature, which destroys as much as it creates, is therefore, according to the laws and rules of civilized society, criminal in that it can kill and destroy without remorse. For example, the devastation caused by an earthquake or a hurricane has the power to decimate a population without reason or guilt, the phenomenon itself remaining completely unaffected. Likewise, if within the course of libertine activity a person comes to harm in some way, neither does the libertine feel anything for having caused it.

The superiority of the libertine over his or her victims is similar to the power that royalty has over its subjects. The libertines are no longer a part of society because they feel that they are, in fact, sovereign over it. Therefore, they are free to use those that they view as beneath them in whatever way they please. Because they are so removed from other people, they have absolutely no compassion, nor any other feelings for them. They are completely apathetic and think only about their own pleasure.

What defines Sade's sexual scenarios is the inequality of the participants. Sex is not an expression of love for another but a source of individual pleasure. The aim is to find what best satisfies one's own desires. This cannot be achieved with an equal, as this would lead to a conflict of interests; the other, too preoccupied with his/her own pleasure, will not be thinking of one's own. Just as a person sacrifices his/her own wants and needs in order to serve his/her god or king, so a person must put his/her own wants, needs and pleasure aside when in service of the Sadean libertine.

The apathy of the libertine means that in order to achieve pleasure she/he must participate in more extreme and excessive activities. Due to their apathy, Sade's libertines feel nothing, and instead experience pleasure through the thought of acts committed. The realization that they have transgressed a taboo and have participated in an act that is thought to be wholly evil and reprehensible — and have done it without the least sense of guilt and remorse — is what gives the libertines pleasure and a sense of achievement. The apathy that Sade describes in his books leads to the ability to gain sexual gratification through crime and violence, which is the

Introduction

most controversial aspect of Sade's philosophy. Sex and violence — two elements for which cinema is renowned — are, in Sade, shown to be connected. These two urges, which in Sade represent the base instincts of the human subject, are trained to be suppressed in order for society to function. In contrast, Sade sought the expression of these instincts. As one of his characters, Madame Delbene (his libertines were not exclusively male), states:

> This capricious portion of our mind is so libertine nothing can restrain it: its greatest triumph, its most eminent delights come of exceeding all limits imposed upon it; of all regularity it is an enemy, it worships disorder, idolizes whatever wears the brand of crime ... what is of the filthiest, the most infamous, the most forbidden, 'tis that which best rouses the intellect ... 'tis that which causes us most deliciously to discharge.[6]

Since the Sadean libertines' only loyalty is to their own pleasure, they feel no kinship with their fellow humans. In fact, they seek only to exploit, abuse and offend others. This selfish tendency allows them to explore the sexual aspects of violence and transgression.

What drives these activities is the thrill that accompanies transgression. As one character claims, "It is not the object of libertine intentions which fires us, but the idea of evil."[7] The object is irrelevant because, for the Sadean libertine, the sexual partner is inherently inferior. Those classified as inferior are labeled so because they follow society's repressive forces instead of embracing nature's instincts. By not giving in to nature, they are destined to become the victims of someone else's base desires.

In Sade's view, society's norms are cultural constructions imposed upon the body and not naturally exhibited by it. In order to stem the natural urges—carnal desires and violent impulses—both church and state have condemned them as evil. Therefore, for Sade, to do evil not only satisfies natural urges, it also delivers the thrill that accompanies acts that are forbidden by or transgressive of civil and moral norms. This is, for example, illustrated in the many acts of blasphemy described in his works. Indeed, Sade's libertines repeatedly insist that there is no God:

> The universe runs itself, and the eternal laws inherent in Nature suffice, without any first cause or prime mover, to produce all that is and all that we know; the perpetual movement of matter explains everything: why need we supply a motor to that which is ever in motion?[8]

By blaspheming, the Sadean libertine publicly pronounces that he/she is no longer subject to God or his laws. The fact that the majority of society

Introduction

does believe in God makes blasphemy an outrageous and transgressive act, and therefore a thrilling one. In breaking this taboo, the libertines gain further pleasure.

These views on religion — namely, that God does not exist and that religious repression should be cast off — positioned Sade outside mainstream society. As indicated above, rather than pursue religion and its restrictions on carnality, Sade followed nature. Sade believed that because we are all created by nature, any urges or desires that we feel are from nature and in consequence must not be ignored or repressed: "Absurd to say the mania offends nature; can it be so, when 'tis she who puts it in our head? Can she dictate what degrades her?"[9]

Contrary to Christian religion, which preaches to love one's neighbor, in nature there is only the survival of the fittest. For Sade, other people are competition: either potential oppressors or victims to be abused. Because he saw no bond between people and no God presiding above, Sade instead looked to nature and the instincts that come from it. He understood our instincts and desires to be like messages from nature, urges that it needs us to express in order to ensure its survival. Yet, these urges are both creative and destructive. Indeed, we experience the desire for both sex and violence, and on occasion these desires are expressed within the same act. While society rules that these desires are base, animalistic and in some cases criminal, the church views them as evil. In general, there is a distinct opposition established in Western culture between nature and religion, which Sade embraces. As church and society viewed the natural as antithetical to the idea of the good and the virtuous, Sade, and his characters, aligned themselves with all that was seen as reprehensible, blasphemous and evil.

However, in contradiction to his view that nature's instincts must be followed, Sade also thought that nature's designs should be thwarted, because as well as being creative, natural forces also lead to destruction and death. Hence, by destroying nature and going against its designs, the Sadean libertine paradoxically perpetuates it. Accordingly, homosexuality and abortion are condoned and celebrated by Sade as strategies that neutralize the chances of conception inherent in sexual intercourse. For example, one of Sade's characters advises that "there are milder means for keeping the population trimmed to neat and sensible dimensions: they would be by encouraging and recompensing *sapphism*, *sodomy* and *infanticide*."[10] These three activities ensure that the only thing to be produced from libertine activity is the libertine's own pleasure.

Introduction

Another way of thwarting nature is to impose rules and methods while exercising nature's urges: "Let us put a little order in these revels; measure is required even in the depths of infamy and delirium."[11] Pleasure is gained not only from performing an act it is gained also by thinking through and analyzing all aspects of the act, in order to ensure that the full potential of each situation is realized and no chance to break any further taboos has been missed. Thus, Juliette is admonished by one of her mentors, Clairwil, for committing crimes only in the heat of passion:

> Whenever Juliette commits a crime, it is enthusiastically. ... One must proceed calmly, deliberately, lucidly. Crime is the torch that should fire the passions, that is a commonplace; but I have the suspicion that with her it is the reverse, passion firing her to crime.[12]

It is crucial to emphasize at this point that although nature has given the Sadean libertine the desire to commit violent, carnal or criminal acts, for Sade it is the *idea* of these actions and the transgressiveness of the activity that create pleasure. These actions should not simply be the result of an immediate impulse; rather, the impulse must be felt, then analyzed and then carried out. For Sade's characters, nature's urges are followed, but only after they are subjected to intellectual reflection. In an expression of their sovereignty, they follow nature yet also conquer it.

Thus, whenever a group of libertines meet for debaucheries, their activities are always meticulously planned and organized. Although the four Masters in *The 120 Days of Sodom* hide themselves in a château away from the outside world, their first address to everyone in their household is a list of rules that must be followed and a routine that is set out for each day. In *Justine*, Justine is taken prisoner by another group of four men: an order of monks who keep their female captives locked within their monastery. Both groups of libertines have rigid systems of conduct set in place, with their victims divided into different classes and subgroups. One of the most important voices in the critical debates concerning Sade's transgressive literature, the American author and scholar Camille Paglia, is correct when she describes the libertines as being similar to "colonies of ants": the libertines follow a natural order in which every person has a certain place and a certain duty to perform.[13] The hierarchy is like a food chain, with those who are stronger presiding over — and feeding off — those who are weaker.

But while following nature, the libertines also subvert it. Rather than succumb completely to the urges that almost overwhelm them,

Introduction

once they are engaged in carnal activities the libertines simultaneously engage in philosophical debate: "There's more to it than just experiencing sensations, they must also be analyzed. Sometimes it is as pleasant to discuss as to undergo them."[14] This intermingling of sex and thought is a trait common to all of Sade's sexual scenes, with descriptions of sexual acts presented alongside lengthy dialogues. For example, *Philosophy in the Bedroom* is made up of nothing but dialogue, being set out more like a play than prose. The activities of the characters are known to the reader only because the characters narrate what they are experiencing.[15] This, again, represents an obedience to nature's laws, followed by their subversion.

Natural processes are also perverted by Sade's libertines through the practice of sodomy. The sexuality depicted in Sade's works is very fixated on the anal, with sodomy as common as vaginal intercourse. This use of sodomy carries a symbolic function, representing the fundamental aspects of Sadean sexuality. While vaginal intercourse has the capacity to create life, with anal intercourse there is no chance of reproduction. The anus is the orifice through which waste is excreted, from which toxins, bacteria and all that the body no longer needs is expelled. Without such expulsion, the body becomes poisoned and begins to die. These connections with waste and filth set anal intercourse in opposition to the regenerative and reproductive aspects of vaginal intercourse. Vaginal intercourse leads to life; therefore, anal intercourse is linked with death.

It should be noted that the idea of anal sex being linked to death is a rather old-fashioned and outdated view, which risks sounding homophobic. Certainly the fact that contraception is now widely available means that all forms of sex can now be non-procreative. Yet, in Sade's time this was one of the only full proof forms of contraception available; therefore, it was valued, as it was conquering nature and its procreative will. The prevalence of anal sexuality also goes against what Leo Bersani describes as the "taboo on 'passive' anal sex," where "[t]o be penetrated is to abdicate power."[16] Throughout his novels all his libertines engage in passive anal sex as a form of pleasure while still maintaining power. Just as one gains power from conquering nature, power also comes from conquering, and then embracing, a social taboo.

Yet, for all their power, there is still a linking between sex and death in Sade's works and philosophy. These forces of sex and death both exert great power over the drives and urges of the body and mind, and certainly there are points where the two become intimately connected. In Sade's

Introduction

native language, French, the orgasm is also referred to as *"la petite mort"* — the "little death." In fact, death is present in all of Sade's sexual scenarios, as he explores a sexuality that is apart from reproduction. All of his libertines spend a good deal of time thinking about and planning their sexual exploits, yet gain very little from the experience because nothing is produced from their efforts. Their excess has only a numbing effect, as if they were playing out their inevitable demise. It is all for nothing because eventually in death they too will be nothing.

Another aspect of anal sexuality in Sade is its effects on gender. While the genitals of male and female are different, men and women are alike in that they both possess an anus: "Male/female differences are annulled in anal equivalence."[17] Therefore, in Sade's works people are no longer divided by gender but by their place in the natural hierarchy of master/mistress and slave. To demonstrate this gender equality, Sade has both women and men take active and passive roles in sodomy. Many of his male characters are effeminate, possessed of soft, rounded bodies, with appetites for passive sodomy and penetration (for example, Durcet in *The 120 Days of Sodom*).

Likewise, many of his female characters have masculine attributes. Even females not in possession of physical anomalies participate in active sodomy through the use of dildos and other implements. Again, this highlights the unnatural aspects of the Sadean libertine's sexuality, as the phallus in these scenarios is artificial. For the libertine, it is not the act that brings the most pleasure, it is the idea. But, of course, there is no idea without the body: the female asserts her dominance over her victim by using their bodies to perform transgressive and unnatural deeds.

From a Freudian perspective, this anal fixation also represents the Sadean libertine as infantile, since playing with the body's filth and waste is a childlike gesture. It is only as the child develops that it is taught that the body's waste is a source of disgust which must be hidden. Although this book does not rely on psychoanalysis, it is interesting to note that Sigmund Freud writes of certain people whose character and eroticism can be said to be "anal" in nature, a condition which he believes stems from childhood experience:

> As infants, they seem to have belonged to the class who refuse to empty their bowels when they are put on the pot because they derive a subsidiary pleasure from defecating; for they tell us that even in somewhat later years they enjoyed holding back their stool, and they remember ... doing all sorts of unseemly things with the feces that had been passed.[18]

Introduction

This behavior is certainly displayed by most of Sade's libertines. Freud states further that many children hold back their stools as an act of defiance. This is in keeping with Sadean sexuality, where playing with the stool is an expression of defiance of societal norms and taboos. There is a celebration of all that is disgusting and shameful. In *The 120 Days of Sodom* several days are devoted to coprophilia and coprophagy: these perversions are discussed, their merits analyzed, and then the activity is publicly performed.[19] This demonstrates that the Sadean libertine has an infantile sexuality, as the emotions of disgust and shame have not yet developed. Feelings of empathy or compassion for others are undeveloped also. Like the infant, the Sadean libertine is selfish and apathetic and thinks only of his/her own pleasure and survival.

Another trait of the libertines' infantile sexuality is its polymorphously perverse nature. In Freudian theory, this means that the sexuality of the child is not yet centered on the genitals, but is, instead, felt throughout the body. It is thus a transgressive sexuality in that it is expressed and felt in areas that do not serve the sexual function. The Sadean libertine's desire is polymorphous, as his/her sexual activities incorporate many different parts of the body (for example, the ingestion through the mouth of the waste product of the anus or being whipped on the back). As well as situating themselves as apart from mainstream society, and casting off the prevailing morals concerning behavior, the bodies of the Sadean libertines also function differently. Their polymorphous perversity is a symbol of their divergence from societal norms. While the Church and the State teach that sexuality is something to be repressed, for the Sadean libertines it envelops their whole being: it is felt throughout the bodies, consumes their thoughts and is expressed through everything they do.

As indicated earlier, sodomy is most notable in that it is a non-reproductive form of intercourse. For men, it is another form of pleasure (one for which Sade obviously has a personal preference); and for women, it ensures that conception will not take place. One character in *Juliette* warns, "Pregnancies are damaging to the health, spoil the figure, wither the charms."[20] Throughout Sade's works the figure of the mother is an object of scorn and revulsion. Sade's own mother was frequently ill, and she later secluded herself in a convent until her death. Consequently, in his childhood he was close to his father, who made no secret of his own libertine activities. Thus, while his father sought pleasure and invited his son to join him in a world of decadence and excess, his mother became a symbol of religious repression. Many biographers have therefore pointed to Sade's relationship with his own mostly absent mother, as well as his ongoing battle of wills with his mother-in-law, who was largely responsible for keeping him incarcerated throughout his lifetime, as reasons why the figure of the mother is repeatedly reviled and violated in his stories.[21] Many of the mothers in Sade's works are hence represented as obstacles to pleasure, voices that preach the virtues of chastity and piety. As his characters choose to live in opposition to these teachings, they must take revenge on the mother, the key person to assert this oppressive power over them.

As well as this violation of the mother, Sade's work also nullifies all other traditional bonds of family. In *The 120 Days of Sodom*, in which four fathers subject their daughters to sexual and physical abuse, and include them in their debaucheries, Sade states:

> It is madness to suppose one owes something to one's mother. And upon what, then, would gratitude be based? Is one to be thankful that she discharged when someone once fucked her? ... As for myself, I see therein naught but grounds for hatred and scorn. Does that mother of ours give us happiness in giving us life? ... Hardly. She casts us into a world beset with dangers, and once in it, 'tis for us to manage as best we can.[22]

Again, there is a conscious rejection of all institutions that are integral to civilized society. The family is completely destroyed in Sade's works; all familial homes are revealed to be the setting for either incest or murder. In order to break the long-held belief in the bond between mother and child, Sade frequently depicts its violation. In *Philosophy in the Bedroom*, Eugénie takes part in the rape of her mother, and then has her mother's vagina sewn up with thread; in *Juliette*, the protagonist actually murders one of her own children.

This emotional detachment on the part of the libertine is reflected by the writing techniques that Sade employs. Renowned for a cold, clinical and descriptive style that focuses chiefly on the physical act, Sade pays no attention to the emotions of his characters. Throughout his novels, long passages are given to philosophical debate, where again the emotions are ignored and only cold intellectual reflection is noted. One gains an insight into Sade's writing process by examining the unfinished *The 120 Days of Sodom*, which, toward the end of the book, degenerates into a list of perversions. This catalogue of the acts that the four Masters will perform on their captives demonstrates that, for Sade, these acts are what is most important in the story—the rest of the narrative being only secondary to the description of sexual exploits. However, it becomes apparent, from

Introduction

the sheer number of actions listed, that no specific act is important; it is the repetition and accumulation of these transgressions that gives the Sadean libertine satisfaction. For the libertine it is quantity, not quality, that counts. This is because it is the idea behind the action that is most important. It is better to have a long list of transgressions than a short list of pleasures.

Once a boundary is transgressed, a new limit is put into place, setting the scene for new possibilities of transgression. This accounts for the somewhat monotonous pace of Sade's novels. While *The 120 Days of Sodom* is unfinished (and one wonders if such a work ever could be brought to a close) and becomes an almost unbearably long list instead of a story, the completed *Juliette* runs to over a thousand pages. The length, as well as the contents of these works, demonstrates the never-ending cycle of transgression. This is because the exploration of base instincts is also an intellectual exercise. It is this aspect of Sade that situates him as an important figure in the intellectual discussion of the body and transgression.

PART ONE

The Monster in Horror

The most extreme example of the transgressive body is the monster. The monsters found in the horror genre are manifestations of all that is thought of as disgusting, frightening and predatory; yet many are also possessed of certain traits that are all too human. Through its unnatural appearance, the horror film monster is constructed as the "Other," representing all that is rejected by society. Yet, simultaneously, the monster retains qualities that mark it either physically or emotionally as still human. As the Other of the Western self, the monster is both outside and within the subject's identity, leading to it being simultaneously rejected and embraced as a source of fascination.

While the characters in Sade's novels commit monstrous acts, they do not physically appear to be monsters (although some are in possession of certain physical anomalies). However, there are striking similarities between what the monsters in the horror film genre and what the Sadean libertine *represent*: a challenge to social and cultural norms, as their transgressions become a source of power. This is because the monster and the libertine choose instead to follow their own instincts and natural urges.

The figure of the monster is constructed as unnatural, as it transgresses natural laws such as death and the human/animal divide. However, these so-called natural laws are actually social constructions, for in Sade's view there are no laws in nature, only transgression. Violations of nature are thus meaningless in the grand scheme of Mother Nature, which Sade sees as being in a state of perpetual motion, forever creating and destroying its creatures without a care for trivial human concerns (such as emotion or consent). As Sade writes, "There is thus, veritably, no crime, no thinkable way or means for outraging a Nature in ceaseless flux and action."[1] The monster is also constantly changing; for example, the vampire is regenerated through its blood-drinking, the zombie is in the process of decomposition, and the werewolf metamorphoses from human to animal and vice versa. It can be stated further that while the vampire represents

Part One: The Monster in Horror

the body's refusal of its own mortality, the zombie represents the body's refusal of the effects of its own mortality, and the werewolf represents the refusal of the limitations of a single body. From a Sadean viewpoint, such transgressions are positive and creative, precisely because they violate and destroy previous cultural constructions of the body.

Both Sade's libertine and the horror movie's monster turn out, despite their common apparent "unnaturalness" and their unlikely pairing, to be founded on similar conceptions of nature. For Sade, nature is already a monster, destructive and cannibalistic, constantly producing in its perpetual metamorphoses what might be perceived as unnatural mutation. The examination of the monstrous body thus ironically reveals that the transgressive body is a challenge — not to norms of nature, but to those of society and culture — and therein lies the power and fascination of the monster's body.

1

Vampires

There are many similarities between vampire films and Sade's novels. For example, both take the link between sex and violence as their key subject. Also, both center on figures who represent all that church and society perceive as indecent, criminal and evil. There is, however, a significant difference that separates them: whereas the Sadean libertine exists in a world where God is dead and the defiance of religious teaching is merely a tool used in the pursuit of pleasure, in the vampire's world God does exist, and the vampire's defiance leads to its damnation and eternal life. Nevertheless, even though the element of the supernatural is absent in Sade's works, both the vampire and the Sadean libertine use their transgressive body to seduce and dominate their victims for pleasure and sustenance. Their play with the boundaries of death is the ultimate expression of their transgressive power.

The two main ingredients of a vampire film are undoubtedly sex and blood, two elements that French theorist Marcel Henaff has pointed out as also being essential to the Sadean novel.[1] For the vampire, the act of blood-drinking takes on connotations of the sexual act (this connection is shown literally in *Female Vampire* [Jess Franco, 1973], in which the vampire fellates her victims to death and feeds on their sexual fluids), thus illuminating the similarities at play within the forces of both sex and death. As Henaff explains, although "from the Bible to classical tragedy, there has never been anything other than sex and blood," these elements are usually "there for some other reason ... as effects or stakes in some cause (honor, justice, love, faith, the state) whose attainment 'elevates' and 'legitimates' them."[2] In other words, in these traditional stories the elements of sex and blood are situated within a larger lesson which teaches that these things, although titillating and entertaining, are bad and wrong. This good versus evil morality can also be seen in the vampire narrative, where the vampire, a creature driven by a thirst for sex and blood, is the villain who must ultimately be destroyed. In contrast, Henaff elaborates,

Part One: The Monster in Horror

Sade's novels are "texts hallucinated by sex and blood, making sex and blood run gratuitously through the narrative, relating sex and blood to nothing outside themselves, and formulating this self-sufficiency as the blunt fact of sexual pleasure."[3]

The two elements of sex and blood are central to Francis Ford Coppola's adaptation of *Dracula* (1992). Not only is it the most sexually explicit of all the film versions, it is also the bloodiest. In fact, the movie is almost saturated in blood. But what marks the film as truly transgressive and Sadean is that the blood is not only spilt in scenes of horror and violence but is the central element that both drives and constitutes the film's notion of sexual subjectivity. Coppola's version departs from earlier ones in that it is a Sadean text in which sex and blood are not indicative of something else, but significant for and by themselves. These natural urges for sex and blood, embodied in the form of the vampire, are set in opposition to societal forces, especially those of the Christian church.

The Vampire Lovers: Bram Stoker's Dracula

Francis Ford Coppola's *Bram Stoker's Dracula* is a modern retelling of the most popular vampire tale. In Coppola's film there is a focus on the sexual aspects of the story, aspects that have been toned down in previous film versions. The sexuality of the vampire directly contrasts with the Victorian society, ruled by the repressive force of the church, in which the story is set. Like the Sadean libertine, the vampire follows its sexual yearnings rather than religious teachings. Sade renounced religion, seeing it as an oppressive tool that was in opposition to nature. While the church preaches chastity, purity and love of one's neighbor, Sade instead follows nature's principles of destruction, fornication, transgression and selfish apathy. The vampire, although characterized as an unnatural aberration that cannot die, also follows these same principles, committing murder without remorse in order to ensure its own survival.

Coppola's film is rife with religious imagery, with Dracula depicted as an anti–Christ figure. This is represented through his ability to transform himself into several incarnations. He is a transgressive body who uses the power of evil to manipulate his body into other forms. Dracula first appears in the guise of an elderly man, deathly pale and clad in long robes, whose shadow moves independently of his body. During the course of the film he is also seen as a dashing young prince, a hairy beast,

1. Vampires

a wolf, a being that seems to be part man and part bat, a pile of rats, and a green mist; at several points in the narrative he is completely invisible.

The vampire Dracula is a supernatural creature, a being that has turned against God and so is able to transgress the laws that govern beings that have been created by Him. He transgresses by incorporating aspects from what Van Helsing calls "the meaner things in life: the bat, the rodent, the wolf. He can appear as mist, as vapor, as fog, and vanish at will." In Dracula's castle, Jonathan opens what seems to be a bottle of perfume, but the drips fall out in an upward direction; later out of his window he glimpses Dracula scurrying up a wall like a lizard. Dracula has transgressed to the point where even the law of gravity does not apply to him. Dracula can thus be understood as a Sadean natural being because he follows nature's transgressive flow by violating what had been deemed as an inherent natural law.

This idea of evil is also embraced by Sade's libertines, who purposely express evil thoughts and commit evil deeds. In both Sade's novels and vampire stories, something is evil if it goes against the teachings of Christianity. However, Sade did not believe that evil exists, for he observed that in nature there is always cruelty and destruction. If an animal kills another for food, or if a hurricane wipes out a particular area of land, the event is not evil — the animal or the hurricane is just following its natural inclinations. Yet the Sadean libertine still uses the socially sanctioned idea of evil as a way of gaining pleasure.

Blasphemy, in particular, plays a part in many of his sexual scenes. For the libertines, pronouncing blasphemies during the sexual act is part of the foul language used to enhance the experience. In *The 120 Days of Sodom* it is actually a strict rule that blasphemy be uttered during libertine activity: "Messieurs are expressly enjoined at all gatherings to employ none but the most lascivious language, remarks indicative of the greatest debauchery, expressions of the filthiest, the most harsh, and the most blasphemous."[4] Coercing their victims into participation in blasphemous acts demonstrates the libertines' power, as they are forcing a person to go against that which he or she most devoutly believes in.

Likewise, scenes in which Dracula renounces God are also scenes where he displays his power. Since his beloved has committed suicide and has been damned by the church for all eternity, Dracula decides to damn himself also. He exclaims, "I renounce God!" as he drives his sword into a crucifix, an act which causes the religious icons around him to begin to bleed. Gathering the blood into a goblet, Dracula drinks it and becomes immortal, signaling that God has abandoned him. The church becomes saturated in blood, symbolizing how it has become corrupted. Dracula has besmirched this sacred place with his evil.

Blood plays a significant role in the film, as it is present within all of the sexual scenes. For the vampire, blood is a sexual fluid: it is drawn from another person in order to give life. This transference of blood blurs the border between one person and another, just as two people become connected and entwined during sexual intercourse. However, the vampire's blood-drinking is essentially a violent act, which results in death (or "un-death" if the victim is turned into a vampire).[5] For within this action is a clear hierarchy of victim and predator, as the person whose blood is drunk does not usually consent to the exchange. The vampire, like the Sadean libertine, thinks only of its own survival and satisfaction, with its very existence depending on its ability to seduce and kill.

This merging of seduction and murder is symbolized in the film through the visual motif of blood, which denotes sexual passion as well as violence. Red is thus a dominant color throughout: Dracula is first seen in red armor, and in his incarnation as an old man he wears vibrant red robes. Furthermore, the act of blood-drinking is shown in the form of a sex scene—for example, Jonathan's seduction by the Brides of Dracula (which will be discussed below), Lucy's meetings with Dracula (which are presented as scenes of bestiality), and Mina's drinking of Dracula's blood. Through this mingling of blood-drinking with kissing, caressing and cunnilingus, the presence of the blood-smeared mouth of the vampire introduces violence into the sexual scene.

Through his renunciation of God, Dracula, like the Sadean libertine, has freed himself from the societal and religious constraints that restrict him from experimenting with carnal pleasure. Seen as a libertine, Dracula is able to explore both the possibilities and limitations of the body, and express a sexuality that goes beyond the idea of sexual intercourse for solely reproductive purposes (an idea in opposition to the sexual mores of the Victorian era). His sexual impropriety is also aided by his status as a member of the aristocracy.

In Sade, libertines are also from the upper classes, or else they work their way up through devious and debaucherous means. Their superiority within the social hierarchy is symbolic of how they see themselves as above the masses and above the law. Yet it is this appearance of sophistication and civilization that allows both the vampire and the libertine to carry

1. Vampires

out their dark and base desires. As the Duc de Blangis, one of the four libertines in *The 120 Days of Sodom*, proclaims, "Thus, nothing but the law stands in my way, but I defy the law, my gold and my prestige keep me well beyond reach of those vulgar instruments of repression which should be employed only upon the common sort."[6] Their social power is wielded in order to undermine the very system that allows them to thrive. Thus, Coppola seems to exploit the figure of the libertine in his depiction of Stoker's character of Dracula, presenting him as a dashing man of pleasure — traits which are missing from Stoker's source novel.

The bite from the vampire Dracula is a catalyst for the unleashing of the previously repressed sexual and aggressive appetites of his female prey. In Coppola's film, the sexual scenes involving Dracula and his brides, although explicit, do not show them engaging in genital intercourse; instead, the vampires tend to incorporate "perverse" practices, such as bisexuality and group sex, blood-letting and blood-drinking, necrophilia and even bestiality (in one scene Mina walks outside to find Dracula, in the form of a hairy beast, with his head between Lucy's legs). As Cynthia Freeland notes in her study of the cinematic vampire, through the juxtaposition of scenes, Coppola demonstrates the opposition of polymorphous eroticism to religious practice: "Scenes of intense eroticism or violence are intercut here with scenes of stately religious ritual."[7]

For example, two crucial scenes, the wedding of Mina and Jonathan, and the death of Lucy at the hands of Dracula, are intercut together, so they seem to happen simultaneously. Just as Mina and Jonathan kiss after their wedding vows, we see Dracula, in the form of a wolf, burst into Lucy's bedroom and bite her neck. There are striking differences between the two rituals: Jonathan and Mina are married in a church in an Eastern European Orthodox ceremony, with a color scheme in muted tones of grey and white; in contrast, the scene with Lucy and Dracula takes place in a bedroom, Dracula in animal form and Lucy barely able to stop coming out of her flimsy nightgown, and by the end of the scene the room is awash in blood. Yet, despite these differences, the two rituals bring about the same result: two people are "wedded" together. The shot after the scene's end shows Lucy lying in a coffin, wearing the wedding dress that she was to be married in.

Just as Sade has his characters mock religious ritual by staging pretend marriage ceremonies, Dracula also has his own rituals that are perverted versions of established religious ceremonies. In Sade's *The 120 Days of Sodom* and *Juliette* there are wedding ceremonies in which the bride and groom dress as the other gender, and parents are wedded to their children. Instead of an expression of deep commitment, these weddings are jokes performed on a whim. The introduction of incest and gender switching illustrates that these ceremonies are a perversion of all that is held sacred about marriage, such as the ideas of pure love and traditional gender roles. In *The 120 Days of Sodom*, marriages are frequent and arbitrary: "On the 30th, for the thirteenth week's festival, the Duc shall take Hercule for his husband and Zéphyr for his wife, and the marriage shall be both accomplished and consummated before the eyes of everyone, as shall be the three others that follow."[8] While these libertine ceremonies are expressions of the death of God and the meaninglessness of religious practice, Dracula's rituals seem to put him in opposition to God — that is, Dracula exists as God's antithesis.

However, there are fundamental elements that disavow the traditional moral dichotomy and invite a reading of this Dracula as a Sadean libertine. Most importantly, we have it that at the heart of both Sade's and Coppola's narratives are the elements of sex and blood. Furthermore, both the libertines and Dracula contradict monogamy by "marrying" several people, an expression of their promiscuous natures. While a Christian wedding is concluded with the phrase "You may now kiss the bride," Dracula's wedding concludes with a kiss that brings death instead of a new life. All of his female victims are referred to as the Brides of Dracula, just as nuns are called the Brides of Christ (which again suggests the notion of Dracula as an anti–Christ figure). However, while nuns are known for their chastity, the Brides of Dracula are known for their carnality. The libertine and vampire weddings thus constitute a complete inversion and perversion of Christian wedding ceremonies.

These vampire weddings are an initiation ritual which awakens thirsts and desires in Dracula's victims. In this respect, David Pirie writes:

> Dracula ... can be seen as the great submerged force of Victorian libido breaking out to punish the repressive society which had imprisoned it; one of the most appalling things Dracula does to the matronly women of his Victorian enemies (in the novel as in the film) is to make them sensual.[9]

Just as Dracula follows his urge to kill, he also unleashes sexual desires in others. In Coppola's film adaptation, the women infected with Dracula's bite are shown to behave wantonly, flaunting their bodies and attempting to seduce any man near them. This is shown most explicitly when Jonathan is visited by three Brides of Dracula. These women are shown as supremely

1. Vampires

The Brides of Dracula (Michaela Bercu, Florina Kendrick, Monica Belluci) drink from Jonathan Harker (Keanu Reeves) in *Bram Stoker's Dracula* (1992).

evil. Upon seeing the crucifix hanging around Jonathan's neck, the gaze of the vampire women causes it to dissolve on his chest, and toward the end of the scene the hair of one vampire becomes a nest of snakes, a reference to both Medusa, whose gaze caused men to turn to stone (in a sense, becoming "stiff"), and to Eve, who, with the help of a snake, tempted Adam in the Garden of Eden.[10] The woman and the snake represent temptation to carnal delights, to "forbidden fruit" outside the institution of marriage.

The vampire women refuse to conform to the idea of the chaste, pure female. Dracula instills in his female victims a newfound desire to explore their sexuality — in order, of course, to seduce men to their deaths. Dracula's bite unleashes a fierce lust within them, freeing them from their previous role of passive nurturer. This is represented most extremely when Dracula casts the Brides from the bed and gives them something else to feed on: a crying infant. Instead of mothering babies, they murder them. Thus, transgressive sexuality leads to a transgression of all rules of behavior.

Part One: The Monster in Horror

Despite his status as evil and unnatural, Dracula is compelled by the natural and instinctual drives of sex and aggression; and he is able to arouse violent and carnal desires in others. His transgressions become a source of power, which he enforces on others and also incites within his victims. The vampire and the libertine transgress the socially constructed notions of nature as a harmonic cosmos—an idea put in place by cultural forces in order to keep natural forces at bay—in order to unleash the unruly, chaotic, destructive force of nature: they are true to "nature's nature." This is demonstrated in *Bram Stoker's Dracula* through Dracula's transgression of the so-called "laws of nature," such as the defiance of gravity and, most significantly, the barrier between life and death.

While past readings have already established how the vampire embodies the transgressive natural urges that society teaches us to repress, a Sadean reading reveals that the vampire is such a seductive and attractive figure because it shows transgression to be a positive, creative force that leads to new, more heightened pleasures. This aspect of the vampire further reveals that sexuality itself is a transgressive force, which can be expressed beyond social sexual norms, which characterize the sexual instinct as the desire for heterosexual reproduction and monogamy, and the upholding of strict gender roles. How the vampire transgresses these norms is discussed in the next section.

Sex and the Vampire

By transgressing the border separating life from death, the vampire becomes one of the "undead." This major transgression leads to other boundaries also becoming unfixed. For example, the vampire is a transgressive body taking on aspects of both genders and defying the traditional distinctions between male and female. In cinematic representations of vampires the gender of the vampire is central to the trajectory of the vampire narrative. While classical Hollywood films tend to show vampires as male, European cinema tends to focus on the vampire as female. The latter is typically shown as a sexually voracious creature who, like the Sadean libertine, also incorporates blood and violence into her sexual expression. Furthermore, in contrast to Hollywood's lowbrow, mainstream films, European cinema has often been associated with a higher level of cultural sophistication.

However, the European female vampire film demonstrates a merging

1. Vampires

of so-called high and low cultures, as both in form and content it incorporates images and themes from these two cultural spectrums. Indeed, European female vampire films follow a tradition in European art where high culture forms utilize themes and images often associated with lower cultural expression. Sade has become a central figure in this respect, with his texts, which combine an obsession with the sexual and the violent with philosophical ideas, being the subject of much intellectual discussion and debate.

As Freeland points out in *The Naked and the Undead*, in contrast to European film, Hollywood movies usually characterize the vampire as a handsome and seductive male.[11] The immortality of the Hollywood movie star correlates with the immortality of the vampire — both will be forever young and beautiful. Both the male star and the male vampire seduce women with their devastatingly good looks and hypnotic gaze. Freeland goes on to observe that "female vampires lag somewhat behind in prevalence."[12] Certainly in mainstream cinema the female vampire is usually a supporting role. For example, Claudia in *Interview with the Vampire* (Neil Jordan, 1994) and Abby in *Let Me In* (Matt Reeves, 2010) are placed in a sexual out-of-bounds through their eternal childhoods, while other films present the female vampire as a temporary spectacle, such as the Brides of Dracula in *Bram Stoker's Dracula*, Queen Akasha in *Queen of the Damned* (Michael Rymer, 2002) or Santanico Pandemonium, a stripper who performs a dance with a snake in *From Dusk Till Dawn* (Robert Rodriguez, 1996). These are characters possessed of an almost overwhelming and outrageous sexuality, who stand out and perform for one scene and are then promptly vanquished. It seems that mainstream cinema is unable to deal with the consequences of a character as strong and sexually voracious as the female vampire. They therefore become mere sideshow acts, momentary distractions from the main narrative.

By contrast, where Hollywood's male vampires are charming and romantic (and female vampires evanescent curiosities), the female vampire in European cinema is sexually aggressive and ferocious when attacking her prey. In Jose Larraz's film *Vampyres* (1974), the two female vampires attack their victims like wild animals, and feast on the bodies more like cannibals than elegant creatures of the night. And whereas male vampires often dress elegantly and seduce their victims with words, female vampires are frequently mute and apt to dispense with their clothes at the first opportunity. Highly attractive and (seemingly) sexually available, the female vampire is also a fierce killer with an appetite for blood. Her sexuality is inseparable from her instinct for violence and murder. She dispenses to her victims both pleasure and pain, but it is ultimately *her* pleasure alone that is important.

Just like the libertines in Sade's novels, the vampire in contemporary film is sexually perverse in that he or she gains sexual pleasure from seemingly "non-sexual" body parts, acts, and objects. They are also bisexual creatures that carry traits from both genders. This bisexuality is expressed in the vampire's urge to seduce and feed on anyone, regardless of gender. Yet, while they do use their fangs to penetrate the victim, during the act of blood drinking they receive fluids instead of spending them, as a man does with semen. This trait highlights the male vampires' feminine aspects. Furthermore, not unlike Sade's libertines, the vampires' pleasure is not centered on the genitals; it is diffused throughout their bodies, infiltrating ordinarily non-sexual acts.

Gender transgression and homosexual undertones are thus rife throughout most vampire cinema. Even in conservative Hollywood the male vampire has more recently been portrayed as possessing traits normally associated with the feminine. He is "beautiful," with long hair and elegant clothes, and usually portrayed by Hollywood sex symbols, men whose popularity is based on their beauty (for example, Brad Pitt, Tom Cruise and Antonio Banderas in *Interview with the Vampire*; or, more recently, Robert Pattinson in *Twilight* [Catherine Hardwicke, 2008] and its phenomenally successful sequels). That these gender transgressions are embodied in the form of such an attractive and seductive creature as the vampire—and are portrayed by people who are defined as "sex symbols"—demonstrates the Sadean notion that transgression is a highly positive force that leads to opportunities for new and greater sexual pleasures.

Vampires are similar to Sade's libertines in that they are situated outside of society and as a result do not have to conform to its sexual norms. In fact, they actively transgress society's restrictive gender stereotypes. For example, as Camille Paglia states, "Sade's libertines are often double-sexed."[13] Indeed, in Sade's novels there are women who rape, and some are even endowed with elongated clitorises which they use to penetrate their victims. On the other hand, Sade describes men who have a "softness which properly belongs only to women," and through this acquisition of "the attributes of the feminine sex, Nature had introduced its tastes into him as well."[14] While the male vampire finds himself in the position of receiving fluids instead of spending them, the female vampire is able to

1. Vampires

penetrate victims with her fangs. And since vampires bite the neck, the act of blood-drinking is always the same, regardless of the gender of the vampire or the victim. Sade's "double-sexing" relates to the vampire's gender transgression, as both represent transgression as a creative force, which leads to the creation of new sexual pleasures. Thus, a Sadean reading reveals that the vampire, a creature that has been deemed unnatural, actually represents nature and its propensity for transgression.

It is in representations of the female vampire that these connections to nature and to transgression are more explicitly expressed in films that, due to their transgressiveness, have been defined as exploitative and "trashy." This is so even though many similarities can be seen in films characterized as part of low culture and works belonging to the avant-garde or high culture. Both areas are often obsessed with testing the boundaries of good taste and acceptable behavior, and both often explore subjects deemed taboo by the mainstream. Joan Hawkins examines these similarities in *Cutting Edge: Art-Horror and the Horrific Avant-Garde*. She cites one director who illustrates this parallel: Jean-Luc Godard, a filmmaker held in high regard as a serious auteur, whose films not only incorporate "scenes from art film masterpieces ... prints of impressionist paintings, [and] Mozart concertos," but also contain "magazine advertisements, billboards, nude shots from erotica magazines, [and] excerpts from pornographic writings."[15] He not only engages his audience in intellectual debate, he also titillates and horrifies them with images of a more visceral nature.

Similarly, Eurotrash filmmaker Jess Franco, in conjunction with images of explicit sexuality and bloody violence, has his characters converse on subjects such as Surrealism, Godard films, and classic literature. And, as he is an accomplished jazz musician, Franco's films always involve a complicated jazz score. In fact, many parallels can be seen in the themes and images of arthouse directors such as Godard, Peter Greenaway, Luis Buñuel, Derek Jarman and Michael Haneke, and low culture horror directors such as Franco, Mario Bava, Lucio Fulci, Jose Larraz and Jean Rollin.[16]

What separates these directors is genre, with the horror genre traditionally categorized as a low cultural form. Here is another parallel between horror and the work of Sade, which was also originally perceived as a dangerous influence on behavior, and banned in most countries. It wasn't until the last century, when many artists, intellectuals and philosophers acknowledged Sade as an important philosophical and artistic figure, that this opinion changed. Sade, too, incorporates aspects of high and low culture, intercutting his pornographic scenes with philosophical debate. On this point, Hawkins comments:

> The works of the Marquis de Sade ... are sold in mainstream bookstores and adult bookstores and housed in university libraries. Sade's works, which the intellectual elite view as masterful analyses of the mechanisms of power and economics, are also — at least if we are to take their presence in adult bookstores and magazines seriously — still regarded as sexually arousing, as masturbatory aids.[17]

The transgressive body thus invites attention at both a sexual and an intellectual level, and there is a body of works, including those by Sade, that provide a context for this.

Filmmakers, such as Rollin, Franco and Larraz, who use the figure of the female vampire as a site of transgressive sexuality and shocking violence, draw on literary, and especially poetic, tradition. Franco Moretti points out that the gender of a vampire changes according to its cultural context; thus, while mass-culture, mainstream literature, such as Bram Stoker's *Dracula,* and movies from Hollywood portray vampires as predominantly male, in high or "elite" culture, such as the poetry of Baudelaire and Coleridge, the literature of Poe and Hoffman, and European film, the vampire is female.[18] Moretti then goes on to argue that the mainstream vampire is male in order to further repress and hide the unconscious fear and desire that vampires embody — namely, "the ambivalent impulse of the child toward its mother."[19]

Moretti's psychoanalytic view contrasts with the Sadean reading of the vampire. A Sadean reading gives its attention less to how the vampire (male or female) may represent repressions of desire, and instead focuses on how all representations of vampires, Hollywood or arthouse, contain to a greater or lesser degree transgressions of fixed gender roles and sexual identity. From this, even the male vampire of mainstream cinema can be seen to undermine and transgress its own supposed masculinity. This new perspective thus offers a powerful instance to reflect on our own constructedness as gendered and sexed subjects.

Furthermore, in comparison to the psychoanalytic view described earlier, in Sade's literature the figure of the mother becomes a great and powerful source of transgression. At some point a child must begin to assert his/her independence from the mother or risk being under her control forever. In Sade's representation of the maternal figure, the mother is a symbol of repressive societal forces and an obstacle to sexual exploration. However, Sade does not fear the mother and is not repressed by her. Sade destroys the socially sanctioned notion of the nurturing mother and produces in its place a bestial one, which follows nature's transgressive forces. This idea can be seen as manifest in the form of the female vampire: instead of giving birth, the female vampire gives death. One recalls the scene in Coppola's film when the vampire women are shown to eat babies.

In summary, the female vampire's transgressive body is represented in films that themselves transgress cultural borders, incorporating aspects of high and low culture. This transgressiveness, which begins with her defiance of death, includes the transgression of gender and sexual practice. The female vampire represents a woman who embraces her sexual instincts and uses them to seek pleasure for herself only. Sex with a female vampire can only bring death, not life. This is demonstrated further by closely examining Jess Franco's film *Female Vampire*, a movie which clearly presents the aggressive sexuality of this transgressive body.

The Loves of Irina: Female Vampire

Jess Franco's *Female Vampire* is a typical example of how the female vampire is portrayed in European film. Franco himself has indicated that Sade is a major influence on his work, and has directed several adaptations of Sade's novels: *Marquis de Sade's Justine* (1968), *Juliette* (1975), *Eugenie ... the Story of Her Journey Into Perversion* (1969; based on *Philosophy in the Bedroom*), and *Eugenie de Sade* (1970; based on Sade's short story *Eugenie de Franval*). One might therefore expect to find traces of Sadean elements in his work. In fact, in his article about the films of Jess Franco, Xavier Mendik argues that Sade is a direct influence on *Female Vampire*, as well as many other Franco films.[20] In *Female Vampire* the protagonist, Irina Karlstein, fellates her victims to death, an act that clearly realizes the sexual nature of the vampire's bite. Irina is in a constant state of sexual arousal which can never be satisfied. She uses each partner until he or she is dead, and then moves on to her next victim. This sexual compulsion, which drives her unrelenting abuse of others, reveals her as a Sadean libertine.

That the film's protagonist is a vampire who is shown participating in many acts of sexual transgression situates the film within the area of low horror. Yet, as revealed in the previous section, the genre of low horror cinema, with the works of Jess Franco being prime examples, exhibits traits which link it with high culture and the avant-garde. In fact, in her book

Part One: The Monster in Horror

Cutting Edge: Art-Horror and the Horrific Avant-Garde, Joan Hawkins makes a case for the consideration of Jess Franco as a serious auteur. According to Hawkins, Franco's films draw on the idea of "cultural accumulation," meaning that they employ aspects of both high and low culture.[21] In order to fully enjoy and experience a Franco film, one must be familiar with high art forms such as jazz and classical literature, while also being attuned to the lower "body genres" of horror and pornography. By utilizing aspects from both cultural spectrums, a unique style is created, but one which takes time and repeated viewings in order to understand. Hawkins even cites the remark made by Tim Lucas that "you can't see one [of Franco's films] until you've seen them all. A degree of immersion is essential."[22]

That one has to "learn" to watch Franco's films situates them outside of mass culture's desire to satisfy the lowest common denominator. Instead, Franco's films can be seen to occupy a similar place within the cultural scale as the one occupied by Sade's literature. In fact, earlier in her book Hawkins uses the example of Sade to highlight similarities within high and low culture,[23] and then later cites Sade directly as one of Franco's key influences.[24]

This mingling of high and low culture can be found in *Female Vampire*. Franco observes that for him, as for Sade, "intellect is bound up with the vulgar and the ability to entertain. The two should not be divided."[25] This statement illustrates Sade's more general influence on a style of storytelling that incorporates both intellectual and bodily, or "vulgar," representation.[26] This style is certainly employed in *Female Vampire*, where scenes of sexual activity are interspersed with scenes in which the libertine-like protagonist discusses and analyzes her actions.

Female Vampire opens with shots of Irina (portrayed by Lina Romay) walking through the misty woods, naked except for a cape, belt and boots. Franco's camera tilts up and down her body, and at one point even zooms into her pubic hair, as though it longed to disappear into this region, one normally kept hidden from view. Tohill and Tombs remark, "When asked why he keeps zooming towards this ... area of female anatomy, he [Franco] disarmingly admits: 'It's the first place my eye looks.'"[27] By focusing so intently on Irina's nudity, Franco highlights its attractiveness, its ability to arouse sexual desire.

Yet he also shows Irina using this ability as a tactic to lure victims: for after traversing the length and breadth of Irina's body, the camera captures her in the act of seduction and murder. A man spies Irina walking

1. Vampires

and asks if she needs help. As Irina is mute, in answer to his question she kisses him, then falls to her knees and begins to fellate him as he leans against a chicken-wire fence. As she brings him to climax, Franco intercuts shots of birds flapping and flying in the coop next to them. At the moment of orgasm, the man screams and expires: the height of pleasure brings the terror and realization of death. Transgressive in her nudity and her sexual promiscuity, Irina is powerful, and this power makes her a danger to others.

The linking of Irina with birds continues: after her kill there is a shot of Irina flapping her cape as though it were a pair of wings. The next scene then consists of one shot from Irina's point of view, looking from within a car over its hood, which is adorned with an ornament in the shape of a bird that flaps its wings. Later in the film, when she appears to a female journalist, the squawking of birds is heard. Following her base carnal and violent desires, Irina is an animal, a creature of instinct; yet it is these very instincts that have turned her into a monster. That she uses other people as her victims reflects Sade's view of the animal kingdom: "[C]ruelty is stamped in animals, in whom, as I think I have said, Nature's laws are more emphatically to be read than in ourselves."[28] Irina's family wealth allows her to travel and thus evade having to face the consequences of her actions in a civilized society. The flapping of birds' wings also suggests freedom: Irina is mute and thus free of language and other bonds of civilization, an animal who communicates through the socially taboo acts of sex and murder.

Irina's ferocious carnality, so at odds with traditional attitudes toward sexual discretion, is demonstrated throughout the film. When Irina is not seducing victims (both male and female), she is shown masturbating almost constantly. Again, Franco's camera takes the opportunity to zoom into Irina's genitals. As Irina, Lina Romay gives a performance that borders on the exhibitionist — almost every scene has her perform a highly sexual act. This fascination with the genitals (both male and female) transgresses mainstream representation, where full-frontal nudity is usually avoided or at least kept brief—close-ups of the genitals are usually only seen in pornographic films.

Yet such images are what exploitation films, which lack both a substantial budget and big stars, use to lure audiences— offering what mainstream cinema can only hint at. Hollywood vampire films such as *Interview with the Vampire* usually refrain from showing any explicitly sexual scenes. In contrast, the European vampire film typically contains many sex scenes; and the homosexuality that is merely hinted at in *Interview with the Vam-*

Part One: The Monster in Horror

pire is an essential part of the European exploitation picture. The female vampire is always either a lesbian or bisexual (even in the Brides of Dracula scene in *Bram Stoker's Dracula* the vampire women are seen kissing each other).

While being interviewed by a female journalist, who is to become a victim, Irina is asked about "being the descendant of a family of vampires." Irina's surname is Karlstein, a reference to Carmilla Karlstein, the heroine of Sheridan Le Fanu's novella *Carmilla* and fiction's first female vampire. This intertextual reference suggests that the curse is handed down from mother to daughter (which also brings to mind another blood "curse" which afflicts both mother and daughter). Irina turns the interview into a scene of seduction, with the female journalist becoming entranced by her, demonstrating Irina's ability to arouse any person, regardless of gender or sexual orientation.

Due to its sexual explicitness, the film plays with the boundaries of pornography; but is it, in fact, pornographic? Like Sade, who mingles descriptions of sexual acts with intellectual discussion, Franco intercuts his sexual scenes with scenes of contemplation, during which the audience hears Irina's thoughts about her existence. In these scenes she confronts her sadistic nature: "Why has my body once again desired of death? Why can't my senses survive without the last breath of a victim?" Although she does not revel in her actions, as do most of Sade's characters, it is only through the kill that she can gain pleasure — and, indeed, her very survival depends on that kill. That sex climaxes with death is another Sadean trait, and it is this philosophical preoccupation with death that separates the film from most cinematic pornography.

While Franco's version does not present actual sexual intercourse and fellatio, many versions of *Female Vampire* were distributed that included inserts of hardcore sex. Within this area of exploitation filmmaking, movies were regularly cut and re-edited in order to cater to a certain market. *Female Vampire* was also released under the title *Erotikill*, which was a straight horror film where Irina drank blood from the neck, and *The Loves of Irina*, which catered to the sex film market (it has also been released as *The Bare Breasted Countess*, *La Comtesse Noire* and in hardcore pornographic form — with all traces of the vampire narrative removed — with the title *Insatiable Lust*). *Female Vampire* is therefore a version that transgresses both the genres of horror and porn, and incorporates aspects of both.

What this film makes clear is the linking of sex with death, and, more

1. Vampires

specifically, the fearsome yet seductive power of female sexuality. When asked directly about Sade's influence on female characters such as Irina, Franco commented, "What Sade does is depict women who have power, I think these films do the same."[29] Sade can thus be read as an influence on the European female vampire film, which presents female characters who are highly sexual and prone to violence. They think only of themselves and their own survival and pleasure, and then are able to kill others and drink their blood without remorse.

This linking of violence and murder with sexual fulfillment aligns them with Sade's female libertines, such as Juliette. These characters have also freed themselves from societal constraints, their behavior the complete antithesis to the way females of their time were supposed to behave. But this freedom is attained through violent means, as Angela Carter points out about the Sadean woman:

> A free woman in an unfree society will be a monster. Her freedom will be a condition of personal privilege that deprives those on which she exercises it of their own freedom. The most extreme kind of this deprivation is murder. These women murder.[30]

This view of freedom also applies to the female vampire. In order to be completely free, Irina has become an animal — that is, a creature of nature and instinct. The vampire Irina can thus be understood as a Sadean woman, of whom Sade himself remarked:

> I say then that women, having been endowed with considerably more violent penchants for carnal pleasure than we, will be able to give themselves over to it wholeheartedly, absolutely free of all encumbering hymeneal ties, of all false notions of modesty, absolutely restored to a state of Nature.[31]

In order to attain this "state of Nature," Irina has become transgressive. Through her defiance of the boundary which separates life from death, Irina is brought closer to nature.

This correlation of the natural with the female has a long history in Western culture. Camille Paglia links the feminine with the chthonian and the Dionysian, arguing that "mythology's identification of woman with nature is correct."[32] The chthonian "means 'of the earth'— but earth's bowels, not its surface,"[33] and the Dionysian refers to the Greek god Dionysus, who was often represented as a youth, sometimes cross-dressed, and is "identified with liquids — blood, milk, sap, wine. The Dionysian is nature's chthonian fluidity."[34] Irina in *Female Vampire* is frequently connected with the body's fluids — namely, blood and sexual fluids. As a vam-

Part One: The Monster in Horror

pire, Irina is obviously linked with blood, especially since she inherits her vampirism. After killing the only man she has ever loved (her instincts have overpowered emotion), Irina decides to end her life, and she is seen dying in a bath of blood.

But just as she finds pleasure in the death of others, her own death proves to be the ultimate pleasure. As she dies, her body undulates in the throes of ecstasy *and* of death, in a bloody fluid reminiscent of the primal soup from which humanity emerged, and to which Irina now returns. The representation of bodily fluids, especially sexual fluids, is usually banished from mainstream film — even in films containing sex scenes.[35] Conversely, Irina kills through fellatio, consuming semen and female fluid in order to survive. After killing the female journalist, Irina raises her head, and her mouth is seen dripping with sexual fluid. The fluids that create life help Irina's to continue, but their consumption also leads to the death of her partners. In consequence, in *Female Vampire* we see that the forces of sex and death, of creation and destruction, are not opposed but actually run and mix into each other. Irina has become one with the fluidity of nature.

But despite her fluid nature, Irina also follows the Sadean hierarchy by which people are separated into master and slave. In fact, while she generally dominates her victims and thinks only of her own pleasure, sometimes she allows herself to take on a subaltern, passive position. In one scene she visits a dominatrix in a room that is filled with the accoutrements of sadomasochism. Irina allows herself to be chained and whipped with a cane (the camera zooms in to show the blood splattering over her flesh), as for her, even punishment becomes pleasure. Yet, despite her temporary masochistic position, Irina remains in control of the situation, and the scene ends as she turns the tables and begins to strip and molest the dominatrix. This scene confirms Irina's status of power, her heightened sexuality being a source of strength that overtakes and inverts other systems of power.

Female Vampire presents many forms of transgression: the transgression of genre in its fusion of pornography and horror; the transgression between sex and death, as orgasm becomes death throes; and its presentation of body fluids which illustrate Irina's all-encompassing and enveloping powers. Like the Sadean libertine, the female vampire is a transgressive body that not only violates the taboos against murder, cannibalism, and the use of bodily fluids, but also *sexualizes* these taboos, gaining both sustenance and pleasure from them.

2

Zombies

In contrast to the beauty of the vampire, the zombie is nothing if not ugly. It is a dead body that has come back to life, completely devoid of all personality, thriving only on the instinct to kill and feed on human flesh. Even though it has gained the ability to move, it still retains the physical effects of death, the rotting and decomposition, as well as showing the signs of what killed it in the first place. Therefore, the body of the zombie causes only revulsion and disgust in those that see it.

This disgust stems from the zombie being a creature of abjection. In Julia Kristeva's influential study on horror, the abject is seen to symbolize all that "disturbs identity, system, order. What does not respect borders, positions, rules. The in-between, the ambiguous, the composite."[1] The zombie certainly falls into this category, for while it retains the form of the person it once was, it is a body that has ceased to be a living thing. With its aimless shuffling and blank expression, it is devoid of all that made that individual a "personality." In fact, Kristeva designates the corpse as "the utmost of abjection," for it is in it where "[t]he border has become an object."[2] In the case of the zombie, Kristeva's notion of abjection can be carried even further, as this creature is the physical manifestation of *several* borders: not only the boundary separating life and death, but also the inside from the outside of the body, as well as the boundary between instinctual and civilized behavior.

In fact, it is in the transgression of boundaries that we may trace a direct correlation between the zombie and the Sadean libertine. Indeed, the zombie can be categorized as Sadean not only through its corpse state but through its animated body, which is simultaneously open and decomposing. For this reason, as its survival can only be ensured through violence and the death of others, the coming of the zombie often signals and/or brings about the end of civilization.

The zombie is an abject creature insofar as, according to Kristeva's definition, it disturbs established order; yet its undead but actively destructive nature, seen through the philosophy of Sade, signifies the complete demise of all borders and rules. This clearly conforms to Sade's view of nature as simultaneously self-destructive and self-productive: as a creature of pure instinct, the zombie brings about the destruction of all kind of law, rule or boundary, whether social or natural. Thus, a Sadean reading lets us see something about the zombie figure that psychoanalysis does not: while the abject passively signifies ambiguity, the zombie, as a Sadean creature, both actively and productively (while also violently and bestially) destroys one order so that it can inaugurate a new one — its own. This notion will be developed through the textual analysis of two key films by two auteurs who have helped define the rules of the zombie genre: George Romero and Lucio Fulci.

Inside, Outside, and The Beyond

Italian director Lucio Fulci is mostly known for his cycle of zombie films: *Zombie Flesh Eaters* (1979), *The City of the Living Dead* (1980), *The Beyond* (1981), *The House by the Cemetery* (1981) and *Zombie Flesh Eaters 2* (1988). Although light on plot and character development, these films are renowned instead for their extreme violence, being filled with graphic representations of the body being torn open by assorted weapons, as well as scenes of zombie cannibalism. In centering on the act of violence rather than the plot that motivates it, these films lay bare the essential elements that define the genre. These movies thus cater to a fascination with the limitations and possibilities of the body, and with how violence affects and destroys it. Such an investigation of the body can be traced back to Sade's novels, which also explore the body's reaction to pain and violence.

Indeed, like Sade, Fulci returns again and again to the same obsessions. *City of the Living Dead*, *The Beyond* and *The House by the Cemetery* form a trilogy that all carry similar themes and images. In these films the protagonist (played in all three by Catriona McColl) moves to a new house that is the dwelling of zombies, where she will live among the dead. It is this space that will take precedence over a linear plot and character development. For it is in this space that all boundaries become unfixed, and transgression becomes the only law. In *The Beyond*, for instance, time actually begins to fold back on itself. The film's prologue takes place in the past, yet the two timeframes begin to merge, shown in the character of

2. Zombies

Emily, who exists in both eras but does not seem to age. The narrative instead consists of a series of violent scenes, with the emphasis being placed on spectacle rather than narrative cohesion. The repetition of violence is emblematic of a time that continuously circles back on itself.

The circular temporality of *The Beyond* mirrors the use of repetition in Sade, where narrative progression is secondary to the exhaustion of all sexual possibilities. As Leo Bersani writes: "[Sade] exemplifies a tendency in art ... whose violence is not only anecdotal but also intrinsic, structural."[3] In Fulci's films, too, violence is the "intrinsic" driving force: his films are structured in order to show the full effect of the violence rather than to present a neatly plotted storyline. Similarly, Bersani points out that Sade's narratives do not follow a linear timeframe:

> Like much erotic literature, *The 120 Days of Sodom* moves from comparatively mild sexual anecdotes to orgies of erotic violence. But Sade points out that this is not the order in which his characters have the experience being related. We are told that on a particular day, for instance, Sade's heroes were engaged in activities which will be narrated only as part of the record of a later day. In other words, the progress from one day to the next in Sade's book is not determined by "real" chronology ... rather, the work is organized in order to produce a certain type of narrative progression which is itself erotically stimulating.[4]

Both Fulci and Sade thus structure their stories in order to evoke a visceral response, even at the expense of narrative consistency and believability. Character is not as important as the body itself and the transformations it undergoes. In this transgressive space, the body's boundaries are shattered and then opened up to new possibili-

Zombie Flesh Eaters (1979).

ties. It is bodily transgression and transformation that is the main focus in both Fulci's and Sade's representations and narratives.

The social marginality of the zombie is emphasized through Fulci's use of space, as well as the appearance and behavior of the zombie within it. In fact, all the zombies in Fulci's films originate from beneath the ground before moving into civilization. By the same token, the character of Madame Delbene, in Sade's *Juliette*, says of moving underground:

> If we thus burrow far down into the realm of the dead, it is to be at the greatest possible remove from the living. When one is a libertine, as depraved, as vicious as are we, one likes to be in the bowels of the earth so as the better to avoid the interference of man and their ridiculous law.[5]

This dwelling underground helps avoid detection, as well as taking on a symbolic significance: it signifies the libertine's and the zombie's status as being apart from society (as it doesn't live among the public), and yet still dwelling "beneath" it (within the fears and desires of those above).

In this sense, most of Sade's libertines choose to engage in their activities in places that are situated away from civilization. For example, the four libertines in *The 120 Days of Sodom* seclude themselves and their victims in the Château of Silling, while the lascivious monks in *Justine* live in a monastery situated deep in the woods. Although the zombie does walk among the living, it always goes back to rest in these lower depths. In Fulci's *The Beyond* and *The House by the Cemetery*, the zombies live in the protagonists' basements. In fact, in *The House by the Cemetery* Lucy pulls up a rug to reveal that the floor underneath is made from a tombstone: her house, in fact, *is* a cemetery!

This connection between the zombie and the base matter of the earth signifies that the zombie is a manifestation of basic desires and urges, as it does not speak or engage in any social interaction, but seeks only to feed and survive. The zombie is also associated with other symbols of the base and the abject, such as dirt, filth, waste, rats, and maggots. "Horrific metonymy," whereby connections are made between bodies and objects, is a technique designating the monster's body as transgressive and impure.[6] At once dead and living, the body of the zombie is often shown crawling with the vermin that feed on dead matter, in places where such vermin are known to inhabit. The dwellings of the zombie signal it as a base creature, part of the underworld. It emerges not from the womb but rather from the tomb, crawling out of its coffin under the ground, born from the dirt.

2. Zombies

By interpreting the zombie through Sadean philosophy, the zombie's association with filth and dirt takes on a sexual aspect: "'tis most voluptuous to wallow, so to speak, in filth ... these exercises offer the completest abandon, the most monstrous intemperance, the most total abasement."[7] This obsession with excrement and anal sexuality symbolizes a mixing of sex and death. In anal intercourse there is no chance of reproduction: indeed, the fluid that helps bring life, sperm, is expended into the orifice that is filled with waste matter. Nature's designs are thus thwarted.

The zombie also spreads death instead of creating life, as their bite causes their victim to die and then return as one of the undead. The linking with filth, therefore, represents the antithesis of reproduction — sex instead equals death. And for the zombie it could be said that death equals sex; it is not shown engaging in sexual acts, but is seen, instead, partaking in elaborate acts of murder, which are shown in almost pornographic detail. This graphic representation suggests that the zombie takes pleasure in these actions.

While the zombie brings about death, it also brings about the end of civilization, and it achieves this through acts of sickening and unremorseful violence that infects others: this is a violence that both destroys *and* creates. Furthermore, Fulci's camera revels in the carnage, taking every opportunity to document the violence and its resulting gore in extreme close-up. For instance, the very first scene of *The Beyond* climaxes with a violent act: as an artist finishes a painting that depicts a barren landscape littered with corpses, an angry mob bursts into the hotel where he is staying and begin to attack him. As soon as he is hit with a chain, the camera zooms in to document the tearing of the flesh and the spurt of blood. This camera movement — a quick zoom into close-up — is repeated in almost every gory scene throughout Fulci's filmography.

In these horrific close-ups, Fulci focuses attention on the blood and viscera bursting from under the skin and into the frame, an act symbolizing how all previous boundaries are about to be violated. The close-up is a cinematic equivalent to Sade's graphic descriptions of the violence that his libertines perpetrate on the bodies of their victims. Fulci's close-up focuses on the wounds caused by violence, while blocking out the person as a whole; in Sade, too, there is an emphasis on the act itself, while the victims themselves are largely ignored: "her arms are burned, so are her thighs in six different places, two teeth are extracted from her mouth, she is flogged...."[8]

The body of the victim in Sade and Fulci is thus fragmented; attention

Part One: The Monster in Horror

is paid rather to the different parts of the body violated and opened. Just as the close-up dissects and fragments the body, with the frame of the picture cutting out the body around it, so too in Sade there is no focus on the person as a whole. The site and act of transgression is emphasized, so that the boundaries between the inside and the outside of the body are blurred and erased. By dispensing with elements that signify "good" filmmaking, Fulci's films instead focus on the spectacle of violence. By showing the opening of the body in graphic detail, these movies force us to confront our innate fear and anxiety about our bodies, how they are subject to disease, accident and, most frighteningly of all, death — incidents that we have absolutely no control over.

Because of their non-conformity to traditional narrative tropes, these films are scornfully denigrated and dismissed by the mainstream. By seeking to provoke "scandal and outrage," these movies continue the countertradition of Sade's transgression of social taboos. These taboos are put on screen in order to shock and offend. Therefore, these films are contemporary equivalents of Sade's works in function as well as effect.[9]

This lack of restraint in representation can lead to an exhaustion of spectacle, as Sade's own work demonstrates. In *The 120 Days of Sodom* an excess of repetition degenerates the narrative into a mere catalogue of atrocities, as Georges Bataille points out:

> Sade ... only had one occupation in his long life which really absorbed him — that of enumerating to the point of exhaustion the possibilities of destroying human beings, of destroying them and of enjoying the thought of their death and suffering.[10]

Just like the numerous murder and torture scenes in countless horror movies, Sade's works also seek to demonstrate the myriad ways that the human body can be violated and executed. It is therefore not surprising that *The 120 Days of Sodom* is an unfinished work, as it would take an eternity to write a book which encapsulated every method through which a body can be destroyed. This also explains the repetitious structure of the horror film, and the genre's reliance on sequels and series.

For as Sade's books and Fulci's films make clear, once the cycle of transgression is begun, it is fated to be repeated over and over. One transgression will always lead to another, a fact that is demonstrated by how these stories are structured. In the films of Fulci, transgression takes place in scenes in which the body is opened, whether through violence (as the result of a person or zombie being attacked), or as part of the process of

2. Zombies

decomposition: the rotting and bodily decay that comes after death is constantly highlighted. And in one scene of *City of the Living Dead*, just the *sight* of a zombie causes one woman to vomit up her internal organs!

The transgression that the zombie represents causes all borders to be destabilized. As the dead are no longer underground, separate from the living, all other borders, such as that which separates and keeps in place the corporeal interior and exterior of the body, are now subject to collapse. In this space of confusion, all that had previously been denied as impossible now becomes distinctly possible; and what was always thought of as supernatural is shown as perfectly natural.

Not only do the zombies from Hell return to Earth, they also bring with them the power to end civilization completely: all of Fulci's zombie films feature bleak, apocalyptic endings. In *The Beyond*, the film closes with Earth becoming a living Hell, depicted as a barren desert, a wasteland without color or life. It is nothing, without boundaries or form. Even time and space are transgressed, for this landscape is actually the painting that was completed in the film's first scene, and the protagonists now find themselves trapped within it. Not only have all boundaries been transgressed, they have been obliterated completely. There is no separation, as everything has become part of "an eternity of negation."[11]

As stated earlier, the idea of complete negation is a central theme in Sade's works. In this respect, Gilles Deleuze asserts, "The sadistic hero appears to have set himself the task of thinking out the Death Instinct (pure negation) in a demonstrative form."[12] Pure negation is, however, impossible, as it is a "delusion; but it is a delusion of reason itself."[13] As negation has to be expressed and experienced as an event, it is only a partial negation — that is, total negation exists only as an idea: the idea of Nothing. However, the endless repetition in Sade's works is an attempt to reach this state, as it is only through "multiplying and condensing the activities of component negative or destructive instincts" that negation can be demonstrated.[14] Through repetition, events are drained of their meaning, becoming a series of movements without reason.

In Sade and Fulci, this repetition serves to reduce ideas of narrative and character to a destruction of the body. The body, the base physical self, is opened up, broken down, shown to be Nothing. In *The Beyond*, the place of negation is reached at the end of the film, represented visually as a physical space. It is the climax to the accumulation of one scene of extreme and graphic violence after another. Yet it is also an anti-climax, as the protagonists suddenly find themselves in a world of Nothing, barren and endless. A close-up shows that their eyes have turned white, so that they can no longer see or be able to differentiate one object from another. In this place they have reached "the beyond," a place without boundaries, of pure transgression, where Nothing exists.

Through Sade's ideas, Fulci's fascination with the body and the many ways it can be destroyed are read as visual representations of the power and pleasure that emerges from the transgressive body. Focusing so intently on the violence that the zombie creates illustrates its power to change and destroy the world around it. Furthermore, Sadean concepts help to identify the sexual aspects of the graphic representations of violence inherent in the zombie film. Like the horror movies that are condemned for their focus on violence rather than narrative, Sade's work degenerates into a sequence of atrocities, which are designed not to disgust but to arouse.

This structure, found in both cinema and literature, highlights body over character and violence over plot, thus laying bare the key elements that drive most narratives—the power of and fascination with the transgressive body. Thus, a Sadean reading reveals how the monster is a natural creature that represents nature's constant transgression. This is evidenced through the creativity with which the zombie violently destroys the established social order. The creativity of transgression can be explored further through the analysis of George Romero's *Dawn of the Dead*, a film in which the zombie destroys civilization completely, creating a new world driven by nature's urges.

Romero's Living Dead: Dawn of the Dead

While Fulci's zombies take on religious connotations, the zombies in the films of Romero comment instead on the apathy and complacency of humanity. Just as Sade depicted a world where one must look after one's own selfish interests in order to survive, Romero shows that human relations have reached the point where civilization can no longer continue. Not unlike Sade's works of fiction, Romero's *Dawn of the Dead* (1979) and his Living Dead series (totaling six films at last count) contain a broader philosophical comment on the human condition and our future directions. The application of a Sadean reading to this series of films, which depict the breakdown of human relations, reveals an affinity with Sade's idea of "isolism."

In Sade, success comes to those who cast off the bonds of human

2. Zombies

relationships. His libertines feel no emotion or compassion for their fellow man, instead caring only about themselves and their own pleasure. In contrast to the Christian ideal of loving one's neighbor, Sade's philosophy of "isolism" (derived from the word "isolation") is based on the idea that humans are not connected but are isolated individuals who must think only of themselves and their own needs and desires: "*isolisme* has become a philosophical thesis, which no longer designates a circumstantial lack, but rather the human condition *per se*."[15]

Sade understands the idea of a brotherhood of man as a construct that has been imposed upon us by Christianity, as a way of making the strong protect the weak. In Sade's words: "he who is neither weak nor Christian subject himself to such restrictions, voluntarily entangle himself in this mythical snarl of brotherly relationships which without benefiting him in the least deprive him enormously."[16] The Christian idea of loving one another is seen by Sade as unnatural. In nature, all creatures struggle purely for their own survival and supremacy. Sade believes that humans are not different: the idea of sacrificing one's own well-being for the sake of others is a religious idea that goes against all human instinct.

It can be argued, then, that in the figure of the zombie the idea of isolism is exemplified, since it is motivated only by selfish instinct, and is completely apathetic and devoid of emotion. In fact, the zombie is completely unable to communicate with others, even those of its own kind. For Romero, the isolism of the zombie represents the present and the future of humankind. Rather than depicting these zombies as monsters or the Other, Romero makes pointed observations on how the zombies are really just like us. In *Dawn of the Dead*, in particular, Romero uses the zombies to satirize modern consumer culture: when one character asks, "What the hell are they?" the reply she receives is, "They're us." And they effectively are: they wear modern clothes, which help define the zombies' (former) personality (some zombies are in business suits or work uniforms, others in casual outfits like jeans and T-shirts, and one is even dressed as a Hare Krishna); they gather into groups; and they all flock to the local shopping mall. One character muses that they must be drawn there by "Memory. Instinct. What they used to do. This was an important place in their lives." The zombie represents our own selfish, isolationist tendencies. Once they are in the mall, Romero shows that the zombies really *do* behave in the same way as when they were alive: they shuffle around the stores meaninglessly, while irritating Muzak plays over the speakers.

What is most significant is that, even though they move in groups,

Part One: The Monster in Horror

the zombies do not interact with each other. They are completely isolated beings. Once a person becomes a zombie, former attachments no longer apply. A zombie will attack friends and family members without realization or remorse. Like the Sadean libertine, the zombie is motivated solely by its own self-interest and instinct. It cannot empathize with others or feel anything outside of its own cravings. The zombie sees the human as nothing more than meat.

Romero illustrates this through the use of gore effects. In his films, the zombies rip open their victims' bodies and feast on the flesh. Shots focus on the entrails being removed and eaten: internal organs are no longer part of the body but look more like raw meat products. In this consumer world we even consume each other and reduce our victims to products. This conforms to Sade's view of the place of the victim as a thing to be used and discarded: "The victims have been erased from the world and now live ... in a world where the function of their own flesh is to ... demonstrate the shocking tragedy of mortality itself, that all flesh may be transformed, at any moment, to meat."[17] This is the possibility that all the humans in Romero's films face: that they may become meat. Most of the characters will become either zombies or the meat that they feed on.

For those left in a human state, the future is still very uncertain. Normality is never restored in Romero's films, a factor that has allowed him to return to the genre again and again over a period of five decades. Like Fulci and Sade, the repetition of themes and (violent) images uncovers the truths usually hidden by plot and character. In the case of Romero, it is the human body, radically transgressed and reduced to meat, that is displayed in endless repetition.

This endless repetition involves the stripping of all social veneers. As Shaviro states, the zombies "continue to participate in human, social rituals and processes—but only just long enough to drain them of their power and meaning."[18] They are symbols of the modern person's complacency; they may appear normal, repeating the same motions over and over, but they are dead, soulless. They are walking meat. Yet even one of the human survivors complains that those still alive have become "hypnotized by this place. It's so bright and neatly wrapped that you don't see this is a prison." The film features montages of the four survivors dressing up and playing with the mall's wares—they have everything they could need and so make no attempt to leave. Like the zombies, they are trapped into repeating the same motions over and over, reliving the memory of their

2. Zombies

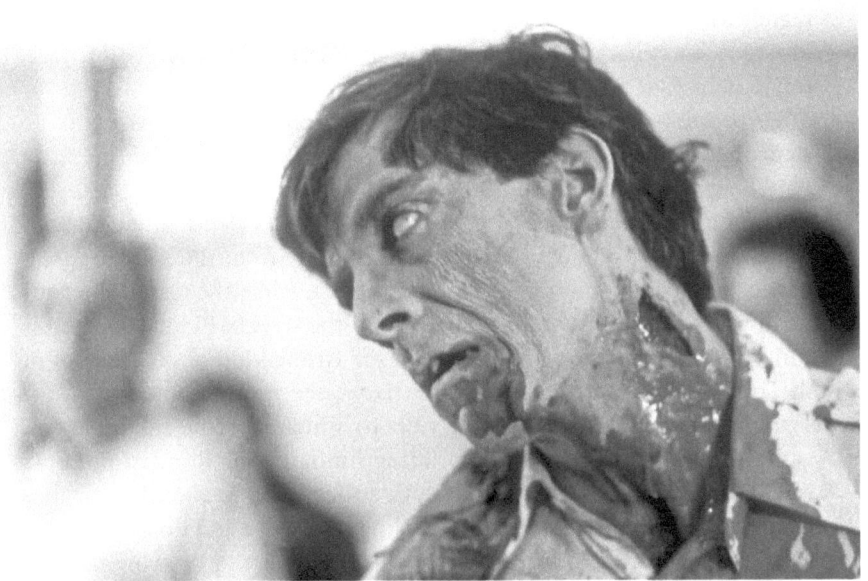

Stephen (David Emge) becomes a zombie in *Dawn of the Dead* (1979).

past lives. This demonstrates how humanity has been reduced and how civilization is ultimately futile.

For it is the zombies, characterized in the film by an expert on the television as "nothing but pure, motorized instinct," who always triumph. The humans' attempts to fight them and rebuild society always fail because, like the zombies, they are not communal but rather selfish and self-serving beings. The inability of the human survivors in Romero's films to work together is continually highlighted.

For example, in *Day of the Dead* (1985), human relations are shown to have completely disintegrated: the protagonists are not trying to save each other, they are using each other. Even though they are bound by a common enemy, the military characters assert their dominance over the others through brute force. They may keep the other characters around for their skills in medicine and so on, but they really need them in order to illustrate their superior hierarchical status.

Even the sanctity of the family is broken. For instance, in *Night of the Living Dead* (1968) a mother, father and young daughter come to the cabin to escape the zombies. Once inside, the father tries to retain his dominant

Part One: The Monster in Horror

position, bullying and shouting at his family and the others. Yet he is ultimately killed by his own daughter: only as a zombie can she escape from him and assert her own dominance. What these situations reveal is that, implicit in Sade's proposal of isolism, there is a fundamental need for other people — in the sense that if one is to dominate, there needs to be someone who is dominated.

This idea is continued in the more recent installments in the series. In *Land of the Dead* (2005) we see a society that is clearly divided, with those who are rich and powerful secluded away from the zombie threat in the planned community of Fiddler's Green, while the rest of the population is forced to fight for their lives on the streets. Fiddler's Green is run by Kaufman, who strives to keep "the wrong kind of people" out of the area. Meanwhile, out on the streets we see an amusement park (of sorts) where people indulge their vices by watching topless dancers and gambling on zombie fights with living human bait. Romero presents isolism in action here, a post-apocalyptic society where people feel no allegiance to each other and are all struggling to survive and dominate. This is in direct contrast to the zombies, who are shown to be evolving, and who actually begin to band together rather than turning on each other as the living humans do. The isolism of the zombies has, in fact, been surpassed by the sadism and selfishness of humanity.

The role of the media within a society in which people are becoming more distanced from each other is explored in *Diary of the Dead* (2007). Shot in the increasingly prevalent "found footage" style popularized by *The Blair Witch Project* (Daniel Myrick and Eduardo Sanchez, 1999), this film demonstrates how people are isolated from each other through their escalating engagement with reality through a camera or a screen, at the expense of actual physical interaction. The film ends with a mock youtube video showing two rednecks shooting zombies, culminating in a shot of a female zombie who is tied to a tree by her hair and shot in the face. As Kim Newman notes in his review, this scene "revives the Vietnam-era violence of *Night* but also evokes new horrors such as Abu Ghraib and Guantánamo."[19] What is referenced here are recent real-life incidents of torture and sadism which have been perpetrated by Americans in order to preserve the "American" way of life. What is significant is that the voiceover spoken over this scene asks the question: Are we really worth saving? As with all the films of his series, Romero seems to be suggesting that humans naturally use power to dominate and violate others, rather than seeking to help those who are weak or different. Unlike Sade, Romero sees this as an indictment

2. Zombies

of humanity (as well as an indictment of actual events within recent American history), while Sade sees this as a natural fact that should be embraced.

As these examples demonstrate, Romero has presented a universe which operates at a base Sadean level, where people are separated into master and slave in a world that bids one eat or be eaten. In *Dawn of the Dead*, the only contact that the four protagonists have with other living humans comes at the end of the film when an unruly motorcycle gang bursts into the mall and attempts to take over. Like the army characters in *Day of the Dead*, they are interested not in cooperation but in domination. In retaliation, while the gang is busy trashing the mall and looting the stores, the protagonists shoot at them. The protagonists must protect themselves even more actively from the gang than from the zombies, for the gang is the more savage opponent: they are armed with guns; and, while the zombies kill for food, the gang torments them for fun, throwing pies into the zombies' faces and spraying them with seltzer bottles.

Romero himself has remarked, "In my films the villains are always the living."[20] In Romero's films the humans transgress the laws of civilization even more than the "living dead" zombies. In a Sadean universe such as Romero's, true monstrosity is always found within humanity. The zombie in Romero's films thus acts as an indictment of the current state of humanity. In a world where civilization has crumbled and human relations have failed, the arrival of the zombie signals a return to instinct, a state where primal aggression and selfish survival reign supreme. For Sade, such an upheaval would return relations to a more natural state, a state of isolism. In isolism one thinks or acts upon one's own needs and desires; other people are needed, but only to be used and dominated. In Romero's films, in which civilization is destroyed, the human survivors have no choice but to rely on these long-repressed instincts for survival.

However, this *regression* from civilization to nature is actually viewed as a *progression* in a Sadean universe. This is because what is defined as "regression" in a real human subject in psychoanalytical terms can be understood as a progressive and creative (insofar as it is transgressive) transformation. This Sadean interpretation of regression as progressive is taken even further in the next chapter through the discussion of the werewolf.

3

Werewolves

Given Sade's construction of behavior in nature and the animal kingdom, the libertines in his narratives view themselves as not only being above the misled masses but also as a different species. In the werewolf film this idea of the transformation of a person into a different species is dramatized through the hybridization of a human and a wolf, an animal synonymous with violent instinct and lustful drives. The acquisition of wolf characteristics leads the character to become something other than human — unnatural but embodying the primal, natural drives. In this sense the werewolf can also be understood as a Sadean being — that is, as a creature of instinct who through transgression of natural law transforms itself into something completely other. This transgression places the werewolf outside of society, as the werewolf represents all that society seeks to repress.

While the vampire and zombie gain power by transgressing the borders of life and death, the werewolf is still mortal but able to wield great power. This power comes from embracing one's "animal" nature, a part of ourselves that is denied in order to function in civilized society. In the figure of the werewolf the idea of animal nature is expressed in sexual and violent behavior that may bring us momentary gratification but which in "normal" subjects is repressed so that social order is maintained.

Not unlike the Sadean libertine, who chooses to subvert all these restrictions and live outside of society, those cursed with the bite of a werewolf are no longer able to control these urges and become a different species altogether. Their loss of the markers of civilization is symbolized by the assumption of the characteristics of the wolf, a creature that represents the "wild" and the predatory. W. Herz summarizes the connotations of the wolf:

> If we now consider the wolf ... that insatiably murderous beast of prey, especially dangerous at night and in winter, he would appear to be the natural symbol of night, of winter, and of death.... But the wolf is not only the most

3. Werewolves

bloodthirsty, he is also the swiftest and lustiest of our larger quadrupeds. This hardiness, his fierce boldness, his cruel lust for fight and blood, together with his hunger for the flesh of corpses which makes him a night visitor of battlefields, make the wolf the companion of the God of Battles.[1]

Characterized as a wild beast, "insatiably murderous," "bloodthirsty," "the swiftest and lustiest," and "fierce," the wolf follows its instincts for sex and blood. While Herz's comment may not necessarily state the truth about actual wolves, it nevertheless summarizes how the wolf has been portrayed in mythology and traditional representation. And it is this view of the wolf that continues to shape the representation of the werewolf in both literature and films. Through the Sadean analysis of two of these werewolf texts, the transgression of the werewolf can be interpreted as an expression of nature, which can be understood as a positive progression away from societal repression.

Growing Pains: The Company of Wolves

In Neil Jordan's *The Company of Wolves* (1985), the hybrid nature of the werewolf is an analogue of the dual nature of adolescence, in which there are elements of both the child and the adult (the transgressive nature of the adolescent is further explored in Part Three). The film is constructed as the dream of the protagonist, Rosaleen; and while the mise-en-scène reflects her childlike view of the world, the narrative itself is one of curiosity about adult sexuality.

In this view, the torments of lycanthropy reflect the torments of puberty. Rosaleen is ultimately seduced by a werewolf, a symbol of her acceptance of sexual maturity, which is potentially both dangerous and pleasurable. To become adult one must also become a wolf. The wolf thus represents the sexual instincts awakened at this time of life. The coincidence of the awakening of the werewolf with the awakening of sexuality corresponds to Sade's view that sexual desire is linked to feelings of aggression. The transgression of the werewolf is therefore also a regression, as the person is reduced to a primal, animal state. However, as stated earlier, this psychoanalytical view of regression conflicts with the Sadean perspective, in which it is seen as a progression.

The connections between lycanthropy and puberty have been consistently highlighted in several werewolf films. The first to do this was the B-movie *I Was a Teenage Werewolf* (Gene Fowler Jr., 1957), which combined elements of horror with the "teen explosion" occurring at the time, so that film was marketed chiefly to teenagers who were flocking to the drive-ins. As Jonathan Ross states, the film was "like a low-budget, black-and-white remake of *Rebel Without a Cause* [Nicholas Ray, 1955], with fangs, brawls and dancing to rock'n'roll."[2] The figure of the teenage werewolf is also the focus of *Teen Wolf* (Rod Daniel, 1985), in which the character of Scott Howard, who complains of feeling "average," discovers that the men in his family have the ability to change into werewolves, a secret that, when revealed to his classmates, is a ticket to fame and popularity. In *Ginger Snaps* (John Fawcett, 2000) a teenage girl, Ginger, is bitten by a werewolf on the same day that she begins to menstruate; and as she transforms into a werewolf, she becomes correspondingly more violent and sexually aggressive.[3]

In these films the process of becoming a werewolf heightens the physical and emotional changes of puberty. Instead of growing pubic hair, hair begins to grow all over the body, and mood swings have the potential to become murderous rages. As John Landis, director of *An American Werewolf in London* (1981), explains:

> Essentially, it's an erection metaphor. A lot of it has to do with adolescence.... The whole thing of metamorphosis, when your body is changing — that's what puberty is about. You're getting hairy. All of a sudden, your dick is getting hard. All of a sudden, these weird things are happening to you. And you're hungry, you're horny, and your hormones are raging.[4]

Like Sade's incorporation of violence into his stories of sexual exploration, the werewolf narrative also highlights how the awakening of the sexual instinct awakens the instincts for aggression and dominance, an idea explored in his work *Philosophy in the Bedroom*.

The changes of adolescence are something one has no control over, changes that turn one from a child into someone else: an adult. While this metamorphosis is a slow and gradual process over a period of years, the metamorphosis into the wolf is shown in the key transformation scene that is a part of all werewolf films. These scenes are usually triumphs of special effects, showing how a human can turn into another creature before our very eyes. Each movie puts its own spin on how the transformation occurs, but there is one technique that is used in almost every transformation sequence: the close-up. The close-up serves to fragment the body so that attention is focused on one part as it changes: for example, nails grow and become claws, incisors become fangs, the ears lengthen into

3. Werewolves

pointed canine ears, hairs sprout and grows all over, the face elongates into a muzzle. The close-up makes every change a spectacle, revealing the full extent to which the body has been changed from human to animal.

Furthermore, as with Fulci's zombie films, the close-up in the werewolf movie focuses attention on the site of transgression. This focus echoes in cinematic form Sade's literary strategy of fragmenting and destroying the body of the victim, while also focusing on parts of the bodies of his libertines, in order to illustrate their power and dominance. For example, much is made of the penis size of his male libertines, most of them being in possession of impressively large members. For instance, in *The 120 Days of Sodom* the Duc de Blangis' physical attributes symbolize his position of power:

> That *dreadful colossus* did indeed make one think of a Hercules or a *centaur*; Blangis stood 5 feet 11 inches tall, had limbs of great strength and energy, powerful sinews ... the strength of a *horse*, the member of a veritable *mule*, *wondrously hirsute*, blessed with the ability to eject its sperm any number of times within a given day and at will ... a virtually constant erection in this member whose dimensions were an exact 8 inches for circumference and 12 for length overall.[5]

This statement demonstrates how Sade's choices of terms reference the animal or bestial character of this man, as well as the monstrous nature of his features. Description and emphasis on body parts increases their significance.

In the werewolf narrative the close-up serves to illustrate the power and transgression of the transformation, a feature that is implicit in Sade's character description, which focuses on each separate body part. Through this perspective, both the werewolf and the libertine become bigger and stronger, more powerful and more dangerous. The transformation scene in the werewolf film focuses on the claws and teeth — that is, on the werewolf's new capacity to cause hurt and damage to others. This scene represents the annihilation of those boundaries and signs of the human.

The Company of Wolves is set in an exaggerated, purposely fake fairytale world, taking much of its storyline from the folk tale "Little Red Riding Hood," a story that details the meeting between an innocent young girl and the Big Bad Wolf. At the climax of the tale the wolf disguises itself as the girl's grandmother in order to get close to her and eat her up. The grandmother represents the older generation which seeks to impose its morality and values upon the young. Due to her advanced age, the grandmother is perceived as sexless, while the wolf is forceful and lusty. She is replaced by the werewolf, and the young girl must defeat the wolf (that is, the forces of nature), or she will be consumed by it. While in the traditional folk tale the wolf is killed, in *The Company of Wolves* Rosaleen ultimately becomes a wolf herself. With the narrative taking on a Sadean turn, the girl will not deny the desires and urges that her meeting with the wolf has aroused in her. Rather, she will embrace them fully and in doing so will become transformed into a new, bestial being.

In Sade, indeed, the figure of the older, maternal woman represents the repression of sexuality, a repression that she tries to force onto the young women in her care. *Philosophy in the Bedroom*, which dramatizes a young woman's introduction to carnal delight, climaxes with the daughter's violation and destruction of her mother. Eugénie rapes her mother with a dildo and then sews up her vagina. As Angela Carter, author of the study *The Sadeian Woman*, as well as the short story on which the film *The Company of Wolves* is based, states, "[S]he must effectively annihilate her mother's sexuality before she herself can be free."[6] Eugénie does to her mother what the latter wanted to do to Eugénie—force her to act as though her vagina was closed up. For Eugénie, this act of rebellion is a triumph: "Here I am: at one stroke incestuous, adulterous, sodomite, and all that in a girl who only lost her maidenhead today!"[7] With this act of violence she has thrown off her mother's control over her. She has transformed and become a transgressive body, as she has systematically transgressed all the sexual taboos of her time (incest, bisexuality, group sex, sodomy, rape).

Similarly, in *The Company of Wolves*, transgression causes Rosaleen's body to change, as she assumes the form of a wolf. Both of these stories depict the bodily changes of puberty as transgressive, with sexual awakening accompanied by violence and the destruction of a mother figure (Rosaleen chooses to join the werewolf who kills her grandmother). Through Sade's ideas, the transformation in *The Company of Wolves* can be read as an act of defiance against societal normativity and repression. In the film, transgression brings Rosaleen power, pleasure and freedom.

On the other hand, Rosaleen's grandmother teaches the girl to be wary of sex, warning her that "a wolf may be more than he seems. He may come in many disguises.... The worst kinds of wolves are hairy on the inside." All men are beasts; any man has the potential to be a wolf in disguise, as Granny repeatedly tells Rosaleen. Therefore, it is up to Rosaleen to control herself and not give in to their seductive wiles. Granny can thus be understood as representing denial and repression of the sexual appetite.

3. Werewolves

Accordingly, when she is killed by a werewolf he knocks off her head, which smashes as though made of porcelain. This symbolizes Granny's lack of flesh: even when she is opened up she is clean and hollow. She does not feel the desires of the flesh because she is not made of flesh.

This scene contrasts with the beheading of a werewolf earlier in the film, where the head lands in a bucket of milk and floats back up in human form, the blood turning the milk pink. This illustrates that although the werewolf is seen as a monster, he is ultimately just a flesh-and-blood man. His death in bodily fluids, blood and milk, is a visualization of his transgression. The werewolf confuses the insides and the outsides of the body, as its inner urges take on an outside form.

Earlier in the scene the man's transformation into werewolf had been precipitated by his tearing off of his flesh, revealing a skinless and bloody dog-like face. The body's fluids symbolize transgression, as they pass from the inside to the outside of the body. A source of disgust, they disturb boundaries and ideas of cleanliness and purity. Likewise, the libertines in Sade's novels, consciously transgressing all taboos, delight in playing with bodily fluids. His sexual scenes are awash with vomit, blood, urine and feces; his libertines see these fluids as an integral part of the sexual act. Not unlike Sade's fiction and the werewolf scene discussed above, all of the monsters in this chapter are visually associated with fluids, which constitute a powerful representation of their transgressive nature.

As well as fluids, Sade's sexual scenes are also stimulated by the telling of stories. Granny, too, teaches Rosaleen through the telling of tales, each of which she stresses as the absolute truth. Storytelling is an activity wherein adults instill in children certain lessons, as a way of teaching them about the world and how to behave in it. Granny uses stories to teach Rosaleen to be wary of men and wolves. However, in Sade's works many of his characters also tell stories—not to teach but to incite the listener, arouse their curiosity and inflame feelings of desire. In *The 120 Days of Sodom*, four prostitutes are hired for exactly this purpose—to tell stories of their past exploits just before the orgies commence. These stories are used to stir the imagination of the libertines while they are engaged in sexual activity.

All the stories told in *The Company of Wolves* are, of course, about werewolves, and they serve to arouse curiosity in Rosaleen. While it is Granny who first tells stories about wolves, by the end of the film Rosaleen has also become a storyteller, although a transgressive one. Two of the stories told (one by Granny and then one by Rosaleen) are set at weddings, the day when girls traditionally lose their virginity. That the wolf arrives at this time illustrates its connection to sexual awakening.

In these stories the wolf is symbolic of a more primal state. The transgression constituted by the werewolf leads to progression. In Rosaleen's wolf/wedding story a poor peasant girl shows up at the wedding of the aristocrat who has impregnated her and magically turns him and all of his fancy guests into wolves. They are then forced to live in the forest, and must serenade her and her baby each night. They have regressed to a primal form, which contrasts with their upper-class status but more adequately suits their behavior. Rosaleen's mother asks, "What would be the pleasure in that?" Rosaleen replies, "The pleasure will come from the feeling of power that she had." This statement certainly reveals a Sadean point of view. Power over others brings pleasure to the self.

The regression into werewolf brings its own potential for power, which mirrors the process that Eugénie goes through in *Philosophy in the Bedroom*. As Angela Carter explains, "[T]he purpose of the gathering is primarily this: to strip Eugénie of all her socialized virtues and to restore her to the primal and vicious state of nature. Her education has regression rather than maturation as its goal."[8] Of course, in Sadean terms regression from society to nature in fact becomes a positive progression. In following Sade, Carter presents puberty as a time when one's maturation implies that one also face one's primal instincts. Sade felt that one must answer this "call from nature"[9] and use the changing body as an instrument for its bidding. Thus, *The Company of Wolves* shows that in order to do this, one must progress to nature, denying humanity and fully embracing animality.

In *The Company of Wolves*, the body of the werewolf symbolizes the changes of adolescence, as well as the allure, and danger, of adult sexuality. In her dream Rosaleen becomes a wolf, and the film ends with a pack of wolves entering her bedroom, suggesting that she herself has come face-to-face with her own wolf nature. The change into wolf involves a change in the body, much like the changes Rosaleen will go through during puberty. In the werewolf narrative the awakening of sexual feelings also causes the heightening of other, more violent impulses. As in Sade's novels, transgression in the werewolf film also involves regression, which is in fact a progression, with both the werewolf and the libertine actively embracing nature and the realm of instinct. This is further investigated in Mike Nichols' *Wolf* (1994), in which regression is shown to be a positive and creative progression, a move that leads to the fulfillment of all that one desires.

3. Werewolves

The Young Groom (Stephen Rea) transforms from man to werewolf in *The Company of Wolves* (1985).

Will-to-Power: Wolf

While many werewolf films deal with the problems of adolescence, in Mike Nichols' *Wolf* the protagonist is undergoing a mid-life crisis. Here the process of becoming a werewolf provides a new lease on life for the browbeaten and aging Will Randall. The bite of the werewolf releases in him all the desires and impulses that he has been denying himself for so many years. By shaking off constraints on behavior, etiquette and fair play, Will achieves success at work and a renewed virility in the bedroom. The constraints of society are cast off, and the natural instincts of lust and aggression are embraced.

Though this leads to an improvement in Will's quality of life, the change in his behavior is due to a change in his body, a change that will ultimately remove him from society altogether. His transgressive body frees him from all that has beaten him down, but it is at the expense of his humanity. The experiences in this narrative of becoming werewolf mirror the Sadean libertine's casting off of societal constraints in order to

Part One: The Monster in Horror

achieve greater power and pleasure. In both *Wolf* and Sade's novels this process is a progression to a natural state, situating the subject as a predator at the top of the natural hierarchy.

We first meet Will when he is at his lowest point. His encounter with the wolf catalyses his rise to the top of the natural hierarchy, and also the corporate hierarchy (although Nichols demonstrates how the two are almost identical). Will works in publishing, is fast approaching retirement, and is increasingly out of touch with today's fast-paced corporate world. He is constructed as a meek and timid man: when his wife asks him how he got an author to sign a contract, his answer is "I begged." While attending a business function held by his boss, Mr. Alden (who is going to take over the publishing firm at which Will works, and is in charge of deciding who gets fired), he is referred to as "a man of taste and originality" and "a nice person," all of which is actually a "handicap" and leads to him being offered a job in Eastern Europe, "a job no one would want." To add to this humiliation, as Will walks away from the meeting with Alden, he suddenly experiences chest pains and is tended to by Alden's daughter, Laura. When he apologizes for his state, Laura asks, "What are you? The last civilized man?"

It is precisely his "civilized" behavior that has put Will at such a disadvantage in both his work and home life. His circumstances echo Sade's views of society as an oppressive force:

> As a human sentiment, virtue is not by any means spontaneous or naturally sanctioned; it is rather nothing but the sacrifice the obligation to live in society squeezes out of a man, an internal enforced sacrifice he makes to considerations the observation whereof will bring him, in return, a certain minimal pittance of happiness.[10]

Will's niceness and generosity have led to his being exploited by others. He has achieved a "minimal pittance of happiness" in that he has a comfortable but very mediocre existence. He goes against his own instincts of self-preservation and dominance in order not to rock the boat or to direct any unwanted attention to himself. In order to maintain his safe yet boring life, he represses his sexual desire for women by staying in a stale marriage, and suppresses his hateful feelings toward the work colleagues who betray him.

Will's personal sacrifices are precisely the sacrifices that, according to Freud, all civilized humans must make in order for society to function. Freud argues that in order for civilization to thrive, we must repress our base desires and instincts for lust and aggression: "Sublimation of instinct is an especially conspicuous feature of cultural development, it is what

3. Werewolves

makes it possible for higher psychical activities, scientific, artistic or ideological, to play such an important part in civilized life."[11] Through this repression and sublimation a person can instead devote him or herself to higher purposes and long-term goals which may bring with them wealth and success, but which, more importantly, reinforce the status quo and avoid the creation of tension or violence. But with this repression comes a certain unhappiness and, in some cases, neurosis.

Well before Freud's theories, Sade, too, was of the opinion that the repression of selfish instinct leads to a population that is weak, dissatisfied and unhappy. Pleasure can be gained only through the casting off of this repression. According to one of Sade's characters:

> Social ordinances in virtually every instance are promulgated by those who never deign to consult the members of society, they are restrictions we all of us cordially hate, they are common sense's contradictions: absurd myths lacking any reality save in the eyes of fools who don't mind submitting to them.[12]

Repression of instinct is thus something that has been instilled in us but which does not bring us pleasure. This is certainly how Will is presented in *Wolf*. Initially shown as a perfect example of the civilized man — which is another way of saying he is a wimp — he accepts his demotion and does not confront his supposed protégé, Stewart Swinton, when he realizes it is he who has stolen his job. At the expense of his own happiness he is willing to accept both the demotion and the betrayal in order to avoid the creation of conflict. He is a man who suppresses his aggression — as well as his lust.

Just as Landis stresses that his werewolf film was an erection metaphor, Nichols maintains that his film is also "about a hard-on."[13] In the beginning Will is represented as impotent: he loses his job and his wife cheats on him. It is only through his embracing of the wolf within that he finds the courage to fight for his job and pursue the young and beautiful Laura Alden. Throughout *Wolf* the "curse" of the werewolf is shown to be a gift, bringing with it a renewed vitality and virility for Will.

After sleeping for twenty hours, Will claims to feel "twenty years younger;" and after a night of lovemaking with his wife Charlotte, he walks into work and realizes that his senses have been acutely sharpened: he can smell alcohol on someone's breath, he can hear conversations in other rooms, and he no longer needs his glasses. When he returns home there is a message from his wife, who mentions "last night" and calls Will an "animal." This increased virility leads to increased dominance in all aspects of Will's life. He gains power through his wolf-ness, and by fol-

Part One: The Monster in Horror

lowing his instincts he finds success. In Sade's world this is the way that one rises to the top of the natural hierarchy.

It becomes clear that these changes are actually manifestations of desires that Will has always been harboring. The wolf is merely a reflection of the man. The changes in Will occur because he no longer suppresses a part of himself that was there all along. As Will is told, "The demon wolf is not evil, unless the man he has bitten is evil." It simply unleashes the animal part of the self; and since animals are creatures of instinct they are amoral, following the laws of nature. While under the influence of the wolf, Will is shown prowling through Central Park. With its grass and trees it is like a small jungle within the heart of the city. It is in this place that natural law still prevails. At night the park is populated by street gangs, people who rule with violence. Will is confronted by a gang who demands his wallet and begins to attack him. That Will retaliates with violence may be explained by his instinct for self-preservation.

As Will attacks, the rapid editing highlights both the swiftness and the exhilaration of what is essentially a "hunt" (an instinct earlier explored when Will chased and brought down a deer on Laura's property)—for

Will Randall (Jack Nicholson) behind bars in *Wolf* (1994).

3. Werewolves

surely prowling in the park at night in New York is an invitation to trouble and violence. Perhaps, along with "instinct," there is also a desire on Will's part to seek out danger. As Sade writes, instinct is driven by the need to feel pleasure—for Will, going on the hunt satisfies certain urges, with both power and pleasure gained from the experience.

What *Wolf* and most other werewolf narratives ultimately show is that while the wolf is a creature capable of violence, it is no match for the evil that men (and women) are capable of when they, too, tap into this instinctual aggression. As Freud attests, "The element of truth behind all this, which people are so ready to disavow, is that men are not gentle creatures who want to be loved. *Homo homini lupus*— man is a wolf to man."[14] The characteristics of the wolf should be more properly attributed to ourselves. In *Civilization and Its Discontents* Freud presents a Sadean view of humankind in its natural, instinctual state. Without the constraints of civilized society, humans become vicious and brutal. We do not naturally seek to help others; we instead think of how we can take what the other has, whether it be his or her body or possessions.

This view of mankind is identical to a quote from Sade's *Juliette*:

> The more atrocious the hurt he inflicts upon the helpless, the greater shall be the voluptuous vibrations in him; injustice is his delectation, he glories in the tears his heavy hand wrings from the unlucky; the more he persecutes him, the happier the despot feels, for it is now that he makes the greater use of the gifts Nature has bestowed upon him.[15]

For Sade, the only things that stops us from going forth and acting on these desires is legal retribution and our own conscience (although Sade feels this aspect of the self has been instilled in us by outside forces).

Once Will opens up to his instinct and acts upon it, it precipitates a change that will see him unable to return to civilized life. When forced to fight for the life of Laura, Will turns to the wolf side of his nature in order to save her from Stewart, who is also turning into a wolf. By using his wolf side to save her, Will is in a sense sacrificing himself, as it is the full moon (the point when the wolf has the power to take over both body and mind). By taking Stewart's life and committing murder, Will sets himself outside society. If he stays, he will be incarcerated. Will instead turns into a wolf completely and runs into the woods. The film ends with the Sadean suggestion that Will and Laura (who is also revealed to be turning into a wolf) might have a better chance at happiness by leaving this hectic world, progressing to nature and becoming animal.

Part Two

Monstrous Humans

Like the monster, the monstrous human is both threatening and impure, but it hides its monstrous behavior behind a face that is undeniably, and unexceptionally, human. Because it perpetrates violence and sexual transgression in order to satisfy its own selfish desires, the monstrous human has no consideration for the law or the wellbeing of others. Sade's writing suggests that such behavior causes a cycle of transgression to be put into effect, one transgression always leading to another: transgression of body leads to transgression of behavior and transgression of societal law.

Sade's libertines give no thought to ideas of the soul and instead live life through the body, listening only to their desires for corporeal satisfaction and pleasure. Having transgressed with their bodies, the libertines see themselves as different from those who are perceived as normal. They feel that they are no longer subject to the laws that govern the masses, and use their bodies to further transgress societal taboos. The monstrous human can be understood as also following this pattern of behavior. The transgressive bodies examined in this part partake in the repetition of acts defined as taboo, whether it be the willful murder of another human, the eating of human flesh, or the participation in new and dangerous sexual acts.

4

Serial Killers

The serial killer is a relatively new addition to the horror genre, which has risen to popularity over the past three decades. The serial killer film first came to prominence in the 1960s with the release of Michael Powell's *Peeping Tom* (1960) and, more notably, Alfred Hitchcock's *Psycho* (1960). These two films set the precedent for how the serial killer is portrayed onscreen: not grotesque in the manner of the zombie or werewolf, but a completely normal human being. Just as Sade's libertines are pillars of society whose wealth and status allows them to indulge themselves in secrecy, it is this appearance of normalcy that allows the serial killer to continue his or her murderous rampage.[1]

The serial killer is different from the killers found in slasher films. For example, in both *The Texas Chainsaw Massacre* (Tobe Hooper, 1974) and *Friday the 13th* (Sean S. Cunningham, 1980) the killers wear masks and wield huge, phallic weapons (a chainsaw and a machete, respectively), picking off individually anyone (usually oversexed teens) who enters their territory. In contrast, the cinematic serial killer is often based on research into real serial killers, defined by Mark Seltzer as those "associated with the killings of at least four victims, over a period greater than seventy-two hours."[2] Seltzer adds that a "'cooling off period'—distributing the murders repetitively and serially over time—has come to provide the working distinction between serial and mass murder."[3]

Likewise, Sade's libertines also engage in a "cooling off period," during which they carefully plan and execute their misdeeds. Thus, through the lens of Sadean philosophy, serial murder can be read as a sexual act. While Leatherface and Jason continue their slaughter until everyone around them is killed, the serial killer plans and pre-meditates, carefully choosing a victim and slowly building up the thirst for the kill, so that the murder itself is like the climax of an orgasm. In fact, as both *American Psycho* (Mary Harron, 2000) and *Henry: Portrait of a Serial Killer* (John

4. Serial Killers

McNaughton, 1990) illustrate, for the serial killer the repeated act of murder becomes the only means of sexual expression.

The Serial Killer as Sovereign Man: American Psycho

Patrick Bateman in *American Psycho* is represented as having it all: wealth, a good job, friends, good looks and a well-toned body. However, the film goes on to reveal that it is precisely these things that make Patrick a monster, a serial killer who can feel satisfaction only through the act of murder. His lifestyle of wealth and excess has numbed Patrick to feelings of compassion or empathy, his status at the top of the social hierarchy encouraging him to view those beneath him as less than human, playthings that he can use at his leisure. Patrick thus personifies what Georges Bataille and Maurice Blanchot define as the Sadean idea of the sovereign man.

Patrick's all-consuming apathy, which only increases with each killing rather than being released by it, is seen in many true-life serial killers, as well as reflecting that of the libertines of Sade's fictions. In fact, both the serial killer and the Sadean libertine feel no kinship with other people; rather, they view themselves as above the masses, as being sovereign over them. As Maurice Blanchot states:

> Sade's cast of characters is composed primarily of a tiny number of omnipotent men who have had the energy and initiative to raise themselves above the law and place themselves outside the pale of prejudice, men who feel that Nature has singled them out and, feeling themselves worthy of this distinction, strive to assuage their passions by any and all means.[4]

This state of being sovereign, whereby one is not equal to others but superior, requires that other people "are to be victims, not partners."[5]

This idea is exemplified by a scene in which Patrick has sex with two prostitutes. He gives the girls names that he will call them by, as their real names are completely irrelevant. He sets up a camera and directs their actions: they are to do exactly as he says. Yet, for all the trouble he takes to control what the girls do, it becomes apparent that the girls are really not that important. They are merely objects used to make Patrick appear more attractive to the camera. In one shot, as Patrick is thrusting away, he constantly looks at himself in the mirror next to his bed, pointing at himself, flexing his muscles, trying to find the most perfect angle that shows his body to full effect, as if he were getting himself off on his own image.

That the women are victims and not equal partners is further realized when Patrick declares that they are "not through yet" and gets out a wire coat hanger and a box of surgical instruments. In the next shot the girls leave his apartment, one storming out angrily and the other walking dazedly with a bloodied nose, while Patrick looks nonchalant. As a sovereign man, Patrick is able to abuse those of a lower class for the purpose of sexual satisfaction. Indeed, murder and the sexual mistreatment of women are his main criminal activities.

This scene illustrates that, due to his emotional detachment, the sovereign man must turn to more extreme pursuits in order to achieve satisfaction. For Sade, the one activity that is certain to provide this pleasure and excitement is crime: "Crime is the soul of lust. What would pleasure be if it were not accompanied by crime? It is not the object of debauchery that excites us, rather the idea of evil."[6] Sade's libertines indulge in all manner of criminal activity, such as theft, rape, kidnapping and, on occasion, murder.

That Patrick turns to murder illustrates the numbing effect of his excessive lifestyle — he has to go to the extremes of taking another's life in order to feel. Like Sade's libertines, the pursuit of pleasure has led to Patrick being unable to feel it; when he is shown killing, Patrick is not shown as overly happy or joyful. While in the act of slaughtering his colleague Paul Allen with an axe, the camera is focused on Patrick throughout, as he chops down at Paul who is below the frame. As he hits Paul repeatedly, he shouts in anger, but as soon as he is finished he instantly regains his composure, removes his plastic coat, sits down and lights a cigar. Only the blood that has splattered on his face and the slight dishevelment of his hair betray what he has done. As he sits and smokes, a long shot shows Paul's bloody corpse on the floor, yet Patrick continues to puff away as though it is not even there. He does not look sated or satisfied; he looks as though he feels nothing at all.

Patrick's apathy increases to the point where he is unable to feel any emotion whatsoever. He himself admits in voiceover:

> There is an idea of Patrick Bateman, some kind of abstraction, but there is no real me, only an entity, something illusory. And though I can hide my cold gaze, and you can shake my hand and feel flesh gripping yours, and maybe you can even sense our lifestyles are probably comparable.... I simply am not there.

4. Serial Killers

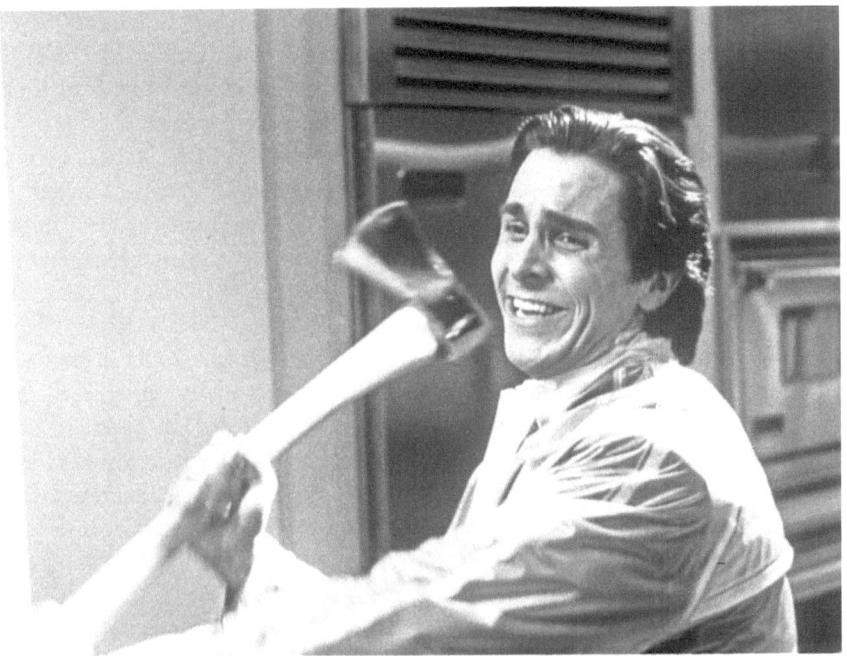

Patrick Bateman (Christian Bale) attacks in *American Psycho* (2000).

Although he is simply "not there," a trace of him remains: his physical, outward self. His surname, Bateman, not only refers to the character of Norman Bates from Hitchcock's *Psycho*, but also plays on the word "bait," for it is his appearance (toned body, designer clothes, perfect haircut, good manners) that he uses to bait and capture his (mostly female) victims.

Throughout the film, Patrick changes his personality from scene to scene. This is because he has no personality as such, and so is able to change himself to suit every situation. He contradicts himself constantly: while with his male friends he joins in on their derogatory comments about women; but when in mixed company he advocates equal rights for women, the homeless, and racial minorities. Yet, in a later scene, he taunts a homeless African-American man and stabs him to death. In one scene he shows he is capable of mercy when he chooses not to kill his secretary Jean, but he has no qualms about mistreating and then killing a prostitute. While in the act of killing, instead of realizing the magnitude of what he is doing, he lectures his victims on the merits of contemporary pop music

Part Two: Monstrous Humans

acts such as Phil Collins, Whitney Houston and Huey Lewis and the News, which illustrates the extent to which he has become numb to atrocity.

Furthermore, it becomes apparent that what is most important for Patrick in all of these situations is the way he looks. For the killing of Paul Allen, Patrick thinks ahead and covers his apartment with plastic sheeting and puts on a plastic raincoat, which will prevent any traces of evidence being left behind. Yet it is not difficult to see that Patrick is even more concerned with preventing blood from splattering his expensive couches and designer suit. For as his inner, emotional self has atrophied, Patrick has become obsessed with outward appearances.

Thus, Patrick can be understood as a transgressive body in that his body is all that he is, being all surface with no humanity underneath. As Patrick introduces himself in voiceover ("My name is Patrick Bateman. I'm twenty-seven years old"), a montage shows his daily beauty regime, which he narrates, listing all the products that he uses. This sequence shows off to full effect the perfect body that he has cultivated. His sovereignty is illustrated through his perfect exterior. For Patrick, events such as his daily workout or a trip to the solarium are as important to him as his nightly pursuit of blood and carnage. It is all a part of his routine of consumption.

This meaningless pattern of consumption — of both products and people — contributes to Patrick's lack of emotional depth. All of his desires and instincts, which in most people are repressed and hidden, can be followed through in the outside world. Patrick and his peers are part of the "yuppie" generation that flourished in America in the 1980s. Yuppies were young, rich businessmen and women whose wealth and youth meant that they were able to indulge all their heart's desires, whether for drugs, casual sex, cars, appliances or other material possessions. In this atmosphere of decadence and excess, greed, ruthlessness and selfishness were seen as admirable traits that one needed in order to be successful. *American Psycho*, both book and film, functions as a satire of this time, as it constructs Patrick Bateman as the epitome of the yuppie, with his good looks, high-paying job, and interests in popular music and designer clothes, but then reveals that this fine, upstanding young man is actually a serial killer, with bodies stashed all over his stylish apartment.

This use of satire connects *American Psycho* to Sade. Sade depicts a counter-society of libertines who, like the yuppies in *American Psycho*, have wealth and privilege that they use to satisfy their own selfish desires. However, they become locked into a cycle of repetitious transgression, with the cumulative effect being one of numbness rather than satisfaction.

4. Serial Killers

His characters never learn from this repetition, and descend further and further into it. Sade continues this repetition to an absurd degree: for example, Justine continually finds herself victimized by everyone she meets; the libertines in *The 120 Days of Sodom* find themselves committing ever more ridiculous atrocities.

Just as Patrick's killing becomes a part of his daily routine, the libertines' debaucheries also become intermingled with ordinary daily activities:

> Happily, the supper bell sounded, for the financier was getting ready to begin again. But the prospect of a meal changed the disposition of their Lordships' minds, they went to taste different pleasures. A few turds were lodged on a few bubs at the orgies, and a great deal of shit was gleaned from asses; within the assembly's full view, the Duc consumed Duclos' turd, while that splendid girl sucked him, and while the bawdy fellow's hands roamed here and there, his fuck came out in a thick spray; Curval having imitated him with Champville, the friends began to speak of retiring for the night.[7]

In this passage, coprophilia is intercut with the libertines being summoned for dinner and with chatter about when to go to bed. That the libertines indulge in such perversities involving bodily fluids within a strict order and routine serves to highlight the absurdity of the society they have created. It also serves to comment on the society that has created these people. These supposed exaggerations actually mirror society's own faults and inequalities. Satire is used in order to reveal how shallow Sade's libertines are, and this use of satire can be read in *American Psycho*. These people (both the libertines and the yuppies), held up as pillars of the community, are exposed as being completely despicable and apathetic.

However, this apathy and self-absorption, far from being only Patrick's trait, is seen in almost all of the characters in the film. Patrick repeatedly makes reference to his nocturnal activities, but everyone is so preoccupied with admiring his surface charm that they pay no attention. He confesses to Paul Allen, "I like to dissect girls. Did you know I'm utterly insane?" Paul then responds by complimenting Patrick on his "great tan." Later, when he is carrying Paul's body out of his building, he is seen by a work colleague who, rather than questioning his suspicious movements, instead gushes over the Jean-Paul Gaultier bag that the body is held in. Even when he makes a full confession on his lawyer's answering machine, it is ignored. Patrick has done such a good job of fitting in, he is seen as so "normal," that no one believes he would do anything so non-conformist (and unfashionable) as murder.

Part Two: Monstrous Humans

Patrick's perceived blandness results in him being constantly mistaken for other people: he really does seem like everyone else. When he tries to convince his lawyer that the confession is real, the lawyer calls Patrick "Davis" and refuses to believe him. With this dismissal, Patrick realizes he has succeeded in becoming a creature that is all surface and no depth. In voiceover he states, "[E]ven after admitting this, there is no catharsis. My punishment continues to elude me. And I gain no deeper knowledge of myself. No new knowledge can be extracted from my telling. This confession has meant nothing."

Although doubt is cast by the film as to whether Patrick is really committing the murders or just imagining them, this last statement encapsulates the idea of Patrick as a transgressive body because, as stated earlier, he is all body, all surface, with no humanity underneath. No one cares that he is a killer; he is free to continue without consequence, and so the act of killing becomes meaningless. Because there is no catharsis, no knowledge gained, and no punishment, Patrick is instead condemned to the endless repetition of his superficial routine of killing and consumption, the continuation of which will only lead to his being numbed even further because each repetitious act of murder serves only to negate his existence.

Patrick's story echoes Deleuze's assertion that the Sadean hero "appears to have set himself the task of thinking out the Death Instinct (pure negation) in a demonstrative form."[8] But the demonstration of the Death Instinct can only be achieved through repetition, and Patrick's life consists of a routine that is repeated day after day. Even though this routine involves the committing of heinous acts, that these acts are repeated over and over serves to drain them of meaning. Just as Patrick knows that his morning is not complete until he uses his facial scrub and does a certain number of sit-ups, so too is the day not complete without some kind of violent or criminal act. However, as his final monologue demonstrates, this routine of excess leads to nothing. In this perfect world, filled with young, beautiful professionals, there is no place for anything dark or violent. All such things are swept aside or kept hidden. Although everyone hears Patrick's confessions, they seem incapable of understanding them — or, for that matter, understanding anything outside their own routines of consumption.

Having surrendered himself completely to the selfish ideology which has since come to define the 1980s, he has, in fact, negated his own self. His indulgence of every single desire has led to complete apathy and an inability to feel. That he cannot get anyone to listen to or acknowledge his confessions, or even get someone to remember his name and recognize who he is, illustrates how excess and repetition has led to "pure negation." The irony at the heart of this Sadean satire is that the ultimate fate of the sovereign man is self-annihilation.

While *American Psycho* shows a character who conforms to the idea of the Sadean sovereign man, it also satirizes this concept, illustrating how the act of being sovereign is in itself an empty and numbing experience. Sade also uses satire in his works, with his characters becoming locked into a cycle of repetition with no end and no satisfaction. *American Psycho* shows that the continued excess of transgressive pleasure actually creates a numbing effect. Having situated himself above everyone else, and having no limits on behavior, Patrick has not become fulfilled, he has become a void. He is trapped in a cycle of transgression that will ultimately lead to his own negation. As he himself states, "I simply am not there."

The Lone Killer: Henry: Portrait of a Serial Killer

The serial killer has become monstrous because, through the repetition of violent acts, he or she seems to have lost all depth. As *American Psycho* demonstrates, excess leads to negation. By doing everything, the serial killer becomes nothing. He or she is a non-entity floating around with no connection to people or places. In *Henry: Portrait of a Serial Killer* the serial killer is a drifter, someone who roams from place to place, leaving in his wake a trail of bodies. He has no conscience and never realizes the destruction he causes. The film presents the serial killer as a person for whom the act of killing has become the only means of expressing both his emotional and sexual life.

Henry's lack of emotion is reflected through the filmic techniques used, techniques which evoke Sade's descriptions of the activities of his morally bankrupt characters. Both *Henry* and Sade's work are populated by characters who, devoid of emotion, seem completely empty inside. It is their emotional blankness which allows them to go through life committing the most outlandish atrocities. In order to represent this state of mind, the film's actions are presented plainly and matter-of-factly, with no commentary on the moral implications of such behavior.

In contrast to the slickness and glamour portrayed in the world of *American Psycho*, in John McNaughton's *Henry* the milieu in which the

Part Two: Monstrous Humans

serial killer lives and works is that of the lower working class. While Patrick Bateman is a character constructed to satirize the yuppie generation, the character of Henry is based on the real-life confessions of Henry Lee Lucas, a man who claimed to be a serial killer.[9] Hence, the aesthetics of the two films are vastly different: while *American Psycho* creates a world that is heightened and full of excess, *Henry* strives instead for gritty realism.

Henry provides a stark contrast to the majority of serial killer films from mainstream Hollywood, such as *Seven* (David Fincher, 1995), *Copycat* (Jon Amiel, 1995), *Taking Lives* (D.J. Caruso, 2004), *88 Minutes* (Jon Avnet, 2007), *Zodiac* (David Fincher, 2007) and, of course, the Hannibal Lecter trilogy (*The Silence of the Lambs* [Jonathan Demme, 1991], *Hannibal* [Ridley Scott, 2001] and *Red Dragon* [Brett Ratner, 2002]).[10] These films take the form of police procedurals, usually following the formula of a "whodunnit," the audience following the attempts to track down and imprison (and, in most cases, eliminate) the killer. In contrast, low-budget independent films such as *Ed Gein* (Chuck Parello, 2000), *Dahmer* (David Jacobson, 2002), *Gacy* (Clive Saunders, 2003), *Monster* (Patty Jenkins, 2004) and *Henry* eschew the police presence almost entirely (as soon as the cops arrive the film is practically over); rather, it is the killer him/herself who is the protagonist. The aim of the narrative is thus not to hunt down and capture the killer, but rather plainly to present the events of the killer's life. It is the body of the serial killer, and not the bodies that he or she disposes of, that is the focus of these films.

As discussed above, a consistent theme throughout these films (as well as in the fictional *American Psycho*) is the total apathy and emotional detachment of the killer. With no connection or attachment to any other human being, Henry is an example of someone who lives out Sade's idea of isolism, discussed earlier in relation to Romero's *Dawn of the Dead*, in that he has no attachment to other human beings. He has already killed his own mother and, during the course of the film, dispatches his best friend Otis, even though the latter is like-minded and shares Henry's love of the kill. Henry also murders Otis' sister, Becky, who has fallen in love with him. In fact, at the film's end Henry drives off alone, having effectively killed every other character in the movie.

When interacting with other characters, Henry is always represented as quiet, almost blank. Even while being romanced by Becky, or in the middle of a kill, Henry's face never registers a single emotion. His thoughts and emotional state remain completely hidden, with the same calm and controlled exterior retained in every scene. Even his dialogue tells us noth-

4. Serial Killers

ing. Like Patrick Bateman, Henry constantly contradicts himself: when asked about his mother, whom Henry freely admits to having killed, he tells Otis that he killed her with a baseball bat; but later, within the same conversation, he tells Becky that he stabbed her, and still later that he "shot her dead." But mostly Henry says nothing. As Philip L. Simpson attests, "We never do get a true sense of the how or why of a Henry Lucas, as promised by McNaughton's deliberately misleading title."[11] By being both silent and blank, Henry becomes a screen onto which people project whatever it is that they need. In the same heart-to-heart when he admits to killing his mother, Becky nonetheless tells Henry that it is "sure good to talk to you.... 'Cause I know you're not judgmental.... I feel like I've known you forever and ever."

But Henry seems to shy away from sexual contact, and it is always Becky who is the initiator. He also constantly admonishes Otis for his inappropriate sexual advances toward Becky, and even stops him from taking advantage of their prospective victims. That killing has taken the place of the sexual act for Henry is demonstrated in his first onscreen kill, in the back seat of a car after he and Otis pick up two hookers. Although what is taking place is unclear, there are sounds of what appears to be sexual activity. As the camera tracks by the car window, however, we see that Henry is strangling the girl he is with. Instead of a sexual climax Henry seems to prefer the moment of the kill. This is an unmistakably Sadean representation: Sade's works illustrate that the incorporation of violence into the sexual scenario escalates until death and murder replace the "little death" of the orgasm.

Even Henry's potentially redemptive relationship with Becky is to end in murder: after catching Otis raping Becky, Henry kills Otis and disposes of his body. Henry and Becky then take to the road and profess their love for each other. Once at the motel, Henry looks at himself in the mirror, and the camera tracks to the bedroom where Becky is sleeping. This is the moment where Henry has the choice of starting a new, normal life. Yet, instead of a tender love scene, the film suddenly cuts to the next morning, and Henry is shown leaving the motel alone. He later stops on a desolate road, gets a bag from the trunk of his car, dumps it and drives away. As the camera tracks in, it becomes apparent that the bag holds Becky's body. Instead of sexual and romantic love, Henry has chosen to continue his life of drifting and serial murder.

This bleak ending, together with Henry's complete blankness throughout the film, expresses the film's distinct lack of a moral conscience and,

Part Two: Monstrous Humans

Henry Lee Lucas (Michael Rooker) in *Henry: Portrait of a Serial Killer* (1990).

indeed, complete absence of consciousness. With no voiceover, as in *American Psycho*, and no scenes that show Henry feeling remorse for his actions, we are given no insight into Henry's inner life. In fact, Henry's and the film's lack of subjectivity mirror each other in their excessive and heightened corporeality. This unemotional approach contravenes traditional literary and filmic narratives, which often promise such an insight. Instead, *Henry* reflects Sade's writing style in his novels. Sade himself states in his essay "Reflections on the Novel": "Avoid the affectation of moralizing: it has no place in a novel."[12] In *The 120 Days of Sodom*, for instance, Sade simply describes chronologically what takes place in the sexual scenes, offering no comment on how the people involved in the scenario (such as the adolescents who were kidnapped and forced to take part in such events) react or feel. The book ends with a table showing the number of people who were massacred and those who survived, as well as a list of the days that each of the victims was dispatched.[13]

The writing style and elements such as the table create the feeling that the events have been documented and studied by a distant and scientific observer. Likewise, in *Henry* the use of filmic technique creates the effect of a distant observer documenting events. *Henry* ends with the only redeemable character, the too-trusting Becky, dead and dumped on the

4. Serial Killers

side of the road, her killer still on the loose. Henry doesn't get his comeuppance; nor is he made to pay for his crimes. In fact, the film ends with Henry released from any human entanglements and completely free to keep on killing.

It is this moral neutrality (or, even, lack of any moral discourse whatsoever) that led to *Henry* originally being refused a rating in the United States. John McDonough wrote at the time:

> In movies, bad seeds must still suffer, at least through a final reckoning with their conscience. Because Henry the killer cannot feel compassion, he cannot suffer. He is beyond the reach of moral self-awareness. When he kills his girlfriend at the end as coolly as he's dispatched a slew of strangers, the audience is denied its catharsis. The issue, in the eyes of the rating board, wasn't breasts, genitals, or even violence. Most of Henry's killings are off screen anyway. The issue was the film's attitude of neutrality toward Henry.[14]

Thus, McNaughton presents the events in the film plainly, just as Sade simply describes the events in *The 120 Days of Sodom*. Absent are the tricks or techniques commonly used in cinema to provide clues as to the emotional state of the character, or as to how the director perceives (and therefore how the audience is also supposed to perceive) the character's actions. Everything is played out in front of the camera in long takes, with no interference from post-production effects such as music, editing or special effects. Henry's final departure at the end of the film is shown in a matter-of-fact manner, with a long shot that plainly shows Henry opening the trunk of his car, taking out the suitcase that holds Becky's body, dumping it by the side of the road and driving away. No close-ups are used to portray Henry's emotional state, and no non-diegetic music or sound is used as a way to cue the audience as to how they should be feeling about the events. The ending can be understood as a filmic counterpart to the ending of *The 120 Days of Sodom*, for just as the libertines are the only ones who leave the château alive, Henry also is seen leaving the town, having disposed of those he has used for his pleasure.

By the film's end, Henry is still the same person he was at the beginning. Not even the promise of love can change him. Unlike most film protagonists, he does not have a character arc: it is more like a flat line. That the film around him provides no comment on his behavior, that it leaves him before he either finds a conscience or is captured by the forces of justice, differentiates it from most other film narratives. It is, rather, closer to the morally neutral narrative structure of Sade. As I have argued, both Sade and McNaughton employ narrative techniques that emphasize the

Part Two: Monstrous Humans

events in the story over the emotional lives of the characters, which demonstrates that the characters have no emotional life. This supports the chapter's proposition that repetition drives transgression, since it is through the repetition of violent events, and not through the engagement with other characters, that both Henry and the Sadean libertine gain sexual pleasure. The figure of the serial killer also demonstrates that this repetition of transgression is a rejection of society and its rules and laws, an idea which will be expanded in the "Cannibals" chapter to follow, where this shift away from society becomes a shift toward nature.

5

Cannibals

In contrast to the serial killer, where murder is a cold and calculated process, for the cannibal the kill is driven by the instinct for violence and the need to satisfy hunger. Just as the Sadean libertine casts off societal constraints in pursuit of the ultimate sexual pleasure, cannibals are also compelled by base desires which must be satisfied. In being a body untouched by civilization, which has retained its instinctual roots (even when it appears in the guise of the most cultured aesthete), the cannibal is a Sadean transgressive body. Cannibals were originally depicted as symbols of the primitive, beings who were unable to repress their instincts and drives, and so could not participate in civilized society. Through the act of cannibalism he or she transgresses one of modern society's most powerful taboos, for in the ingestion of the flesh of another human, the boundary separating one human from another is transgressed and dissolved. This transgression of body is also a transgression of law: even though the cannibal satisfies the need to eat in order to survive, unlike those who eat the meat of animals, he or she is perceived as a murderer, someone who has killed another human being for selfish purposes. The cannibal has repeatedly transgressed to the point that they are completely outside of society and instead exist in a state of nature.

This is illustrated by the fact that cannibals were initially represented in films as being completely untouched by civilization, whether as native tribes from the jungle, as in *Last Cannibal World*, or as people who live in desolate and unpopulated areas of developed countries, such as *The Hills Have Eyes* (Wes Craven, 1977; Alexandre Aja, 2006) and *Motel Hell* (Kevin Connor, 1980). In recent years, the taboo of cannibalism has been broken by increasingly significant figures in society, culminating in the widely popular figure of Dr. Hannibal Lecter, who is shown to have a fierce intellect as well as a fierce appetite. Even while cooking the brain of a still living human, he prepares it in gourmet style and ensures that all proper etiquette is maintained at the table. But, as the figure of Lecter shows, even those who have acquired the trappings of civilization and high culture may be subject to the same burning desires and instinctual cravings as people who are not as highly regarded. Likewise, Sade portrays his libertines as cultured beings who are, nonetheless, paradoxically close to nature and to the primal instinctual drives. By applying Sadean philosophy in the analysis of the figure of the cannibal, the forces of a brutal and transgressive nature can be seen to lie within every human. This is shown to be the case in Ruggero Deodato's *Last Cannibal World*, which dramatizes how a man who represents Western capitalist society, when confronted with the full force of nature and its urges, is capable of the most heinous transgression.

Getting Back to Nature: Last Cannibal World

The figure of the cannibal came to prominence within the horror genre in the early 1980s with the release of several cannibal films from Italy. With sensationalistic names, such as *Cannibal Apocalypse* (Antonio Margheriti, 1980), *Cannibal Holocaust* (Ruggero Deodato, 1981), *Cannibal Ferox* (Umberto Lenzi, 1981; also known as *Make Them Die Slowly*) and *Last Cannibal World*, these films are set in the untamed jungles of Asia or South America, pitting travelling Westerners against savage cannibal tribes. Reinforcing racial stereotypes, the cannibals in these films are portrayed as brutal and uncivilized people living in, as is claimed in *Last Cannibal World*, "Stone Age conditions." The cannibals are not subject to the same laws and taboos as those who venture into their territory — namely, they do not follow the taboo against the eating of human flesh. However, the European and American protagonists of these films are also shown in an unfavorable light — as greedy opportunists who come to the jungle in order to plunder it.

At some point during the narrative the tourists suddenly find themselves at the mercy of their surroundings, either through injury, the failure of technology, or, in the case of *Cannibal Holocaust*, their own evil deeds. Once they are lost in the jungle and vulnerable to the elements, there is a power struggle between the native inhabitants and the white intruders. In *Last Cannibal World* the main protagonist, Robert Harper, travels to the island of Mindanao in search of oil. After a crash landing he finds that the crew he had sent to work there some time earlier is now missing. He soon realizes that the crew fled from the cannibal tribe that lives in the jungle, who are referred to as "the last cannibals left in the world." After

5. Cannibals

the tribe kills and eats the pilot and his daughter, and he loses his companion Ralph in some river rapids, Robert finds himself alone and lost. When he awakes after passing out from eating poisonous mushrooms, he finds himself surrounded by the tribe and is taken prisoner.

Last Cannibal World focuses on the brutality and cruelty of the natural surroundings, where inhabitants are reduced to an existence based on instinct and the fulfillment of desires both physical and sexual. The film's narrative in this respect follows Sade's philosophy of nature, with the cannibal being a transgressive body driven by instinct and the immediate satisfaction of hungers. In this representation of the cannibal, no thought is given to the morality of one's actions, a notion which echoes Sade's own words: "Absurd to say the mania offends Nature: can it be so, when 'tis she who puts it into our head? Can she dictate what degrades her?"[1] Sade believes that all desires are natural, even those perceived as bad or wrong by society, and not to follow them is a betrayal of nature. The cannibals can thus be read as followers of nature: they not only have a desire to protect their territory from intruders, they also have a need to satisfy their hunger. Throughout all of the animal kingdom, what is killed must then be eaten.

Deodato shows humanity's place in the animal kingdom by intercutting Robert's story with shots of animal life in the jungle, where creatures prey ferociously on each other. This serves to represent humans as operating on the same level of survival as other animals: humans are not superior beings who control the land, they are just an insignificant link in the food chain. In Sade's *Juliette* the question is asked:

> Is there really anything more extraordinary than this superiority to animals which human arrogate to themselves? Ask them upon what basis their superiority rests. "We have a soul"— that is their silly response.... I tell you that I'm not aware of having any soul, that I'm acquainted with and feel nothing but my body; that it is the body which feels, which thinks, which judges, which suffers, which enjoys.[2]

From a Sadean point of view, humans are not superior to animals due to the former's seemingly enlightened consciousness. If anything, such ideals have divorced humans from their connection to the body, the one true, provable fact of existence.

Thus the cannibal narrative, which details the breaking of one of the most basic taboos of modern Western society, is a tale in which a person leaves behind the trappings of civilization and returns to the life of the body and the instincts. Following the dictum "You are what you eat," the act of eating the body becomes a potent metaphor of this return to the flesh and the casting off of culture and civilization, where food is processed and its origins become indeterminate. In *Last Cannibal World* the place of disgust in regards to food and its origins is commented on when, trapped underground, Robert shares his space with a large bird which he must fight in order to eat the meager scraps of meat that are thrown down to him. At first Robert refuses to eat these raw and bloody scraps, but is soon driven through excessive hunger to fight the bird for what remains of them. His need to eat conquers his disgust at the meat's bloodiness, as well as the probability that the flesh may have come from another human.

This process of overcoming disgust is a driving force also of the Sadean narrative, as his libertines incorporate many objects that arouse disgust (mainly bodily fluids and waste) as part of their sexual liaisons. Overcoming disgust is a main ingredient of transgression, since disgust is connected to taboo objects. One feels disgust when confronted with such an object, and it is this feeling that stops one from entering into contact with it. Where the transgressive body is concerned, therefore, taboos are not only broken, they may then also be incorporated back into that body through ingestion or sexual play. From a Sadean viewpoint, taboos and the feelings of disgust that they provoke are not natural; they are social constructs that people are conditioned to accept. To overcome disgust, then, is to enable a return to a more natural state, a trajectory at the heart of the cannibal narrative.

Overcoming his culturally-imposed disgust, Robert consciously commits an act of cannibalism later in the film. After Robert has escaped from the tribe and been reunited with his lost colleague Ralph, they are captured by the tribe again. Having to face a tribesman in a one-on-one fight with spears, Robert kills his opponent. Then, in an act designed to demonstrate his supremacy, Robert cuts open the dead man's chest and removes his heart, and, as the tribe watches, takes a bite and ingests it. By overcoming his disgust and breaking the taboo of cannibalism, Robert saves both Ralph's life and his own, for even though the two men are outnumbered, the tribe does not attack them.

Thus, the only way for Robert to survive is through the adoption of the ways of the jungle, regardless of how brutal or disgusting they may seem. Not only does this lead to his escape, it also provides Robert with moments of sexual pleasure. When he escapes from the tribe he takes with him a tribal girl whom he uses as both a guide and a partner in what Mikita Brottman describes as "atavistic, Stone-Age-style sex."[3] Brottman

5. Cannibals

observes how sex scenes in Italian cannibal movies typically show the man penetrating the woman from behind on all fours, which is the same position taken by animals when they mate. This aligns the humans in the scene with other animals in the jungle, and illustrates that the sex in these films is an expression not of love but of instinctual cravings. In these scenes Robert is able to achieve pleasure without any thought of the societal pressures of marriage or commitment. As in Sade, these sex scenes can be read as natural sexual expressions antithetical to the formation of social structures such as monogamous relationships and family.

However, even though these sexual expressions can be said to be derived from nature, through Sade these desires can be seen as operating within strict guidelines. The tribe in *Last Cannibal World*, although categorized as "Stone Age," follows a set of rules and rituals, evoking Sade's notion of order during transgression. Even though they commit cannibalism, an act that supposedly highlights their status as primitive and uncivilized, the tribe carry out the deed in the form of an ordered ritual, just as Sade's libertines, who, while performing orgies—an activity that also

Rolf (Ivan Rassimov, left) helps Robert Harper (Massimo Foschi) prepare to fight in *Last Cannibal World* (1977).

marks their status as transgressive and unrestrained — also follow certain rules. Although the taboo against cannibalism is one of the most fundamental of modern society, in *Last Cannibal World* it is shown to be part of a solemn ritual. As Ralph admits, "Maybe it's terrible in our world but it's not in theirs. Everyone becomes a link in the chain of survival."

Before their final showdown with Robert, the tribe finds the girl that Robert has kidnapped. Rather than returning her to her home, the tribe kills the girl because she has been corrupted by outside influences. The contamination must not be brought back to tribal ground. The tribe then prepares to eat the girl's body, which entails her being washed (and thereby cleansed of impurities) and her head cut off. Her stomach is cut open and her internal organs are removed, her ribs are cut and opened, and hot rocks are put inside her chest. Several close-ups are used so that the audience misses no detail. The close-ups serve to highlight the refusal to respect the boundaries between the inside and outside of the body, as the girl's intestines are pulled out of the body and into the camera's view: the body has now become meat. The girl, once a part of the tribe, is now a source of food. Her identity is destroyed through this process. Likewise, Sade postulates that in order to use a person as a means to satisfy a desire that is either physical or sexual, all notions of identity must be stripped from the victim.

In his novel *The 120 Days of Sodom*, sixteen adolescents are kidnapped and used for sexual pleasure. When addressing the victims, the kidnappers refer to them as "feeble, enfettered creatures destined solely for our pleasures" and tell them that "the life of a woman — what do I say, the life of a woman? The lives of all women who dwell on the face of the earth, are as insignificant as the crushing of a fly."[4] The cannibals in *Last Cannibal World* also reduce the status of their victim to less than that of an animal. Through their ritual, which entails the cutting up and taking apart of the body, the girl changes from a whole human to pieces of meat — lumps of flesh that are used to satisfy hunger.

This ritual of cannibalism is the climax of *Last Cannibal World*. It is a statement of the supremacy of nature and humanity's place within it. As Sade writes, nature is in a state of constant motion, and we, too, go through many changes and transformations, the final of which is the transition to death. Yet, at all stages we are merely just a part of this cycle, no more important than a fly. Sade's libertines claim that they imitate nature when they strip their victims of all identity and use their bodies as instruments of pleasure. They are acting upon the instincts given to them by

5. Cannibals

nature. The cannibal tribe in *Last Cannibal World* can thus be understood not as evil transgressors but as a part of nature's transgressiveness. Deodato depicts the cannibals as an integral part of the environment, subject to the same instincts and needs as the other creatures who dwell there. In contrast to this natural world, the cannibals in *Trouble Every Day* (Claire Denis, 2001), which will be examined next, exist in a contemporary city setting.

Creating Monsters: Trouble Every Day

While *Last Cannibal World* portrays cannibalism as an instinctual expression, *Trouble Every Day* portrays it as a sexual perversion. The eating of flesh becomes the climax of sexual activity. This perversion is the result of a science experiment gone wrong. The human pursuit of knowledge has brought us full-circle back to our primal origins. The cannibals in *Trouble Every Day* are not part of a Stone Age tribe but are scientists who symbolize human intelligence and superiority. Therefore, they can be read in terms of the Sadean, as they appear to be the pillars of society but are actually driven to commit heinous acts in order to satisfy their base desires. They have transgressed natural laws through scientific manipulation and so have set a cycle of transgression into motion.

Even within the context of director Claire Denis' filmography, this film is transgressive. *Trouble Every Day* contrasts with Denis' more critically acclaimed films, such as *Chocolat* (1988), *Beau Travail* (1999), *35 Shots of Rum* (2008) and *White Material* (2010). When *Trouble Every Day* was first shown at the 2001 Cannes Film Festival, the movie was met with shock and derision, with reports of several people walking out or fainting during the film's violent scenes.[5] In what seemed like a radical departure, Denis had made a film that conformed more to the horror genre than high art drama, a film whose protagonists shared traits with the sexual vampires and cannibals of low art exploitation movies. However, as shown in the previous chapter on vampires, there are many similarities to be found between movies that fit into the category of the high art avant-garde and films from the exploitation and grindhouse circuit. In *Trouble Every Day* Denis focuses on a subject that is usually found in low horror, but she imbues the subject matter with her usual high art style.

If one looks closer at Denis' career, *Trouble Every Day* is, in fact, a logical progression. She had previously taken on the serial killer sub-genre

Part Two: Monstrous Humans

with *I Can't Sleep* (1994), which, instead of focusing on the serial killer's murder spree, centers on the relationship that develops between three immigrants, one of whom is revealed partway through to be a serial killer. As Todd McGowan states, "Denis implicitly cautions the viewer against expecting a satisfying resolution to our desire. The film's emphasis is on desire itself."[6] This is also the case with *Trouble Every Day*, where the emphasis is again on the nature of desire, with the protagonist's cannibalism not the main focus of the film (it contains only two scenes of violent cannibalism, both of which occur toward the end). Cannibalism instead works as a metaphor for desire. When a person is in love or in lust, there is a strong urge to connect and to become one with the object of one's affection. In *Trouble Every Day* this is taken to extremes, where the desire for connection and the longing for another's touch become an urge to devour the other and ingest them so they become part of the self.

The bodies of the cannibals are transgressive in that they physically manifest inner desires. There is a transgression of the bounds between inner thoughts and outer actions, expressed through the tearing open of the sexual partner, in itself a transgression of the boundary separating the insides and the outside of the victim. Like in the case of the serial killer, transgression of the body leads to transgressive behavior, which is also a violation of societal laws. There is also a transgression of the boundary separating sex and violence, a boundary that Sade consciously disregards through his characters' attempts to reach greater heights of sexual pleasure. The two scenes of cannibalism both begin as scenes of consensual sex which gradually gets rougher, and then, with the breaking of skin and the first taste of blood, degenerates into horrific violence.

Unlike earlier cannibal films, in which cannibal tribes use people as a source of food and nutrients, the cannibalism in *Trouble Every Day* is driven by the need for sexual gratification, not by necessity. Therefore, it suggests a Sadean sexuality where lustful desires are inseparable from desires for violence and murder. The mixing of sex and violence also harks back to pagan Dionysian orgies. Camille Paglia claims that in the Dionysian realm beings are not separated but joined together in the primordial slime where existence began. This is expressed in the orgy, where bodies merge together and are awash in bodily fluids. This all-encompassing sexuality has a violent element: "Dionysus' amorality cuts both ways. He is the god of theatre, masked balls, and free love — but also of anarchy, gang rape and mass murder."[7] In this realm all limits and boundaries are melted away, and self-control and restraint are abandoned. Paglia writes: "Diony-

5. Cannibals

sus liberates by destroying.... Dionysian orgy ended in mutilation and dismemberment."[8] The Dionysian overtakes and overwhelms: it is a transgressive energy that cannot stop, only accelerate.

The sexual cannibalism in *Trouble Every Day* thus may be understood as an expression of Dionysian lust, whereby people literally merge together through the ingestion of flesh. If you desire someone, you desire all of them — the inside and the outside — the guts as well as the glamour. Once in the throes of this passion, the cannibal partner cannot stop until the other is obliterated. Transgression can end only in destruction, which a Sadean reading understands is actually a creative act that leads to an opportunity for new forms of pleasure.

True to the Dionysian orgy, these cannibal scenes become saturated in blood, for, as Paglia insists, "Dionysus was identified with liquids"— namely, the fluids emitted from the body.[9] Unlike the ritual seen in *Last Cannibal World*, the cannibalism in *Trouble Every Day* is represented as an orgiastic frenzy in which sex is so uncontrolled that it becomes violence. Surprisingly, it is the supposed "savages" who practice cannibalism in the form of an ordered ritual, with the appropriate reverence, in order to stave off starvation, while the Western scientists succumb to cannibalism in a messy, uncontrollable rage in order to quench sexual longing. Sade's libertines also enter into this Dionysian realm in order to satisfy sexual desire, as Paglia observes:

> Sade's sexual dissenters seek Dionysian lawlessness and abandon themselves to Dionysian fluids.... The libertines eagerly obliterate the body's formal contours, tearing, piercing, scraping, gouging, maiming, slicing, shredding, burning, melting.[10]

The Dionysian is thus the realm of transgression, where all boundaries are obliterated. It is the zone where the body's limits and possibilities are tested. Sade's works explore this zone, his texts becoming a catalogue of the body's functions and perversions. In order to open up the body to new possibilities it must be opened physically, hence the "tearing, piercing, scraping" and so forth.

However, Sade's libertines enter into this realm within a framework of analysis and experimentation, and this self-examination can also be read in *Trouble Every Day*. What really distances this film from most other cannibal movies is that the perpetrators are scientists, intellectuals who are thought to be the epitome of the cultured and civilized human being. The cannibal is not the other, some being that is outside the norm, but is,

Part Two: Monstrous Humans

rather, a person who symbolizes all that people in society strive to be. The character of Shane, for example, is portrayed as an ambitious and talented doctor, someone who has accrued wealth and prestige, and who appears to be vacationing in Paris on his honeymoon. His new wife, June, is young, beautiful, and sweetly innocent. Yet it becomes apparent that Shane is not the typical newlywed: he refuses to have sex with his wife, he is on some form of medication, and he spends much of his spare time trying to track down a former colleague, Dr. Leo Semeneau. Shane, through medication and abstinence, is trying to stop a certain disease or condition from taking over his body — a condition that threatens not only himself but also the safety of his wife. While in bed with June, he gets up and goes into the bathroom to masturbate, and he is plagued by visions of June naked and covered in blood.

Telltale signs, such as a bite mark on June's arm and a faint cut on her lip, reveal that Shane's condition is constantly on the verge of taking over. Such signs of "love-bites" mask a darker desire, as Havelock Ellis observes:

> The result of the love-bite in its extreme form is to shed blood ... the mingled feelings of close contact, of passionate gripping, of symbolic devouring ... the love-bite is really associated with a conscious desire, even if more or less restrained, to draw blood, a real delight in this process, a love of blood.[11]

In Shane's visions he sees a hand that caresses and runs over bloody flesh. This mental image then raises a question: are these visions what Shane fears or what he desires?

It soon becomes apparent that these are desires Shane is valiantly trying to resist, desires that meanwhile have completely taken over Leo's wife Coré. Although Leo keeps Coré locked up, she frequently escapes, and Leo usually finds her covered in blood, delirious, and with a male corpse that must be disposed of. The film reflects Robert Louis Stevenson's classic tale *The Strange Case of Dr. Jekyll and Mr. Hyde*, as it becomes evident that Coré's and Shane's conditions are the result of self-experimentation. They have somehow tapped into the base instinctual and primal part of themselves, and this becomes uncontrollable when they are sexually aroused. Once involved in the sexual act, they begin to devour their partner. Fleshly desires become a desire to eat the flesh. Lust becomes bloodlust.

In keeping with this theme of primal regression (which, as discussed in the analysis of werewolves, from a Sadean viewpoint is seen as a progression leading to new forms of pleasure), the characters are clearly divided into two categories: predator and prey — or, more precisely, the

5. Cannibals

Sadean division of perpetrator and victim. The cannibal Coré is represented as a wild animal, portrayed by Beatrice Dalle in a performance that has been described as "feral."[12] She is mute, expressing herself only through sexual come-ons and violent outbursts. In her equation with the animal, Coré becomes a Sadean creature, totally driven by her desires and the need for immediate satisfaction. It is only after she has killed and fed that she is calm. Leo finds her in the wilderness, hiding in the scrub and long grass; and when she is returned home he gently washes the blood off her skin. Coré is represented as a creature that is unable to take care of herself, someone who no longer knows the difference between right and wrong, and who operates at the base level of hunger and satisfaction. In this, *Trouble Every Day* corresponds to those films in which the cannibal human is associated with a wild animal, acting without conscience or compassion.

Despite this seeming helplessness, Coré is also a ferocious hunter. Even when trapped in her room, many shots show her looking from her window, scouting for future prey. In the film's most shocking scene, a young man enters Coré's room, and in the midst of the sexual act, she begins to bite and tear at his face and chest, eating his flesh while he struggles and screams. This scene shares similarities with the scene of vampirism found in Jose Larraz's film *Vampyres*, where the drinking of blood is shown to be a ferocious act akin to cannibalism. Just like the two women in Larraz's film (and most other female vampires in cinema), Coré has lured her victim through feminine wiles and the promise of sex. And, just as the two female vampires in *Vampyres* kiss and fondle each other while feeding on their prey, in *Trouble Every Day* the act of cannibalism is also shown to be part of the sexual act.

But whereas Larraz shot his scenes of vampirism using a variety of shot sizes, Denis shoots the majority of this scene in close-up, so that a violent intensity is created. Though we see clearly the blood that covers both Coré and her victim, the close-up also blocks much of the action, as well as fragmenting parts of the body so they cannot be identified. The scene begins with a close-up of the young man's armpit; and the camera slowly tracks down his chest, the closeness to the body rendering it almost abstract — as a series of textures and shapes rather than part of a living human being. Like the ritual of cannibalism shown in *Last Cannibal World*, this technique also serves to strip the victim of identity. We do not see the body as a whole, but only pink flesh, brown tendrils of hair and red blood, which would create a beautiful picture if only there were not also the sound of the young man's agonized screams.

Part Two: Monstrous Humans

Throughout the scene Coré's face dominates the framed close-up as she sits on top of her victim. The back of her head frequently blocks part of the action. Within the close-ups we see Coré's blood-smeared mouth and her bared teeth, as she is again characterized by movements that are distinctly animal-like. With her feral licking and slapping, she is like a cat that plays with the mutilated remains of a dying mouse. At one point Coré fingers a flap of skin on the young man's chest, as though she does not recognize that it is a wound that she herself has caused. It becomes apparent that Coré has completely regressed to an animal state, driven by an urge for blood and flesh. She is unable to grasp the cruelty of her actions, bringing to mind a statement made by Sade that "cruelty is stamped in animals, in whom.... Nature's laws are more emphatically to be read than in ourselves."[13] This scene reveals the violence that is inherent in sexual desire, and demonstrates the tenet that surrendering to instinct brings with it a total loss of control. To transgress with the body causes all boundaries to become unfixed.

In contrast to the predator Coré, Denis also presents the prey of these perverse desires—in the form of the hotel maid Christelle, who is portrayed as vulnerable and open to attack. As in Sade, if there are to be perpetrators there must be victims. Christelle is lower in the social hierarchy, a member of the working class whose status differs from that of the doctors and scientists who populate the rest of the film. Christelle is first seen from behind as she carries Shane and June's luggage. The camera is frequently behind Christelle, as though it were stalking her without her knowledge. The camera focuses on the pale white skin of her neck, which seems vulnerable and exposed. When she shows Shane and June into their room, the two newlyweds fall onto the bed and canoodle while Christelle tries to arrange the sheets. She is treated as though she were not even there.

Christelle uses this anonymity to her advantage, as she is shown taking condiments and skincare products that are left unused on room service trays. This again establishes Christelle as lower in both the social and the natural hierarchy: she scavenges among what has been discarded by others. By situating characters in this hierarchy, the film illustrates that people, however cultured or civilized they may be, are still subject to the same natural forces that affect animals. Shane and Coré were once leading scientists, but through their tampering with nature it has returned to them in full force, reminding them of their animal origins.

Having been set up so obviously as an intended victim, it is Christelle who finally drives Shane to give in to the urges he has been fighting to

5. Cannibals

suppress. Starting with a shot that again shows the back of Christelle as she undresses in the servants' locker room, Shane is revealed watching her, and she turns to see him behind her. Like most predators, he has been stalking his prey before he has attacked. Shane grabs her face and holds her up against a locker as the two begin to kiss. What starts as seemingly consensual soon becomes violent, as Shane holds Christelle down on the floor. Just as Coré had been on top during her encounter with the young stranger, this time Shane is also on top of his intended prey. Unlike Coré's scene, this scene uses longer shots, with Shane's body and the placing of the lockers blocking some of the action.

While the scenes are horrific, the blocking of the shots prevents a lot of the actual action being clearly shown, so what becomes most affecting in this sequence is the abundance of blood and the screams of the victim. One of the few close-ups in the scene is of Christelle's face upside down as she begins to scream, the next shot showing Shane's head emerging from her crotch, his mouth smeared in blood. The rest of the scene is obscured by shadow, as Shane continues to fuck and eat, fulfilling two basic needs at the same time. The squence ends with another long shot, as Christelle's now dead body is pulled behind a locker. She is pulled both out of view and out of the narrative.

These scenes can be read as visual representations of the Sadean notion that desire is inherently selfish. Shane and Coré are not satisfied until the one they desire is destroyed. They consume their victims completely. As Lucienne Frappier-Mazur writes, cannibalism in Sade is divorced from earlier religious connotations and is instead an expression of individual satisfaction:

> We may recall the episodes in *Juliette* when pregnant women are crushed to pieces and ground up, or in *Les Cent-vingt journées de Sodome* when fetuses are eaten (13:150, 347). Some of these rituals, such as spermaphagia and, of course, cannibalism, can be found in other so-called primitive societies Sade learned about through his readings. Sade introduces these into the orgy ritual, but strips them of any religious, initiatory significance when he states matter-of-factly that sperm and human flesh are consumed to fortify and strengthen the individual.[14]

The eating of another's flesh or fluids is thus not a communion with the other, but rather a testimony of one's domination over them. This is illustrated by Shane's attempts to refrain from intercourse with his wife and his attack on Christelle, a servant whom he views as socially beneath him. The urge within him becomes too strong, and he finds relief for his own

Part Two: Monstrous Humans

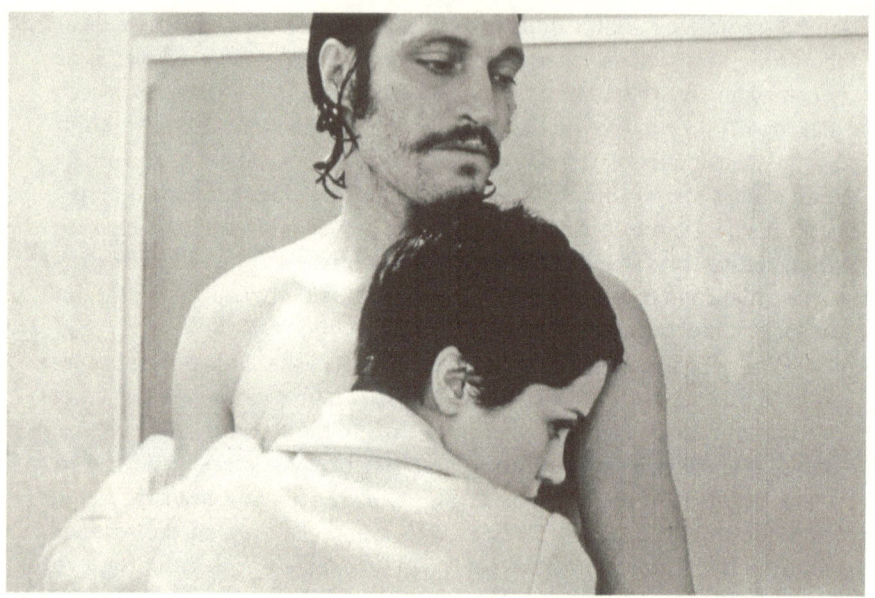

Troubled newlyweds Shane (Vincent Gallo) and June Brown (Tricia Vessey) in *Trouble Every Day* (2001).

selfish reasons, using someone who means nothing to him. It is not a measured ritual, as seen in *Last Cannibal World*, but an act that, as Frappier-Mazur suggests, has been stripped of its religious connotations. Like Sade, who revels in the Dionysian realm but then reframes his activities within strict guidelines (Paglia states that "Sade organizes Dionysian experience into Apollonian patterns"), the cannibalism in *Trouble Every Day* is about individual pleasure, not assimilation into the Dionysian group-body.[15]

With their sexual desire having gone to such extremes, Shane and Coré are not as capable as the Sadean libertine of emerging from the experience with the same control. Having killed Coré, and then succumbing to his own desires, Shane has started his own cycle of transgression. Having tasted blood, the film leaves Shane's and his wife's future uncertain. Emerging from the shower after his first kill, Shane embraces June, who sees a solitary bloody water drop slide down the curtain. This drop of fluid, which combines blood and water, symbolizes the transgression that Shane has begun.

This film thus illustrates the repetitive nature of transgression. Even the title — *Trouble Every Day* — suggests an ongoing, never-ending cycle.

5. Cannibals

The film expresses explicitly the chapter's proposition that the repetition of transgression is a form of violence which brings about a sexual release, a fact illustrated by the way in which the violence is shown only within a sexual context. The film itself, with its mingling of high and low art styles, and confronting scenes of graphic sexual violence, transgresses many cinematic boundaries. The trangressiveness of its form is matched by its content, where sexual desire is presented as a primal force which overrides humanity's scientific attempts to control it. Like the Sadean libertine, the cannibals in *Trouble Every Day* discover that their scientific and intellectual explorations are actually driven by nature's primal urges and instincts. This transgression of science and nature, which is played out within the body, is explored further in the following chapter.

6

The Transhuman

As technology has advanced, the boundary separating the technology that has been produced and the humans that have created them has been transgressed. Technology has been incorporated into the body in an attempt to improve it. This technological evolution is played out in the films of David Cronenberg and Shinya Tsukamoto, where the boundary separating the human body from technology is frequently transgressed, affecting emotional and sexual expression. These films explore the future of the body but also invoke Sade's past exploration of the body and its possibilities. In fact, it can be argued that these filmmakers are continuing Sade's work by exploring the incorporation of technology into the area of perversion and transgression.

The evolution of the body precipitated by technology has led many to believe that we are moving from a human to a posthuman age. The posthuman is defined as a "possible future human being whose basic capacities so radically exceed those of present humans as to be no longer unambiguously human by our current standards."[1] However, before one reaches this stage the body must go through a transhuman phase (short for "transitional human"). At this moment in time, most of humanity is thought to be transiting from the human to the posthuman, demonstrated by the introduction of bodily transformations such as plastic surgery, prostheses, fertility treatment and the concentrated use of communication systems such as digital video and the Internet. While it may also be argued that rather than moving to a posthuman state, this continued fusion of human and machine instead means that we need to reengage with and redefine traditional notions of what it is to be "human." The films analyzed here align more with the concept that humanity is in the process of becoming "something else."

The films of David Cronenberg and Shinya Tsukamoto focus on the idea of the transhuman, using the medium of cinema to visualize and hypothesize the future of the human body, and explore the possibilities

6. The Transhuman

that arise from the fusion of flesh and technology.[2] As Cronenberg himself has suggested, "[W]e are not fully evolved — culturally, physically or in any other way. [My] films are an attempt to try and perceive what, having said that, a fully evolved human being might look like."[3] Cronenberg's films deal with the transhuman by theorizing how the human body will be changed as technology advances. In some instances, such as in his films *Videodrome* (1982) and *The Fly* (1986), technology invades the body and changes it from within; in *eXistenZ* (1999) technological artifacts begin to take on characteristics of the human body (for example, computers take on the form of fleshy pods and are powered by the organic processes of the human body).

In Tsukamoto's films technological artifacts become fetish objects, such as the metal and machinery in *Tetsuo: The Iron Man* (1988), *Tetsuo 2: Body Hammer* (1991) and *Tetsuo: The Bullet Man* (2009); body piercing in *Tokyo Fist* (1995); guns in *Bullet Ballet* (1998); photography equipment in *A Snake of June* (2002); and surgical tools in *Vital* (2004). In all these films technology has invaded sexuality, becoming the means through which the characters' sexuality is expressed. This idea, that technology can become a form of sexuality, is also explicitly addressed in Cronenberg's *Crash*, in which the repetition of transgression is expressed through technological forms, bringing about a new form of sexual pleasure.

Days of Neo-Sodom: Crash

The films of David Cronenberg are unique in that, as well as presenting stories, they also offer scientific explorations into the possible future of the human body. They investigate how aspects of modern life — the technology, the media, the saturation of information — have affected the body. What is common throughout all of Cronenberg's filmography is that his films parallel the style used by Sade, providing a cold, almost medical approach to observing and exploring the possibilities of the human body. And since issues of the body are discussed, issues of sexuality become integral to the investigation. As Cronenberg observes:

> Sexuality is one of those very basic issues. Life and death and sexuality are interlinked. You can't discuss one without in some way discussing the others. Since my films are concerned very much with death and the human body, sexuality is automatically discussed.[4]

This is most thoroughly explored in his film *Crash* (1996), where the event of a car crash becomes a metaphor for the collision of flesh and technology, a collision that unleashes new sexual possibilities. Cronenberg thus continues on from Sade, in that Cronenberg explores new sexual possibilities and opportunities for gaining pleasure, which result from the creation of new technology.

Just as the libertines in Sade's novels are often gathered in groups in order to participate in sexual exploration with those of like minds, *Crash* too shows a group of people joined together through their common search for sexual fulfillment. But in conjunction with this practical experimentation, Sade's libertines also discuss and analyze their actions: "There's more to it than just experiencing sensations, they must also be analyzed. Sometimes it is as pleasant to discuss as to undergo them."[5] This is also mirrored in the group in *Crash*, as they also have a philosophy behind their sexual exploration. As the group's leader, Vaughan, explains:

> There's a benevolent psychopathology that beckons toward us. For example, the car crash is a fertilizing rather than a destructive event, a liberation of sexual energy, mediating the sexuality of those who have died with an intensity that's impossible in any other form. To experience that, to live that — that's my project.

Vaughan refers to the others in the group as his "partners in psychopathology." He shows James his "workshop" and books filled with writing and photographs: his sexual experimentation is also an intellectual study.

The scientific approach taken by the characters is reflected in the film's technique and style. All the people in the group have been involved in near-fatal car crashes, an experience that has profoundly changed them both physically and emotionally, opening them up to new ideas about the body and sexual expression. For just as the crash causes destruction of bodies and property, it also creates new mutations from this collision of flesh and machine. James' leg is wounded, and the camera tracks up his leg, showing in close-up the metal brace that has been attached to him and the pins that penetrate his flesh. The close-up also reveals the bruising that James has sustained as a result of the accident: his skin has changed in color. The motif of bruising — the sign of physical convergence between flesh and machine — is carried throughout the film, with most of the characters wearing clothes in bruise-colored shades (black, blue and purple), suggesting visually that their bodies have incorporated both flesh and technology. In fact, the whole film itself is filtered through blue-grey light. The world around the characters is controlled by technology; there are few sights of trees or parks, only endless roads and traffic, concrete buildings and steel interiors.

6. The Transhuman

This cold, mechanical world has affected human interaction: all the actors deliver somnambulistic performances, never betraying any emotion or affection for each other. For *Crash* hypothesizes that, as the physical self is changed by technology, the sexual, emotional, social and mental aspects of a person also undergoes change and adaptation. Our unconscious desires and emotional needs will be expressed through, as well as be provided by, our use of technology. The technology incorporated into the characters' bodies now infiltrates all aspects of their lives. As JG Ballard, the author of the novel on which the film is based, observes:

> What we're getting is a whole new order of sexual fantasies, involving a different order of experiences, like car crashes, like travelling in jet aircraft, the whole overlay of new technologies, architecture, interior design.... These things are beginning to reach into our lives and change the interior design of our sexual fantasies.[6]

The influence of Ballard is palpable here, as *Crash* focuses on how technology invades the flesh, which is antithetical to Cronenberg's tendency to present technology as becoming more organic (as seen in the swollen, breathing televisions of *Videodrome* and the fleshy computer pods in *eXistenZ*). The colder, more clinical approach seen in *Crash*, with its emphasis on harder, smoother textures, seems more in keeping with the Sadean emphasis on detached, objective analysis and experimentation. Ballard himself remarks, "Think of the film as straightforwardly Sadean."[7] The film's Sadean quality is expressed through its form and content, in the cold and matter-of-fact presentation of a catalogue of the character's sexual exploits. Ballard and Cronenberg extend the work of Sade through their focus on the ways that modern technology has altered and expanded sexual activity. This establishes *Crash* as part of the tradition began by Sade, with Ballard exploring in prose and Cronenberg in cinema all the possibilities and limitations of the body.

In following Sade, neither book nor film focus on plot and character development, but instead propel the narrative through scenes of sexual activity. As Cronenberg remarks, "[S]omeone said, 'A series of sex scenes is not a plot.' And I said, 'Why not? Who says?' ... In *Crash*, very often the sex scenes are *absolutely* the plot and character development."[8] Like Sade's sexually repetitious novels, *Crash* offers an endless repetition of sexual scenarios which, instead of building tension, drain the scenes of their intensity. The focus in these scenes is not the furthering of plot and character development, but rather the way the content of the shot is composed. The sexual position is important, not emotions; so no emotion is conveyed by the characters. Like Sade's texts, the film is an account of sexual experimentation, and so the narrative is really only a catalogue of the sexual activity that takes place.

Nevertheless, in this repetition meaning can be found. For example, although the film follows the sexual exploits of Vaughan and his group, the main protagonists are actually James and Catherine Ballard, a husband and wife who have an open marriage. The film commences with two separate scenes in which the husband and the wife have sex with other people. There are certain similarities between the two scenes, as both take place among technological artifacts. Catherine's scene takes place in an aircraft hangar, and as her partner approaches she exposes her breast and leans against the surface of the airplane in an eroticized juxtaposition of flesh and technology. James' scene, which is shown directly after, occurs at his place of work, a film set, in which he and his partner are surrounded by filming equipment, suggesting a technology of watching and voyeurism. These scenes echo Ballard's statement above, highlighting how the technology around us has become incorporated into our sexual fantasies.

The positioning of the couples in these scenes comments on the relationship between the two protagonists, for although they are with other people, they are connected by the positions that they adopt. At the end of Catherine's scene she is standing, her partner kneeled down behind her, his face poised at her buttocks; when there is a cut to James we first see him behind his partner, in the same position as the man who was with Catherine. That this position is repeated demonstrates that the two people are connected: they are not with each other, but they share the same experience, which is continued in the next scene, where James and Catherine discuss these sexual exploits with each other. The discussion of a sexual act is shown to be an integral part of its enjoyment. The Ballards, therefore, have a distinctly Sadean marriage, not only in their promiscuity, but also in their desire to explore, experiment with, and discuss their sexuality. They are also a transhuman couple: technology has been incorporated into their sex lives, a fact highlighted in the first two scenes.

What these two opening scenes do not incorporate, however, is the film's main focus: the automobile. Since its inception, the car has been imbued with a sexual allure, something that advertisers have capitalized on time and again. As Cronenberg admits:

> A car is not the highest of high-tech. But it has affected us and changed us more than anything else in the last hundred years. We have incorporated it. The weird privacy in public that it gives us. The sexual freedom — which in

6. The Transhuman

the '50s wasn't even subtle! I mean, the first guy who had a convertible in high school was the guy who had the sex.... He had a mobile bedroom.[9]

In *Crash* the car as sexual object takes on a special significance. It is both womb and tomb, a transgressive site where both fertilization and destruction take place. At times during the film the car is a warm, dark, womb-like place in which characters are seen to rest and nestle. For example, after a re-creation of the James Dean car crash, a wounded Seagrave lies in the back seat of Vaughan's car, and an overhead shot shows him in the fetal position. This cinematic strategy is repeated toward the end of the film when Helen and Gabrielle go to Vaughan's car after his death and make love in the back seat: another overhead shot looks down on them entwined together. Both shots take place in Vaughan's car, as he is, in a sense, the leader, or the parent, of the group. It is through his tutelage that the characters begin to explore a new side of their sexuality. And it is in the space of the car that these sexual exploits occur and their new transgressive bodies are born.

The boundary separating Vaughan from his car has thus been violated. They merge into one being, demonstrated by the scars and dents

James (James Spader) and Catherine Ballard (Deborah Kara Unger) cruise for thrills in *Crash* (1996).

Part Two: Monstrous Humans

viewed on both Vaughan and the car — they have imprinted themselves on each other. Vaughan even has what he calls a "prophetic tattoo," an imprint on his chest of the steering wheel. He consciously tries to fuse with the car, to be reborn as a new being. The car thus functions for Vaughan as a sexual organ: he is always seen having sex only in his car, while other characters remark on how it "smells of semen." As an evolving being, Vaughan is represented as possessing both feminine and masculine attributes. When a person enters Vaughan's car to have sex, he or she, in a sense, penetrates his body. As Vaughan's physical body dies, the car becomes the site of Vaughan's rebirth as a being that fuses man with machine.

As Vaughan repeatedly states, a car crash is a "fertilizing event." The car survives but is altered physically by the crash and by "the sexuality of those who have died with an intensity that's impossible in any other form." When James and Catherine pick up Vaughan's car after he has died, his sexual energy is still alive within the vehicle. This echoes Vaughan's earlier display in which he recreates before a live audience the crash that killed James Dean. He observes that it was the crash itself that "created a Hollywood legend," and that "James Dean died of a broken neck and became immortal." This suggests that it is the death of the physical body in a car crash that leads to the creation of a new being, a "legend." This interchanging of creation and destruction is a Sadean motif. The creation of new technology leads to the destruction of the body in its original form. Through Sade, the transhuman stage, where the boundary separating technology and flesh is blurred, can be viewed as a phase that incorporates both creation and destruction.

For Vaughan, the car is eventually his tomb. It is the piece of technology in which his physical body is destroyed. The car has the capability of becoming a metal coffin, a manifestation of the desire for self-destruction. Due to their increasingly dangerous and reckless behavior, it is inevitable that the other characters, by following their leader Vaughan, will also kill themselves while driving on the road. Each time they conduct their sexual experiments, they risk their lives. The car may thus become a physical manifestation of the desire for self-annihilation. In fact, toward the end of the film it becomes apparent that the attainment of orgasm has been replaced by the desire to sustain a wound from a car crash. Thus, Catherine's remark "Maybe the next one" — a response to James' negative answer to her query, after the two scenes in which James and Catherine have sexual encounters with other people, whether his partner achieved

6. The Transhuman

orgasm — is repeated at the end of the film after James runs Catherine, the only member of the group not to have been wounded in a car crash, off the road. When he finds her thrown from her car but still unscathed, he consoles her by repeating "Maybe the next one" as tears fall down her face: she will reach sexual satisfaction only through the acquisition of a crash injury. The cycle of transgression must continue. Like the Sadean libertines, the characters in *Crash* have transgressed to such a point that they can no longer experience pleasure without going to extremes. As Sade remarks, "[O]ne excess leads to another, the imagination, never sated, soon brings us to our destination."[10] This statement highlights the cyclic nature of transgression. In *Crash* the characters have transgressed to the point that an orgasm becomes an act of violence.

Such violence may lead to physical alteration and the creation of a new sexual orifice, with new opportunities for sexual pleasure. In one scene, for instance, James takes Gabrielle, the member of the group most obviously disabled by a car crash, to a car showroom to look at a Mercedes Benz. Gabrielle, although sporting a cane and leg brace, is nonetheless dressed provocatively in fishnet stockings, a black leather skirt and tight top. After limping over to the car, she leans over and runs her hands across the car's surface, exclaiming, "This interests me." As Kauffman notes, this scene suggests there is a

> connection between the female body and the auto body.... Arquette's black leather miniskirt mirrors the leather interior of the Mercedes. The shiny steel chrome on her leg mirror's the car's chrome. Mouth open, she seductively caresses the car the way one might caress a lover. Everything ... duplicates the clichés of thousands of automobile advertisements, but the leg brace (the result of a car accident) adds an incongruous element.[11]

Gabrielle is a transgressive body, representing the collision of car and flesh and their subsequent transformation into a new sexual being, with the incorporation of the car expressed through her clothing and medical aids. Her changed body has altered the way she interacts with the world around her, suggested by her statement that she wants "to see if I can fit into a car designed for a normal body." After the foreplay of touching and caressing the car, she attempts to enter it, with the camera set at crotch level. With Gabrielle's head and torso out of frame, all the viewer sees is an abstract collage of flesh, leather, fishnet, metal and steering wheel, pulling and twisting at each other, a struggle that is at once both violent and, given the placement of the camera and the rhythm of Gabrielle's movements, highly sexual. This interlude illustrates how Gabrielle's body is no longer "normal," having been altered — or, as Vaughan puts it, "reshaped by modern technology."

The next scene demonstrates that this sexual interaction between Gabrielle and car has led to the creation of a new sexual practice. After the visit to the showroom, James and Gabrielle attempt to have sex in a car. The tight mid-shots and close-ups give the appearance that they are trapped in the vehicle, Gabrielle's leg brace making it difficult to find a suitable position, until a close-up shows the long thin wound on Gabrielle's thigh. James rips open her stockings, and in an edit to mid-shot, James seems to be penetrating the wound. Gabrielle's car crash has created a new sexual orifice, as well as a new sexual practice that is pleasurable but not reproductive.

Throughout *Crash*, sex is repeatedly linked with the death instinct, not the urge to continue the species, again positioning the car as a transgressive space that represents both the womb and the tomb. This is expressed through the dominance of both anal and rear-entry vaginal sex between the couples. As Marcel Henaff explains:

> The anathema pronounced against the practice of sodomy (even between spouses) is intended to eliminate the redoubtable competition that the anus poses to the vagina, and therefore to the womb, for, in addition to the sterility ensured by this rejection of procreation, there is the blasphemy of uniting the "fluid of life" with "dead matter" (in the old ecclesiastical terminology).[12]

The prevalence of a distinctly anal eroticism sets the sexuality in *Crash* in direct opposition to the traditional and social sanctioning of sexuality, which dictates that sex take place between monogamous heterosexual couples for the purpose of reproduction and the creation of a nuclear family. Echoing Henaff's words, Mikita Brottman and Christopher Sharrett also state:

> As an act of paraphilia, anal sex is a metaphor for a profoundly degenerate attitude towards human life. The pursuit of satisfactions in *Crash* is the pursuit of the Sadean void; as in Pasolini's *Salò* (1975), anality becomes an emblem of the transmogrification of transgressive sexuality.[13]

As this statement makes clear, anal sexuality in *Crash* is closely linked to Sade, who, time and again, espoused the virtues of sodomy and anal eroticism, if only because it is a sexual practice that shocks and is taboo to the moral majority.[14] The sexual experimentation of the characters in *Crash* thus reflects the experimentation carried out by Sade's libertines. It represents the characters' drive toward self-annihilation and negation.

6. The Transhuman

Both Catherine and Gabrielle represent a new form of femininity, which is a continuation of gender reinvention seen in Sade's character of Juliette. In Angela Carter's study *The Sadeian Woman*, the figure of Juliette is discussed as a new form of womanhood, described as "mechanistic," incorporating "a technological approach to biology" where biology is "amended."[15] This is visualized in *Crash*, with Gabrielle's invention of a new sexual act, as well as Catherine's equal status in her Sadean open marriage. This new form of femininity, though, is not reproductive but destructive: "She uses sex as an instrument of terror; death is more frequently the result of it than birth."[16] Thus the representation of femininity here is one completely removed from its traditionally maternal aspects. The transgressive female must defy both nature and culture's urge to procreate and nurture others. This focus on death rather than birth is manifested through the predominance of anal-centered sexuality.

The gender of the other partner in this connection becomes irrelevant, as both men and women can be sodomized. Of course, there is some imbalance in that it is usually the male character who is the penetrator, but the film also shows the female characters as the equal of their male counterparts. In one scene of sodomy between James and Catherine, James remains completely silent as Catherine talks about the possibility of James having sex with Vaughan. Although she can be read as the passive partner in this scenario, she is, in fact, the more active party, dominating the scene with a monologue in which she describes how masculine and powerful Vaughan is. Again, the sexual activity discussed is anal in nature, with much of the talk centered on Vaughan's anus and what it would be like to penetrate it. Catherine demands that James "tell" and "describe" to her what it would be like with another man.

This scene is transgressive in a number of ways. First, it is the penetrated partner — that is, the one who is usually "passive"— who dominates: this is a transgression of the way power is generally assumed to operate, especially in a situation like this. Second, the scene is transgressive in that a character narrates a completely different sexual situation to the one that is presented, thereby doubling the erotic effect on the viewer and challenging the narrative norms of erotic accounts. It also echoes Sade's statement that it is just "as pleasant to discuss" a sex act as it is to "undergo" it.[17]

Later in the film James does experience an encounter with Vaughan, as well as with all of the other members of the group, both male and female. All are bisexual and frequently swap sexual partners. The focus

Part Two: Monstrous Humans

on anal and rear-entry sex obviates the issue of a partner's gender because the sexual experience is all about individual satisfaction. In *Crash*, interaction with a sexual partner is about as heartfelt as interaction with a toaster or any other technological device that is designed to meet our needs. That the two partners are not facing each other signals their emotional distance from one another. As Cronenberg observes, "It felt right, getting both the actors looking toward the camera and not at each other. It helped that sort of 'disconnected' thing.... It's more, 'How do you have sex when you're not quite having sex with each other?'"[18]

As Cronenberg's observation suggests, the characters experience no connection with each other — even when they are physically joined. As Sade states, the experimenting and exploration of sexual pleasure is a selfish exercise: "What is it one desires when taking one's pleasure? That everything around us to be occupied with nothing but ourselves, think of naught but of us, care for us only."[19] Like the serial killer Patrick Bateman in *American Psycho*, these characters are the result of a culture that is centered on the accumulation and consumption of surface wealth. The Ballards have an ultra-modern apartment, work in the media, and own all the technological mod-cons that one could need. These characters are so materialistic that they are beginning to merge with these surface materials, suggesting in turn that they are all surface, with no deep, emotional core within. Because of their privileged position in society, all their desires may be realized through the objects that they have, rather than in their relationships with each other.

This lack of emotional empathy between the characters leads to what is most disconcerting about *Crash*, which, like *Henry* and Sade's novels, refuses to offer a moral critique of the characters' actions. At the beginning of the film the characters are already part of a non-traditional open marriage, and in the last scene they show no signs of giving up their ways. In fact, since the last line spoken is "Maybe the next one" in the final scene in which James drives Vaughan's car, it seems certain that the characters will continue their sexual exploits, with James now assuming Vaughan's role as leader of the group. Like *Henry*, the film does not employ the device of a voiceover as a way to justify and explain the characters' actions, instead filming the action from a distance, coldly observing and documenting events.

This lack of a subjective viewpoint is similar to the way events are portrayed in Cronenberg's first feature film, *Shivers* (1975), which tells the story of how the population of a high-rise become consumed by a relentless

6. The Transhuman

sexual appetite as the result of a parasite that is cultivated by a scientist. The parasite is designed to pass from person to person through sexual contact, releasing repressed sexual appetites, so all those infected become unable to control their sexual urges. Again, Cronenberg represents technology as a tool to unleash forms of sexual desire usually repressed by society, suggesting that although technology is usually seen as advancing humankind, it can also bring us back into contact with the archaic instincts that we have repressed. In *Shivers*, this heightening of the sex drive leads not only to the rapid spread of the infection, but also to the transgression of all sexual taboos (against rape, incest, pedophilia, group sex, bisexuality), as the infected increasingly have no choice but to act on all of their sexual impulses. The film ends with everyone in the building infected and dispersing into cars, in order to leave the confines of the high-rise and infect the general population.

While this may seem to be a tragic ending, with normality destroyed rather than restored, Cronenberg has remarked that the ending can be seen as triumphant—if only we were to assume the parasite's point of view:

> It's about trying to understand interrelationships among organisms, even those we perceive as disease. To understand it from the disease's point of view, it's just a matter of life. It has nothing to do with disease. I think most diseases would be very shocked to be considered diseases at all.... For them, it's very positive when they take over your body and destroy you. It's a triumph. It's all part of trying to reverse the normal understanding of what goes on physically, psychologically and biologically to us.[20]

Just as *Shivers* shows events from the perspective of the parasite, it could be argued that *Crash* shows events from the perspective of the car — or any of the other technological artifacts that silently contribute to our everyday lives. Since these objects have become incorporated into our bodies, and are used to live out our desires and combat our fears, perhaps humans have changed them just as they have changed us. Therefore, as Vaughan insists, they, too, may view the car crash not as a terrible catastrophe causing only destruction and tragedy, but as an enabling of the object to release its own creative energy.

In *Crash* the erasure of the boundaries between flesh and technology — a blurring which characterizes the transhuman — has led to the emergence of new sexual practices and bodily possibilities. The characters who experiment with this new form of sexuality are direct descendants of Sade's libertines: JG Ballard, the author of the novel that provides the basis for the film version of *Crash*, has stated unequivocally that the film is "Sadean" in structure and content.[21] *Crash* is an example of a Sadean work updated for the twentieth and twenty-first centuries. Through their sexual experimentation, the characters in *Crash* repeatedly transgress taboos and norms—to the point that they begin to physically transform and mutate, thus demonstrating the chapter proposition that it is repetition that is the driving force of transgression. With the aid of new technology, sexual desires and urges can be expressed in new and different ways—but at the expense of human emotional connection.

In *Crash*, Cronenberg presents a commentary on contemporary society as being a transhuman society where technology is invading the human. The result of this is a society populated by Sadean beings, forever striving for the ultimate transgression yet unable to feel the thrill and excitement that they seek through their endless consumption of objects and technology. In contrast, Shinya Tsukamoto's *Tetsuo* shows the shift from the human to the transhuman as having an energetic rather than a numbing effect.

The Body as Machine: Tetsuo: The Iron Man

The films of Shinya Tsukamoto share many similarities with Cronenberg's. For example, in Tsukamoto's films latent desires and feelings are manifested physically on the bodies of the characters. In his debut film, *Tetsuo: The Iron Man*, and its sequel, *Tetsuo 2: Body Hammer*, the characters' repressed sexual and violent desires are expressed through the fusion of flesh with metal and other technological materials. As their bodies change, they express their lust and aggression more freely. Thus, as with the Sadean libertine, it is through the body that the cycle of transgression begins. Through the violation of the boundaries of the body, in the integration of flesh with metal, the characters are enabled to transgress against, and then destroy, all previous norms of body and society.

Unlike Cronenberg, who in films such as *Shivers*, *Rabid*, *The Brood*, and *Videodrome* portrays bodily transgression and transformation as a site of anxiety and disgust, in Tsukamoto such transgressions are met with feelings of joy and delight. Acts of destruction, rage and rebellion are transformative, as they are in Cronenberg, but with more positive and energizing results. This is more in keeping with a Sadean point of view, where transgressions are celebrated as a move away from societal norms

6. The Transhuman

and oppressions. Like the Sadean libertine, Tsukamoto's characters use their bodies to rebel against the prevailing culture, and rejoice in the resulting mayhem and the destruction of ordered society. Tsukamoto himself remarks that in his films there is a recurring obsession with the place of the body within the modern metropolis: "The theme of 'human body and the city' started with *Tetsuo* and ended with *Vital*."[22] Tsukamoto is commenting here primarily on the constraints imposed on those living in the highly populated, highly confined cities of Japan. In the *Tetsuo* films, as well as *Tokyo Fist* and *Snake of June*, characters turn their back on the oppressive, buttoned-down existence that people are forced to live within the cramped spaces of the Japanese metropolis, and embrace a new freedom that comes with sexual exploration and violent aggression. For just as Sade's works present his most extreme fantasies, in the films of Tsukamoto we also see extreme fantasies played out onscreen, fantasies which incorporate technology into the body in order to wreak tremendous destruction.

In *Tetsuo*, man and machine fuse together to create a new being. This is presented as an organic process and not an operation performed by other people who impose change on the body. The body in *Tetsuo* undergoes a transformation, a metamorphosis from within. Metal and mechanical parts grow from flesh, an expression of repressed emotions. These changes in the body then precipitate changes in behavior. The main character, known only as the Salaryman, is a meek, mild-mannered man who one day engages in a transgressive act: he has sex with his girlfriend (known only as the Girlfriend) at the scene of a car accident after having just hit a man (who is called the Fetishist due to his fetishistic desire to insert metal into his flesh) and presumably having killed him.

Through this act the Salaryman transgresses the rigid codes of behavior enforced by the strict and oppressive society around him. Instead of helping someone in need, he thinks only of his own sexual pleasure. Not only do the violence and death excite him instead of repelling him, they turn on something within him that will change him irrevocably. The guilt and the pleasure released by the car accident (an act that, as discussed in the previous section, involves the forced melding of flesh and technology) manifest physically, as metal bursts out and invades his flesh.

The fusion of technology and humanity has been explored in many science fiction stories. It has also become a reality, with many people's bodies having been aided by technology in some way (for example: reading glasses, prosthetics, pacemakers and performance-enhancing drugs). The term "cyborg" has been developed to describe a being that is part human and part machine. As Donna Haraway writes, "A cyborg is a cybernetic organism, a hybrid of machine and organism, a creature of social reality as well as a creature of fiction."[23] It can be argued that, as it is a creature that is made of both metal and flesh, Tetsuo is a cyborg. In her "Cyborg Manifesto," Haraway posits that the cyborg is a creature in which all previous boundaries and rules become unfixed. It is a transgressive body in that all notions of gender, reproduction and sexual orientation are now completely opened to new configurations. The cyborg thus presents an opportunity to destroy all of the old, oppressive and patriarchal ideas about the body.[24] Certainly in *Tetsuo* normative representations of gender, reproduction and sexuality are subverted, climaxing in the vow of this new cyborg being to destroy the "whole fucking world."

Because its very existence focuses on the transgression of bodily norms and the seeking of new bodily possibilities, theories and representations of the cyborg can be read as a continuation of many of Sade's key themes. In fact, many writers have likened the Sadean libertine body to that of a machine[25] in that it is devoid of emotion and works single-mindedly toward a goal — namely, the exhaustion of all possibilities of sexual satisfaction, which in turn requires the taking of the natural urges to such an extreme point that they become almost unnatural. Sade, while following nature, always sought to transcend it and to thwart its will at every turn. Technology, which is artificial and hence non-organic, can thus be used as a tool to combat nature in this way. It has been used to change and transform the body, the self in its most natural form. However, as demonstrated in Sade's novels, all these attempts at thwarting nature are simultaneously used as a means to explore and express natural desires and urges — namely, the sexual and violent instincts.

The introduction of metal into the flesh leads to the release of previously repressed desires. Those who are afflicted can no longer control themselves, acting in bursts of sexualized violence. In an early scene, the Salaryman fantasizes about his girlfriend dancing suggestively. As she dances, a phallic metal pipe emerges from her crotch. The Salaryman is near her, crouched on all fours, and the Girlfriend penetrates him with the pipe as the Salaryman screams. In this scenario, notions of gender and sexuality are subverted, as it is the woman who penetrates and the man who is penetrated. And it is technology (the metal pipe) that has allowed this gender switch to take place.

However, when he awakens, it is the Salaryman who has begun a bodily transformation. After having sex, the Salaryman and the Girlfriend sit

6. The Transhuman

down at the table to eat. As she eats, he hears loud, metallic noises instead of chewing: his whole perception of the world is changing. The organic has become metallic. Suddenly a drill bursts through the table, and the Salaryman runs to the bathroom. When the Girlfriend finds him, she screams, and a medium shot shows the Salaryman's rotating penis/drill. As he walks toward her, the drill cuts her and she runs away. The Salaryman begins to chase her, and she tries to fight him off, using a frying pan and a knife. As they struggle, the Salaryman's body is transformed, as violence creates change. The Girlfriend stabs the Salaryman in the neck, and he drops to the floor. A close-up reveals that the drill has now stopped spinning. The Girlfriend straddles him, and while she holds the knife in his neck they begin to kiss.

Paglia's observation about Sade that "sex and aggression so fuse that not only is sex murderous but murder is sexual" assists in enabling the viewer to view this scene as a constant shifting between sexual satisfaction and attempted murder.[26] There is a brief flashback to the two having sex at the car accident (another incident where murder leads to a sexual climax). This flashback actually causes the Salaryman's penis/drill to start rotating again, and a close-up of the Girlfriend reveals blood spurting all around her, as she is killed by the drill. The traditional heterosexual coupling has now been destroyed, and this destruction will only escalate.

Through the lens of Sade's writing, *Tetsuo* can be understood as a glorification of destruction. Both *Tetsuo* and its sequel, *Tetsuo 2: Body Hammer* (which has different characters and a different protagonist, Tomoo), end with the protagonists hell-bent on destroying the society around them (and in *Tetsuo 2* he actually succeeds). Since their bodies now transgress the division between flesh and machinery, the protagonists no longer exist as part of normal society and so plan to destroy it in order to build a new world that suits them. After the Salaryman and the Fetishist meld together into a huge mound of metal, with only their faces visible, they begin to travel through the streets. The Fetishist declares, "We can mutate the whole world into metal. We can rust the world into the dust of the universe." The Salaryman replies, "Let's do it." The two have joined together to become a completely new being, something that exceeds and transcends the idea of the human. From this creation will come destruction, for at the top of the being, next to the Fetishist's head, is an arm with a gun fused onto it. This being has been created to destroy, and the last line uttered in the film is the Fetishist's proclamation that "our love can destroy this whole fucking world! Get 'em!"

Part Two: Monstrous Humans

Just as Haraway stated in her manifesto, the cyborgs in *Tetsuo* present a whole new form of reproduction that refuses established gender rules because it is practiced by two men. Their fusion begins as an act of violence, with the Fetishist attacking the Salaryman, but as they fight they become merged together. A shot shows them floating, naked and upside down, in what looks like a womb. In close-up their heads emerge from a wall of tissue made up of plastic, metal and a foaming substance, and a pan across the screen reveals that they have been reborn as a combined metal being. From this act of rebirth comes the means to destroy the "whole fucking world." Like Sade's libertines, the characters in *Tetsuo* have imitated the forces of nature, with creation and destruction becoming mixed together. What began as a violent attack has created a new being. Destruction becomes the driving force of nature, as Sade insists:

> [D]estruction is the soil and light that renews her and where she thrives; it is upon crime she subsists, it is, in a word, through death she lives.... Why does she send ... plagues, wars, blights, and dearths, if it were not essential that Nature destroy, and if crime and destruction were not inseparable from her laws?[27]

In *Tetsuo* the destruction of the physical body creates a new body in which all previous ideas about gender, sexuality and reproduction become irrelevant and are instead opened to completely new interpretations. All previous boundaries have been destroyed. The film ends with this new hybrid creature moving through the streets, about to begin its assault on the world. Such an ending speaks of broader cultural and political ideas in which the destruction of old beliefs about the human and the human body, rather than leading to a new, more oppressive society where humans are caged and constrained by technology, can in fact lead us to completely reinvent conceptions of the human and our place in the environment around us.

This destruction of the body and society is continued in *Tetsuo 2*. Destruction follows the protagonist, Tomoo, throughout his life. After his kidnapping by a gang leader, Yatsuo, it is revealed that Tomoo and Yatsuo are actually long-lost brothers. After Tomoo defeats Yatsuo, a black tube bursts out of Yatsuo's head and latches onto Tomoo's. Tomoo's memories are then fed into Yatsuo. He remembers how his father tried to create "the first human weapon," and that he and his brother were used as guinea pigs. They were trained to shoot guns, and Tomoo soon began to assimilate the gun into his own body. Yatsuo comments that Tomoo changed through his own will, and that "his will to kill always beat mine."

6. The Transhuman

The Fetishist (Shinya Tsukamoto) in *Tetsuo: The Iron Man* (1988).

Tomoo changes himself so he can dominate others, a process that parallels the transgression of the Sadean sovereign man, who also uses his body to enforce his superiority over others. Blanchot's comment about the sovereign man seems also to apply to Tomoo's transformation: "To be unique, unique among one's species, is indeed the sign of true sovereignty ... for the Unique Being, being independent of all others who are incapable of harming him, immediately declares complete dominion over them."[28] Once Tomoo changes—when he becomes "unique"—he begins to rule over everyone else. Yatsuo tells a story of how Tomoo's gladioli bulbs were stolen when he was a child. Tomoo, who was usually shy and timid, beat up the children who took them and "most of them died." In the process, the bulbs were crushed also. This suggests that Tomoo brings nothing but destruction into being, and in his new bodily form Tomoo develops from meek and mild-mannered into a creature of destruction: a large, tank-like creature that assimilates other people. So sovereign over them is he that he uses them as fuel to keep himself going.

The defining moment, when Tomoo realizes his power, occurs when he murders his own parents. As children, Tomoo and Yatsuo spy on their parents having sex, during which their father holds a gun to their mother's

Part Two: Monstrous Humans

head, forces it into her mouth and then (accidentally) pulls the trigger. Tomoo bursts in and shoots his father, who is holding nothing but a sheet in front of him, with his gun/hand. Their mother, not yet dead, stands up, and Tomoo begins to shoot her also. In slow-motion, blood bursts from the parents' bullet wounds, the camera showing clearly the damage that guns do to the human body. Yet, over this violence, Yatsuo in voiceover comments: "I don't think he felt sorry he'd killed our parents. He felt ... the beauty in destruction. That scared him and he lost his memory." Yatsuo's parting words before he expires are: "So go ahead, destroy. Destroy the greatest thing of all." The scene then ends with a close-up of the father's face as bullets fly into it: blood sprays, and chunks of flesh are blown off the skull.

Both *Tetsuo* films detail the body being torn open, invaded and destroyed. Yet, as Yatsuo admits, there is a certain "beauty" to the destruction. There is no doubt that Tsukamoto is a stunning visual stylist, and nowhere is this striking visual aesthetic better utilized than in scenes of violence, where the body is damaged and destroyed. In this sense, Tsukamoto continues the work of Sade: not only does he focus on the body, but he also concentrates most intently on the way the body's boundaries may be transgressed and then opened up to new possibilities. Like Sade, his characters follow nature's urges but then transcend them, in this case by merging with technology. Such bodily transformations represent a commentary on the pressures and restrictions that come from living in the modern metropolis. Rather than being oppressed, confined and invaded by the technology that surrounds us, in Tsukamoto's films the human body uses this technology so that it becomes a site of rebellion against restrictions, with rage and destruction bringing feelings of pleasure and delight.

In *Tetsuo*, transgression of the body has led to a mounting transgression of behavior, as the body's changes lead to the release of repressed desires until society itself is destroyed. All previous norms of gender, reproduction and sexuality go through change and mutation: the heterosexual couple descends into violence; two men recreate themselves in a new form; sexual release comes from the bonding of flesh with inanimate metal objects. This process of mutation illustrates this chapter's central argument, as it is through repeated acts of violence and transgression that sexual desire is increased and new forms of pleasure are achieved. Through the use of technology, the characters in these films continue Sade's project in his literature: to destroy society and to embrace nature's chaos.

PART THREE

Victims

In contrast to the bodies of the previous chapters, the victim's transgressive body differs in that it is a body that is also transgressed against. The victim does not actively participate but is, rather, forced either by another person who is stronger, or by circumstances that render the victim powerless. The victim differs from the masochist in that the latter willingly subjects him or herself to pain and suffering for the purpose of his/her own enjoyment. In fact, the masochist has as much, or even more, control over the situation as his/her partner. The victim, on the contrary, is seen by the perpetrator not as an equal but as a thing to be exploited. The body of the victim is thus a consumable product, something to be used and then discarded.

Following this idea that the victim is an object to be exploited, in his works Sade advocates a form of sexuality that is completely self-centered, with the partner viewed as a victim subordinate to one's own will and enjoyment. Thus, the figure of the victim is important within the work of Sade, for although his stories mostly focus on the figure of the libertine, who casts off all societal constraints and personal inhibitions in order to seek the ultimate pleasure, his work also focuses on victims, who are subject to the libertine's more violent desires.

Moreover, for Sade, those who fall into the victim category are victims not only within the sexual realm but in all other aspects of life. Sade's central victim figure is the title character of his novel *Justine*, a virtuous young maiden who seeks only to help others but is repaid with cruelty and abuse. This tale's "moral" is that the way of life extolled by both church and state, which entails that one must put aside one's own lust and greed for the greater good, leads only to poverty and ruin. Instead, Sade depicts a society that follows a natural hierarchy in which those who deny themselves nothing get all that they desire and rise swiftly to power, while those who choose to follow a virtuous path find themselves the victims of nature and its urges. Justine thus serves as an archetype of the victim, for she receives no respite from the continual torrent of abuse from those around her.

Part Three: Victims

For Sade, this victimizer/victim scenario occurs throughout nature, in which there is, according to him, a hierarchy of the strong and the weak. In Sade's words:

> When next we see that Nature has physically distinguished individual persons, that she has made some strong, others weak, what could be more patently evident that, in so making them, she expects the strong to commit the crimes she needs to have committed, just as it is of the essence of the wolf that he devour the lamb.[1]

According to Sade, in human society some are destined to be "wolves," while others, "lambs." In nature there is a primal struggle for domination and supremacy, with the strong overpowering and feeding off those who are weaker. This natural hierarchy of power dominates Sade's works, with his characters divided into the categories of strong and weak, or, more specifically, victimizers and victims. The victimizers are his libertines, who use the victims for their own pleasure.

It is ironic, however, that society is portrayed by Sade as being just as brutal as nature. For Sade always depicts the pillars of society as hypocrites, people who use their power to oppress others. Those beneath them are disadvantaged because they are the only ones who actually follow the path of virtue which has been taught to them. As Camille Paglia observes, "Sweep one hierarchy away, and another one will take its place, perhaps less palatable than the first. There are hierarchies in nature and alternate hierarchies in society."[2] However, the victim's capacity for transgression differs from the libertine's in that the former leads to punishment by societal forces.[3] Justine, for example, repeatedly finds herself accomplice to criminal activities for which she is then imprisoned. Thus, the transgressive bodies in the films discussed below are victimized and punished because they also transgress societal rules and boundaries, either through the breaking of a law or the violation of a moral standard (such as committing adultery, or participating in premarital or underage sex). This transgression is different to that of the Sadean libertine though, in that these transgressions are most often undertaken not for one's own pleasure but for the sake of another. Yet, despite being punished for their transgressions, in both Sade and the films below it becomes clear that the only way to fight or overcome this victimization is through further transgression.

Despite the fact that Sade's texts and the films discussed here belong to different genres and utilize different types of representations, a Sadean reading of these movies will reveal something about the victim which has hitherto remained hidden and unexplored — namely, that the victim is not

Part Three: Victims

a passive figure but a fully transgressive character. I have chosen, therefore, to concentrate my discussion specifically on the victims and the acts of transgression which help release them from their victimization. This allows the analysis to keep with the central idea that transgression can be understood as a positive and creative force, as well as also keeping with the focus on the victim as a transgressive body. In order to begin this Sadean reading of the victim, I will first focus on the figure of the woman in the films of Lars von Trier.

7

Women

The representation of women in cinema has always been under discussion within film theory. That women are often depicted as either sexual objects or damsels in distress has been a source of contention and debate, especially within the field of feminist film writing. Theorists such as Laura Mulvey have claimed that the medium of narrative cinema is an oppressive force which subjugates women, imposing onto them "the dominant patriarchal order."[1] According to this view, the woman onscreen is victimized in order to assuage male fears and anxieties about women being both controlling and castrating.

According to Mulvey, in order to counter these fears, instead of representing the female as castrating, she is shown to be castrated. Because she does not possess the phallus, woman is viewed by patriarchal society as essentially lacking, and it is this lack that not only makes her different from the male but also inferior, or "less than." This view of woman is expressed cinematically in two ways: "The male accepts her difference either by re-establishing her 'castration' and punishing her accordingly or by disavowing her castration by setting up a fetish in place of her 'lack.'"[2] The woman onscreen is thus shown as being punished and victimized, or else turned into a sexual object. In either case she is positioned as the passive victim of the active and sadistic male gaze. As a result, the female spectator is left with only two options: she must either take on the male gaze herself and identify with the male subject onscreen, or she must identify with the female object's passivity and victimization in a masochistic sense.

As this summary suggests, the place of woman as a strictly passive victim is rigidly upheld within this Mulveyan framework. This is a notion that is challenged here, for despite the fact that this section also focuses on the woman-as-victim, a Sadean reading of this figure will differ from previous feminist theory, which relies heavily on a psychoanalytical framework, in that there is a shift in focus from victimization to transgression. By showing the woman victim as transgressive, she is revealed as a complex representation which challenges dominant norms. The female victim is released from her passive position and instead assumes a fully transgressive one.

The films of Lars von Trier directly explore this archetype of woman-as-victim, focusing on female protagonists who are unjustly used and abused by others. While these idealist characters sacrifice their comfort, dignity and in some cases even their lives for what they feel are noble causes, they are always defeated by a selfish and unfeeling society. Thus, the division between victimizer and victim, integral to the Sadean text (as all of his characters are separated into these two categories), can also be applied to the characters in von Trier's films.[3] As a result, it is possible to understand the societies portrayed in these movies in terms of the Sadean hierarchy of nature, for in these films those who are stronger willingly manipulate and exploit those who are weaker, thus punishing those who strive for goodness. However, following the Sadean view that the victim is active and transgressive, the protagonists in von Trier's films, although subject to victimization, can be understood as the dominant force which drives the narrative. These women are active agents who not only transgress societal norms and standards, but also endure incredible punishment and hardship.

Grace/Justine: Dogville

Dogville (2003) is the first installment in Lars von Trier's "American trilogy" (although only one sequel, *Manderlay* [2005], has been made), each film executed in a style that fuses film techniques with theater. These films tell the continuing story of Grace, a woman on the run who, in the first film, is taken in by the people of the small town of Dogville. Although at first Grace and the townspeople live in harmony, soon the townspeople begin to take advantage of Grace's vulnerable position. Because Grace has transgressed by breaking the law, the townspeople see fit to punish her, despite the fact that she tries hard to better herself. Like Sade's Justine, Grace suffers at the hands of others while she strives to be good and put others before herself. This demonstrates the Sadean view that nature is selfish and that those who follow society's teachings of compassion and mercy find themselves in a weaker position within the natural hierarchy. Both *Justine* and *Dogville* reveal society's innate cruelty, as it victimizes those who most valiantly seek to uphold its ideals.

Part Three: Victims

Dogville is filmed on an empty stage, with the enclosed space representing the whole town. The set consists of chalk outlines designating streets and houses where each character lives, with only sparse props, such as doorframes and beds. Even living things, such as Chuck's pet dog Moses, and Ma Ginger's gooseberry bushes, are represented as crude outlines on the floor. The emphasis is therefore on the human body, its movements and placement within the set and within the camera frame. Without walls, *Dogville* shows literally that there are no boundaries within von Trier's world. In this place the rules that govern conduct and good behavior are systematically broken by the townspeople. Faced with a person who makes herself completely open and vulnerable to them, they disregard ideals of altruism and compassion, and instead exploit her to their own ends. In a completely open set, Grace is continually seen and exposed to the townspeople, each of the violations committed upon her carried out in plain view.

The town of Dogville shares many parallels with the society depicted in *Justine*. Like Sade, von Trier depicts a society in which the good are made to be the victims of other people's lascivious and unlawful designs,

Tom Edison Jr. (Paul Bettany) convinces Grace to stay in *Dogville* (2003).

7. Women

and the good nature of a young woman who seeks only to help her fellow humankind and perhaps find some meager happiness for herself is exploited. Although Dogville is a small, impoverished town struggling to survive the Depression, it also serves as a microcosm of modern American society. Directed by a Danish filmmaker who has never set foot on American soil, *Dogville* has led to von Trier being accused of anti–Americanism.[4] Although the people of Dogville are different from the aristocratic libertines in *Justine* who use their wealth and privilege to bend others to their will, they can still be understood as operating within a natural hierarchy where the weak and helpless are preyed upon by those that are stronger. *Dogville* illustrates that exploitation is not the prerogative solely of the rich and powerful; even those who are downtrodden can abuse those that are beneath them.

The first of many violations that Grace endures takes place while she is looking after the children of Chuck and Vera. A police car rolls into town, and when Chuck returns home he mentions the police presence and reminds Grace that her freedom is in his hands. Chuck then rapes Grace, claiming that she "tricks men into feeling that they mean something to you.... It's your own damn fault that I need your respect." During the rape, the camera repeatedly tracks out from the act to a wide shot of the town, showing the townspeople going about their daily business, completely oblivious to the violence taking place among them. While the lack of walls makes Grace vulnerable and open to attack, it also shows that the townspeople are indifferent to Grace's plight, easily willing to turn a blind eye to injustice.

As the body transgressed, Grace's physical appearance changes throughout the story. When she first arrives, Grace, dressed in a long black coat with a fur collar and sporting a blonde bob haircut, is much more glamorous than the working class townspeople. It is as though a cinematic *femme fatale* had wandered away from the city and into America's heartland. Grace is thus represented initially as a transgressive figure, and since the townspeople also view her as dangerous and transgressive, they, as the "normal" majority, seek to punish her for her transgressions. It is therefore ironic that this blonde gangster's moll, the kind of woman who has always symbolized sexual manipulation and deceit, becomes herself the victim of manipulation and exploitation by the good, hard-working folk of a small town, the very people who usually represent honesty, wholesomeness and the American dream. In order to stay under the town's protection, Grace, although remarking that she has never worked a day in her life, must carry out odd jobs for each of the townspeople. When she embarks on her work, she is no longer dressed in the clothes she arrived in, but is from then on dressed in a light pink dress and a dark purple cardigan, clothes in colors that are cute and girly and typical of the town's women.

While Grace is in Ma Ginger's shop, the townswomen remark on her beautiful hands, and Grace advises them on how to keep them in the best condition. However, after several scenes showing Grace hard at work, the narrator explains how "slowly, those alabaster hands turned into a pair of hands that could have belonged to anyone in a small rural community": Grace's body has adapted to the change in lifestyle, and she has become roughened and hardened by it. Grace is portrayed by Nicole Kidman, whose pale complexion, fair hair and slender frame contribute to the character's vulnerability and fragility. Her body is not strong and robust, but slight and completely unsuited to the physical labor (and the subsequent physical assaults) that she must undergo. For example, after an attempted escape from the town, Grace is fitted with an "escape prevention mechanism"—a thick metal collar with an attached bell that Grace must wear around her neck, as well as a heavy chain attached to a large wheel that she must drag behind her. Grace's thin frame is in direct contrast to the heavy metal mechanism that the townspeople have forced her to wear.

However, Kidman also manages to imbue Grace with a strength that endures throughout her ordeals. Even while being molested or assaulted, Grace's face does not betray her emotions. She is able to keep a quiet calm, as the narration insists:

> It was not Grace's pride that kept her going ... but more the trancelike state that descends on animals whose lives are threatened. A state in which the body reacts mechanically, in a low, tough gear, without too much painful reflection. Like a patient, passively letting his disease hold sway.

As this statement is made, the camera is above Grace looking through the window frame of Jack MacKay's house, tracking in to focus on Jack's hand as it rests on her thigh. Both Grace and Jack sit still, neither acknowledging the inappropriate placing of Jack's hand. That this molestation occurs as they sit at the window again illustrates that the townspeople make no attempt to hide their mistreatment of Grace, as well as Grace's acceptance of her position within the group.

The next shot shows yet another sexual assault, the camera tracking out from a close-up of Grace's face as she lies face down on her bed to a

7. Women

wider shot that reveals Bill Henson behind her, using her for his own sexual pleasure. The narration continues:

> Most townspeople of the male sex now visited Grace at night to fulfill their sexual needs.... The harassments in bed didn't have to be kept secret anymore, because they couldn't really be compared to a sexual act. They were embarrassing, in the way it is when a hillbilly has his way with a cow. But no more than that.

Both of these excerpts from the voiceover narration liken Grace to an animal: she is now used by the townspeople in the same way they would use livestock. This is highlighted by the tracking shot of Bill's assault on her, with the camera peering through the headboard of Grace's bed, thus creating the impression that she is behind bars like a caged animal.

The townspeople's use of Grace as though she were a thing to be consumed can be understood in terms of Sade's view of the victim as something less than human, a thing that exists solely to provide others with pleasure. As one of Sade's libertines, the Duc de Blangis, remarks to the intended victims of one hundred and twenty days of debauchery: "[C]onsider that it is not at all as human beings we behold you, but exclusively as animals one feeds in return for their services, and which one withers with blows when they refuse to be put to use."[5] This passage by Sade encapsulates the way in which the people of Dogville come to view Grace. Indeed, the victim in Sadean philosophy is seen as inferior to the victimizer: because he or she is used for the pleasures of others, the victim is treated in whatever way will bring the perpetrator the most enjoyment. As Justine's sister, the libertine Juliette, observes while engaged in a libertine escapade involving the rape of a young girl: "I soon remarked, from the manner the group adopted with her, by the harsh tone in which she was addressed, that the poor little wretch was considered nothing more than a victim whose doom was already sealed."[6] Being designated the victim means that social niceties no longer need apply to the person so designated. The victim is outside society, or below it, and therefore can be violated without regard for societal law.

In von Trier's film, at first it seems that the townspeople of Dogville merely want compensation for the danger in which they put themselves by protecting Grace from gangsters. Yet their later attempts to thwart Grace's escape from the town reveal that they now perceive Grace as their property. She must stay with them in order to attend to their needs. When Grace is accused of stealing, she is not taken to the authorities; instead,

Part Three: Victims

the townspeople impose their own idea of justice, and put the bell and chain around Grace's neck.

Furthermore, von Trier goes on to show that romantic love is merely an exchange based on exploitation. Just prior to Grace's arrival, Tom Edison Junior, a young writer and self-proclaimed "town philosopher," explains to his best friend Bill Henson that the town "has a problem with acceptance," and that the town needs "something for them to accept, something tangible." When Grace arrives, Tom sees her as a "gift" to the town, something that will teach them about being open and accepting. And certainly at the beginning the people welcome Grace into their homes and into their hearts. Even the intellectual and analytical Tom finds himself falling deeply in love with her, claiming, "When I come to decipher you, I get nowhere." This is a telling remark, for Grace's openness and vulnerability does not so much show who she is as it shows who the townspeople really are. Grace only too perfectly illustrates Tom's theory that the town "has a problem with acceptance." Both Tom and Grace become victims of their own ideals, of trying to make people more open and accepting. They try to make Dogville a better place, and both fail miserably. As with all von Trier's protagonists, Grace and Tom are idealists, and in following their ideals they bring about the very evil they are trying to vanquish.[7] Even though Tom claims to love Grace, he is content to use her as part of an experiment that he has devised, an experiment that causes her much harm and eventually leads to the total destruction of the town.

Von Trier highlights the failure of romantic love and high ideals by making Tom the one who betrays Grace to the gangsters. Tom is aware of how the men of the town are using Grace for sex, and Grace feels that she can make love to Tom only when she is free. The scene that leads to Tom's betrayal of Grace is prompted by her refusal to have sex with him. At a town meeting, during which Grace reveals all that she has suffered at their hands, Tom is asked to choose between Grace and the town. When he arrives at Grace's house he tells her, "I've chosen you." He begins to kiss her, but when again she stops him from going further, Tom asks her to "compromise her ideals." In response, Grace lies down on her bed, completely passive "You can have me if you want me," she says. "But do what the others do: threaten me." While she remains in the town, Grace is a victim, a captive in chains, and therefore unable to take part in a sexual act in which she is the equal of her partner. As Tom's anger at her refusal rises, Grace sees that he has "been tempted to join the others and force me. Perhaps that's why you're so upset." Grace has an ability to show people who they really are, which leads them to mistreat her.

Indeed, people seek only to exploit Grace's goodness for their own ends. As Tom walks away from Grace's house, the voiceover explains: "Tom was angry.... It was not because he had been wrongfully accused, but because the charges were true.... The danger Grace was to the town, she was also to him." By observing this, von Trier illustrates that anyone is capable of the acts that the people of Dogville commit. In fact, throughout the film Tom is complicit in the violations of Grace, with several shots showing Tom watching silently as the chain is put around her neck, and standing by as men leave Grace's house in the middle of the night. Tom even lets the people believe that Grace stole his father's money, when it was he who had actually committed the theft. Once he realizes all that he is capable of, he calls the gangsters and tells them where Grace is, aware that they may very well kill Grace if they capture her.

The coming of the gangsters is awaited with trepidation, but also with expectations of rewards. However, when the gangsters arrive they are appalled at Grace's state and immediately remove the chain from around her neck. Ironically, it is the gangsters, figures renowned for their violence and ruthlessness, who are shocked at how Grace has been treated by these honest, simple folk. It is soon revealed, however, that Grace is the daughter of the head gangster, having run away from what she saw as the injustice of their lifestyle. Yet, as her time in Dogville demonstrates, this injustice prevails in all walks of life. Von Trier sees evil as a natural trait of humanity. Even Grace, who endures so much and strives so hard to be good, eventually gives in to the desire for revenge, and gives orders for the town to be burned to the ground and all the inhabitants killed. The only alternative to being a victim, as Sade indicates, is to become a perpetrator: Grace's revenge allows her to take a higher place in the natural hierarchy.

When the gangsters arrive, Grace climbs into the car to see her father, and the two debate the fate of the town. Grace initially defends the people, but her father admonishes her: "[Y]ou sympathize with everyone.... Rapists, murderers may be the victim, according to you." He calls Grace arrogant, for even though she applies high ideals to herself, she does not apply them to others: "[Y]ou forgive others with excuses that you would never permit for yourself.... The penalty you deserve for your transgressions, they deserve for their transgressions." Grace and her father discuss the nature of humanity, her father referring to people as "dogs." Grace agrees with this, replying that "dogs only obey their own nature, so why shouldn't we forgive them?" This statement suggests that, just as the people of Dogville view Grace as an inferior animal, Grace in turn also views them as helpless beasts. They do only what is in their nature to do. This echoes Justine's statement that "it is then true that there are human creatures Nature reduces to the level of wild beasts!"[8] What sets Grace and Justine apart is that they do not follow their natures, and Sade and von Trier demonstrate that the consequence of this is to become a victim. Following her father's advice that the only way to stop a dog "is with the lash," Grace sacrifices her high ideals and decides to deal with her abusers on their own base terms. Grace comes to the conclusion that simply to excuse these actions and forgive them is to allow such injustices to be continually inflicted on other helpless people. But in order to do this, she must — like the townspeople — become a violent perpetrator.

Until this conclusion, Grace is the epitome of the victim, continually used and exploited by others. Like Sade's Justine, Grace seeks to be good, even though it is this very goodness that is the cause of her suffering. Both Sade and von Trier depict humanity as naturally cruel and selfish, the characters of Justine and Grace being anomalies within their worlds. They highlight society's hypocrisy, as they embody society's ideal of the good woman but are then victimized because of this. On the contrary, it is those who follow the natural urge for domination and supremacy who triumph. Grace's luck changes once she realizes this, demonstrating that although one is victimized because they have transgressed, it is only through further transgression that this subjugation can be cast off. This is what separates Grace from the heroines in von Trier's earlier films in his "Golden Heart" trilogy. Like Grace, these women are victims, but they remain so because they deny nature's selfish urges and think only of others.

Bess/Justine: Breaking the Waves

Dogville can be seen as a continuation of, as well as a response to, von Trier's "Golden Heart" trilogy, which consists of the films *Breaking the Waves* (1996), *The Idiots* (1998) and *Dancer in the Dark* (2001). Just as the little girl in the fairy story *Golden Heart* [9] gives to others without any thought for herself, in each of these films the female protagonist must commit a sacrifice for the people she loves, an act that will save others but not herself. The Golden Heart willingly becomes a victim, giving in to suffering for what she believes is a higher purpose — just as, in Sade's work,

7. Women

Justine refuses throughout her ordeal to indulge in revenge or pleasure, believing that her goodness will guarantee her a place in Heaven. The character of Bess in *Breaking the Waves* can thus be understood as a representation of the Sadean idea of the victim. In fact, Bess is ashamed of her sexual allure, and, rather than seeing it as a gift of nature that she must use, she sees it as the reason that she must suffer.

Unlike the conclusion of *Dogville*, in which the female protagonist seeks revenge on those who have wronged her, the women in the Golden Heart trilogy suffer without respite. For example, Karen in *The Idiots* consents to "spass" (the term used by the characters to refer to the act of pretending to have a mental disability) in front of her family. She consents to this in an attempt to keep her group of friends together, even though interviews throughout the film reveal that the group still broke up after Karen humiliated herself. Selma, in *Dancer in the Dark*, refuses to use money that will help her defense in a murder trial, so that the money can be used to pay for an operation to save her son's eyesight. Eventually, her lack of funds leads to her being found guilty and sentenced to death. Finally, in *Breaking the Waves*, Bess, like Grace in *Dogville*, also seeks to be good but finds herself sexually exploited by men.

These women are victimized because they do not conform to societal norms. All four are, ironically, labeled transgressors against the ideal of a good woman who contributes to society: Bess is promiscuous; Karen leaves her family and joins a commune in which the inhabitants pretend to suffer from intellectual disabilities; Selma is a poverty-stricken, progressively blind immigrant who commits murder; and Grace is a criminal wanted by the law. As Thomas Beltzer states, "In *Breaking*, *Idiots* and *Dancer*, the female saints may 'deny themselves' as the gospel tells us to, but all do so in a decidedly un–Christian way — the saint as adulterer, anarchist and murderer."[10] It is because they transgress that these women are victimized.

Likewise, in Sade's work Justine is also labeled a transgressor, and she ends up in jail several times. In fact, she even has the mark of the thief branded onto her body, which identifies her as a criminal. In Sade's book, Justine's transgressiveness is reflected in her punishment. The man who brands her declares:

> [L]et's punish her a thousand times more than we would were we to take her life, let's brand her; this disgrace, joined to all the sorry business about her body, will get her hanged if she does not first die of hunger; until then she will suffer, and our more prolonged vengeance will become the more delicious.[11]

Part Three: Victims

Although this harsh punishment reflects Justine's own transgressions in the past, it is Justine's body that is being transgressed now. Furthermore, it is on her body that her status as victim and outsider is inscribed. Paradoxically though, despite these marks and labels, Justine and the Golden Heart women are represented as epitomes of goodness. Motivated solely by a desire to help others, the women willingly sacrifice their happiness—sometimes even their lives—for those that they love. It is always their labeling by others that causes them suffering and makes them victims. This, and the fact that they choose not to rebel against this oppression, is what separates them from Sade's libertine transgressors.

Bess' torment begins after her husband, Jan, is paralyzed following an accident at work. While lying in his hospital bed, Jan asks Bess to go out and sleep with other men in order to tell him about it: "It will feel like you and me being together again. That will keep me alive." Bess has several encounters with other men, all of which are shown to be degrading and unpleasant for her (for example, after masturbating a man on a bus, she vomits; and during sex with a man from the pub, a close-up reveals that she is crying). Brought up a strict Calvinist, and taught that one must be good on Earth in order to be rewarded in Heaven, Bess sacrifices her place in Heaven in order to save Jan.[12] Portrayed as very innocent and childlike, she frequently has conversations with God in which she herself assumes the voice of God, speaking in low, admonishing tones. Thus, for instance, in church Bess prays to God and asks, "Am I going to Hell?" to which she replies, "Who do you want to save, yourself or Jan?"

Like Sade's Justine, Bess believes that her behavior on Earth will affect her place in the afterlife, and that sexual activity leads to damnation. Furthermore, far from empowering them, the lust that the beauty of these women arouses in others makes them feel "bad." In *The Sadeian Woman*, Angela Carter reflects on this narrative logic while discussing the character of Justine:

> Because she is beautiful, she arouses concupiscence. Therefore she knows in her heart she must be bad. If she is bad, then it is right that she should be punished. She is always ready for more suffering. She is always ready for more suffering because she is always ready to please.[13]

This statement is also relevant to Bess. Because she wants to save Jan, she feels that she has forfeited her place in Heaven and has thus become "bad." Accordingly, she puts herself in increasingly dangerous situations. In the film's seventh chapter, titled "Bess' Sacrifice," she sees local prostitutes

7. Women

being taken out in boats to nearby ships to service the men who work on them. Although she is refused passage to these ships because she will take away business from the regulars, she is warned to avoid the biggest ship. As Jan's condition deteriorates, Bess believes that the only way he can be saved is to continue with what he requested.

However, having failed to consummate a recent encounter on a ship after it turns violent, Bess' whole world falls apart: she is excommunicated from the church and cast out by her mother due to her lewd behavior. She is also told that she is to be committed to a mental institution, from which she later escapes. Once outside she is taunted by local children and faints outside the church. The priest finds her on the ground and, visibly disgusted by her state, simply walks away from her. Just as Justine searched in vain for kindness, Bess also finds that no one will help her in her time of need. And von Trier shows, just as Sade claims throughout all his works, that the church is the last place that one will find salvation and forgiveness. Although the church preaches the repression of natural urges, its representatives are capable of the same cruelty that is to be found in nature.

After the priest leaves Bess passed out on the ground, her sister-in-law, Dorothy, happens by and rushes to her. Unfortunately, she delivers more bad news: Jan is dying. Having been cast out of the church and declared unfit by the medical authorities, Bess has nothing left except what she believes is her ability to save Jan. As she leaves Dorothy, her only wish is that Dorothy prays for Jan to "rise from his bed and walk." In the face of all the suffering she has undergone, she still thinks only of others. Bess believes that she is bad and unable to be saved, so she must be punished. Her plight echoes one of Justine's prayers: "Powerful God! Thou knowst it, I am innocent and weak, I am betrayed and mistreated; I have wished to do well in imitation of Thee, and Thy will hath punished it in me: may Thy will be done, O my God!"[14] Bess is also shown praying to God and asking for His guidance. Both Bess and Justine throw themselves at the mercy of God. They are victims because they do nothing to help themselves, as they feel whatever happens to them is God's will. Consequently, both are continually punished, as neither of them chooses to fight the injustices that befall them. For her sins, Bess realizes the only thing she can do is sacrifice herself for Jan. As a result, she returns to the ship where the two men who had attacked her earlier await her arrival.

The Golden Heart trilogy's preoccupation with suffering and cruelty is matched by the aesthetic approach of each film. All three movies are shot using handheld cameras and edited in a rough style. The shots are

Part Three: Victims

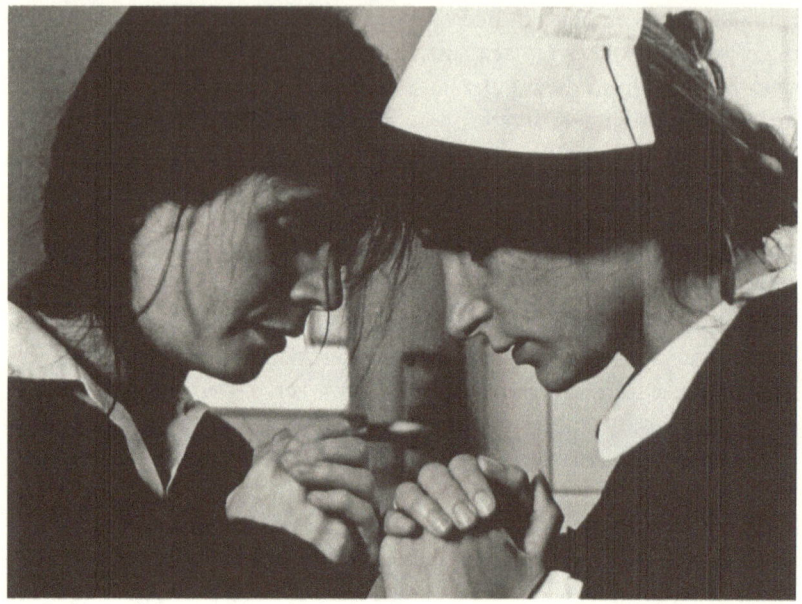

Bess (Emily Watson) and Dorothy (Katrin Cartlidge) pray in *Breaking the Waves* (1996).

thus not framed to look like pretty pictures with expressionistic lighting or elaborate sets, but instead present a gritty portrait of the women's lives, highlighting the harshness and hopelessness of their situations. The world is represented as being as ugly as the treatment the female protagonists receive. Indeed, von Trier himself admits his eye for the ugly, making reference to a character in Hans Christian Andersen's *The Snow Queen* who has a "troll's shard" in his eye: "I remember there is a boy who at some stage gets a troll shard in his eye and sees things ugly."[15] Even the women themselves—Bess in *Breaking the Waves*, Karen in *The Idiots* and Selma in *Dancer in the Dark*—do not fit the stereotype of the glamorous leading lady found in the Hollywood melodrama, a genre full of suffering women. In von Trier's films all women are dressed in drab, cheap clothes, with no make-up, and lit only with natural light. There are, however, brief moments of beauty in the films; for example, in *Breaking the Waves*, postcard chapter headings of misty landscapes divide up the story, while *Dancer in the Dark* possesses characteristic musical numbers. Yet these moments serve only to show that the reality of these women is vastly different from their fantasies of how life should be.[16]

7. Women

Just as Sade creates a world wherein there are only victimizers and their victims, von Trier can be read as presenting a world like Sade's in which people are divided into two classes. However, von Trier is more interested in representing the victims, those with high ideals and the desire to do good, who are systematically destroyed by the society around them. These high ideals are always undercut by the base desires of nature: those who are good are always taken advantage of by those who seek only to dominate and exploit others. This is also true in the case of Sade's Justine, who denies her natural urges and thus becomes their victim. Although forced into transgression by others and for the sake of others, both Justine and the Golden Heart women refuse to transgress for their own pleasure. Thus, they remain victims, proving that victimization can only be overcome through further transgression. This dilemma over whether one should follow one's urges or repress them as society dictates is a central concern in representations of the adolescent, which will be discussed next.

8

Adolescents

The figure of the adolescent is problematic in cinema. Although cinema has obsessively documented young, beautiful faces and bodies, there has always been controversy over the sexualization of bodies that are deemed not yet of the appropriate age to engage in sexual activity. In extreme cases, films have even been charged with inciting pedophilic desires. This matter has been of particular concern over the last decade or so, with many movies that explore the sexuality of adolescents, such as Adrian Lyne's *Lolita* (1997), Gregg Araki's *Mysterious Skin* (2005), and Larry Clark's *Ken Park* (2003), finding it difficult to find distribution, and in some countries have faced censorship and banning.

What is meant by the term "adolescent" is actually hard to define. Each person matures and changes at his or her own individual rate. For the purposes of this study; the "adolescent" refers to a person who is going through the process of puberty, the phase when one is no longer a child physically but not yet a fully grown adult. It is at this stage that a person embarks upon sexual maturity, experiencing sexual feelings that accompany physical changes.

In the work of Sade, this time of sexual initiation is dramatized in his *Philosophy in the Bedroom*. In it, the young Eugénie is schooled in the art of sex by three older libertines, with the story's introduction addressing a message to its younger readers: "You young maidens ... imitate the fiery Eugénie; be as quick as she to destroy, to spurn all those ridiculous precepts inculcated in you by imbecile parents."[1] Sade thus constructs the mother and father as instruments of repression, representatives of a society that instills chastity and shame in its young people. Adolescents are thereby taught to deny nature and their own natural urges, and Sade depicts adolescence as a time when these urges take over. From the view of Sadean philosophy, both *For My Sister* (Catherine Breillat, 2001) and *Ken Park* can be read as depicting the sexual activity of its young characters in an attempt to eradicate the shame and guilt that

8. Adolescents

young people are taught to feel in conjunction with their natural burgeoning sexuality.

"It's sick being a virgin": For My Sister

Just as Sade focused on sexuality and its transgressions, Catherine Breillat has also made a career out of breaking taboos about sexuality. Her films have shattered previous ideas about how sex can be represented in cinema. She has appropriated the techniques of pornography (such as explicit scenes of actual sexual activity, and close-ups of both male and female genitalia while in a state of sexual arousal) and used them to create films that are also intellectual treatises (in this respect she bears similarities to Sade, who, as discussed earlier, likewise mixes pornography and intellectual debate). Since Breillat consciously explores, and then breaks, many of cinema's taboos, she has been labeled the "female de Sade."[2]

There are certainly parallels between the two figures, with Breillat also being subject to censorship and outrage throughout her career. Her first novel, *L'homme facile*, was restricted to readers over the age of eighteen due to its extreme sexual content. Ironically, Breillat was only seventeen when she wrote the book. The content of the book, and its subsequent reception by public authorities, set a pattern that has been repeated throughout her career. All of her films center on female sexuality, depicted in frank and explicit terms. As Breillat maintains, sexuality is taken "as a subject, not as an object."[3]

With her film *For My Sister,* Breillat concentrates on the area of female adolescent sexuality. Her previous film, *Romance* (1999), broke taboos on cinematic sexual representation, and *For My Sister* continues this approach, presenting scenes that contain nudity and sexual activity involving adolescents and teenagers. This is done not for the purposes of titillation, however; the film presents an examination of how adolescents must wrestle with their own natural urges and burgeoning sexual feelings as they enter into conflict with society's restrictions on sexual expression. In this film Breillat presents a character, Anaïs, who transgresses dominant ways of thinking about the adolescent body and sexuality. It is through this transgression that Anaïs is able to overcome victimization. Breillat can thus be understood as presenting a Sadean view of sexuality whereby societal repressions of sexuality are seen as

Part Three: Victims

working in opposition to natural urges. By unflinchingly representing adolescent sexuality, Breillat counters the shame and guilt that has become associated with it.

For My Sister depicts a summer vacation taken by a family with two daughters, twelve-year-old Anaïs and fifteen-year-old Elena. The film opens with a wide shot of the two girls walking through a woodland area. Noticeable immediately is the physical differences between the two girls: while Elena is strikingly beautiful, Anaïs is slightly overweight, a pubescent girl who has yet to shed her puppy fat. What also becomes apparent as the scene progresses is their difference in attitudes toward the opposite sex. Anaïs admonishes her older sister, "When you fall for a boy, you try to pin him down too soon." Anaïs advocates sex without love, saying, "If I meet a man I love I'd want to be broken in.... The first time should be with a nobody.... Guys are all sick." While Elena maintains more romantic notions about her loss of virginity, Anaïs, even at her young age, is able to see through the lies that boys and men tell, and views sex as a physical act rather than part of a love affair.

This echoes the sentiment advanced by Sade, who also sees a separation between sex and love. One of the lessons that Eugénie is taught by her older teachers is: "Never listen to your heart, my child; it is the most untrustworthy guide we have received from Nature."[4] Similarly, what Breillat's film illustrates is that Anaïs' perspective in this first scene will, literally, help her to survive the tribulations that befall her over the summer. By the end of the film Elena will have her heart broken and her life taken away from her, while Anaïs' realistic approach to love and sex allows her to overcome all manner of obstacles, some of which will be life-threatening.

Anaïs' ideals are further expressed through a game that she plays by herself. While swimming in the pool she plays out a scene between a wooden pole and a metal rung, pretending that the objects are two jealous lovers. Holding the wooden pole, she tells it, "[Y]ou're my love, but I don't want to marry you yet," and then swims to the metal rung, kisses it and says, "Now I know that men like me, I want other experiences." This play-acting game reveals what for Anaïs is a perfect scenario—having found love (with the wooden pole), she has also found "nobody" (the metal rung) to whom she can "give it all." She explains these actions to the wooden pole: "I haven't really cheated on you. Women aren't like bars of soap.... They don't wear away. On the contrary, each lover brings them more and you get all the benefit."

8. Adolescents

Anaïs (Anaïs Reboux) playacts an adult scenario in *For My Sister* (2001).

This game illustrates an opinion expressed by Sade:

One can fuck every day in every conceivable manner without diminishing the sentiments of the heart, and without their help. 'Tis the most commonplace thing in the world, to love one man to distraction and to fuck frenziedly with another; you don't give your heart to him, just your body.... There are two manners of loving a man: morally and physically.[5]

The lofty, romantic ideals of love, taught to young girls everywhere through stories, songs and films, are thus represented as being in direct contrast to the natural and lustful urges. Anaïs realizes this through her performance in the pool. The transgressive nature of the adolescent is illustrated by this scene, as Anaïs enacts a very adult, sexual scenario, but in the form of a childish pretending game. Later in the film there is a shot of Anaïs, again by herself, in front of a mirror: in mid and wide shots she lifts up her nightgown and looks at her developing body. While gazing at herself she says out loud "Slut." Although she is a virgin, Anaïs calls herself a "slut" because young girls are taught to be pure and chaste in thought as well as deed. Breillat implies that the thoughts and desires that both Anaïs and Elena experience are actually normal, and that it is only the

Part Three: Victims

shame and guilt imposed by society that sullies what is perfectly natural for any adolescent.

Elena, meanwhile, has moved on from sexual games and adolescent curiosity, and during the course of the summer embarks on her first sexual relationship. Because of her age, her sexual exploration must take place in secret, and, unbeknownst to her parents, Fernando sneaks into her room (which she shares with Anaïs) in the middle of the night. A prolonged scene takes place, as Elena yearns to show her love for Fernando but also wants to keep his respect. The scene is shot in long takes, in either mid or long shots that capture the awkwardness and frustration of the young lovers. They long to express their desire physically but are bound by social convention; for not only is Elena under the age of consent, but there is also the fear that she will be labeled promiscuous by her peers. As the scene begins, the two make small talk, with Fernando promising to visit Elena after the summer ends. The dialogue, however, is insignificant: the wide shots focus attention instead on body language, as Fernando constantly touches and caresses Elena's body, slyly trying to remove clothing. Once Elena refuses to have sex with him, Fernando stops touching her, sits up and lights a cigarette, coldly announcing: "That makes a big difference."

Elena is torn between doing what she desires and doing what she thinks is right. In order to get around these feelings of guilt, Fernando, like so many other young men before him who have found themselves in the same situation, resorts to lying. He tells her that sex will be a "demonstration of love," and that she is "the kind of girl men dream of marrying." During this conversation there is an edit that shows Anaïs awake and listening; in one of the few close-ups of the scene, Anaïs looks on with her hand over her face, peering through her fingers. This shot represents how it is the younger sister who sees through Fernando's lies, and throughout the love affair it is Anaïs who is the voice of reason to which Elena goes for advice. Although Elena is physically older, Anaïs has wisdom beyond her years. Breillat cuts back again to Anaïs later in the scene, after Fernando has convinced Elena to consent to anal sex, telling Elena "all girls take it the back way. That way it doesn't count." By focusing the audience's visual attention on Anaïs, only the sounds of Fernando and Elena are heard, Fernando gasping with pleasure, while Elena's gasps seem to be filled more with pain than delight.

Breillat shows how the stigma attached to the loss of virginity can lead to other sexual activity being explored as an alternative, and in this

8. Adolescents

case it seems to be an alternative that, for Elena at least, is not particularly pleasurable. The next morning Fernando complains that what should be "natural" has become "sinister," and he stops Elena as she falls to her knees, warning her that if they are caught he will be sent to jail because she is underage. If they are to give in to the desire that they both feel and both consent to, they will become criminals. Elena replies, "That's not fair; it's me who wants it." This is a point that Breillat addresses in an interview:

> I don't know why, but the puritan authorities don't want Elena to know that marvelous act [of making love]. The problem is that all governments and all religions have always been determined to make sex something dirty. Religion is afraid of the power of sex — because a person who can find the transfiguration of sex in her life is no longer a person who can be directed.[6]

If Elena becomes sexually active she will be defying the moral conventions that have been taught to her by her parents and by society at large. Consequently, she may be victimized because she has transgressed: Elena risks being labeled as promiscuous and rebellious, someone outside of societal norms which dictate the virtue and purity of young women, who ought to be seeking a husband, not merely a sexual partner. Yet, as Breillat states, through this transgression Elena will be free of repression, she will become someone who can "no longer ... be directed."[7] Breillat's way of thinking is thus aligned with Sade, who also sees sexual experimentation as a form of freedom where one is no longer subject to society's moral teachings.

This scene, which takes up almost a third of the film's running time, is presented not only with a rarely seen truthfulness, but also with the trademark explicitness that has led Breillat to become a controversial figure. As Brian Price observes, Breillat has gained "a reputation as the female de Sade, the new Bataille — a purveyor of transgressive sexuality."[8] The use of mid and long shots in this scene exposes the nudity of both Elena and Fernando. While most films (especially teen sex comedies) focus on female nudity for the purposes of titillation, *For My Sister* presents a situation that is not played for laughs or arousal, but instead strives for realism. It therefore not only shows male nudity but represents the penis in various states of erection. In this respect, Breillat states: "There is no masculine psychology in my cinema. There is only the resentments and desires of women."[9] Just as heterosexual men have been gazing at the female form since cinema began, with female nudity becoming a norm in many film genres (horror, erotic thrillers, sex comedies), Breillat now presents sexual scenes from a female heterosexual point of view.

Part Three: Victims

The explicit sexual scenes in Breillat's films are not intended merely to titillate an audience, but are, rather, intellectual exercises whereby the viewer is confronted with the character's dilemmas. The conflict and narrative drive of the films are found within these scenes. The sequence between Elena and Fernando is typical of this approach. This scene contains two beautiful young people in states of undress, showing explicitly the sexual activity that is taking place. Yet the scene is harrowing, not arousing, illustrating the confusion and frustration of the two young people, which leads not to a sexual climax but, instead, to the young girl participating in a sexual act that brings her no pleasure. This scene is concerned with issues of female sexuality, representing Elena's internal guilt, shame and arousal, as well as Anaïs' curiosity and increasing knowledge of how women are manipulated.

Just as Sade's *The 120 Days of Sodom* is viewed as a precursor to the intellectual and scientific works of Krafft-Ebing and Freud, in the work of Breillat, depictions of sexual scenarios can also be read as studies of human psychology and intellect. In fact, Breillat's film *Romance* has direct links to *The 120 Days of Sodom*, as it concerns the exploits of a young woman's quest for sexual pleasure and fulfillment, and shows her participating in a variety of different sexual acts. In the works of Breillat there is a fascination with sexual acts that deviate from the norm of vaginal intercourse within monogamous relationships. Her characters search for sexual satisfaction and personal fulfillment through the exploration of transgressive sexuality — indeed, this search is the main narrative drive of both *Romance* and Breillat's subsequent film, *The Anatomy of Hell* (2004).

Breillat's point of view encompasses the desires not only of the adult female, but also the adolescent female. The obsession with the loss of virginity, primarily an adolescent concern, has also been explored in Breillat's previous films *A Real Young Lady* (1975) and *36 Fillete* (1988), as well as one of her most recent movies, *Bluebeard* (2009). In cinema, the body of the adolescent is taboo, a body with adult attributes but still obviously childlike. In *For My Sister*, several scenes show the naked body of twelve-year-old actress Anaïs Reboux, most controversially in a rape scene. Breillat herself has referred to the body of the adolescent as a "forbidden body, a blend of a little girl's body and an incredible sexual opulence."[10] This blurring of the child and the adult within the body of the adolescent leads to discomfort among censors about whether showing the body of the adolescent will result in the minor being seen as a sexual object.[11] This censorship of the body represents society's denial of the sexuality of the adolescent.

8. Adolescents

Most Hollywood teen movies are, in fact, populated by actors who are well into their twenties: because they look like adults, it is acceptable to show them as sexual objects. A film like *For My Sister* is different in that the actresses playing the sisters are the same age as their characters. At the age of twelve, a time when many girls experience the beginnings of puberty, Anaïs Reboux changed and matured through the course of filming. In Breillat's own words, "I had a big concern about censorship because in the last scene you could see [Anaïs'] breasts. I actually wanted her not to have breasts, but her body changed between casting and the end of shooting."[12] Unlike Hollywood teen movies such as *American Pie* (1999), the process of adolescence is shown as neither titillating nor amusing, but rather as a painful time when one is pushed and pulled by many opposing factors. It is a time when one strives for independence, and boundaries are tested.

Throughout the film, Anaïs is held back in her own sexual exploration by her mother and her sister. The mother insists that Anaïs always be chaperoned by her older sister, with Elena's beauty leading to all male attention being diverted away from Anaïs (earlier in the film Anaïs complains to Elena, "I'm sick of being your ball and chain"). It is no coincidence, then, that immediately prior to Anaïs' sexual initiation by rape, Elena and her mother are removed from the scenario, killed by an anonymous attacker. This sudden attack comes as a complete surprise, being very different in tone from the rest of the film. The first three quarters of the movie presents a coming-of-age narrative, but as soon as Anaïs and her mother and sister leave their summerhouse, the film becomes more sinister and suspenseful. As they drive back to the city, several wide shots show their car on the busy motorway, which is full of big trucks. The traffic moves very fast, with the trucks dwarfing the women in the car; and when they try to change lanes no one allows them in, a chorus of beeps telling them to keep their place (any woman who has ever overtaken a man in a big/fast/expensive car will know the anger and indignation that such an act can provoke in a male driver!). These shots create a feeling of rising tension and an increased loss of control for the women over their surroundings.

Inside the car, however, mother and daughters are still preoccupied with what took place on their holiday—namely, Elena's loss of virginity. Their conversations also foreshadow their eventual fates. Because Elena is still underage, the mother announces to her that "your father wants you examined." Not only has Elena had her heart broken after realizing that Fernando's proposal was fake, but now she must also face a shaming medical examination, and even a possible court case. This threat to Elena of examination and legal action will most likely become a reality for Anaïs, who is last seen in the film being led away by the police. At one point they pull over to the side of the road so Anaïs can vomit, and Elena tries to comfort her as the mother stands to the side. Elena, still furious with her parents, confides in Anaïs, "I want her to die," and then adds, "I'll die with her." Anaïs states, "I don't want to die," to which Elena replies, "No danger of that. You're not in the dead man's seat," a reference to the front passenger seat, which sustains the most damage in a car crash. Although they are not involved in a car accident, Elena's words become prophetic, as both her and her mother die together while Anaïs survives. The ending, with its sudden and completely unexpected attack, represents a complete genre shift. It is a transgression made by one of cinema's most prolific transgressors.

This sudden genre shift can be viewed as an inherently Sadean trait. In her description of *The 120 Days of Sodom*, Annie LeBrun remarks on Sade's tendency to mix forms and genres: "Here we have a text which begins like a historical novel, moves into a theatrical structure, is transformed into a philosophical dialogue, thins out into a catalogue, and finishes as a balance sheet of those who are massacred and those who survive."[13] The transgressiveness of the bodies in Sade's texts is mirrored by the transgressiveness of Sade's narrative form, a trait that can be found in *For My Sister*. Although Breillat creates a rising tension, when the film does change (with the surprise arrival of the family's attacker), it comes as a complete and violent shock. This sudden turn of events is not in any way in keeping with the movie's narrative trajectory up to that point. Yet, from a Sadean perspective, it is very much in keeping with Breillat's constant transgression of established filmic representations of the body and sexuality. In her exploration of the sexual body, Breillat, like Sade, always includes scenes of violence. And by shifting genres, Breillat captures the sudden, visceral nature of the attack.

As this genre shift in *For My Sister* reveals, Breillat does not shy away from portraying the dangers that come with her characters' sexual explorations: both *For My Sister* and *Romance* not only contain scenes of rape, but the films remain ambiguous about the moral status of these representations. While the films of von Trier clearly designate certain characters as victims—people who are subject to abuse and exploitation—Breillat presents less certain scenarios. Indeed, in the rape scenes in both *For My Sister* and *Romance*, the female victim denies her status as victim. In

8. Adolescents

Romance it is even uncertain whether what takes place can be classified as rape. The protagonist, Marie, is walking up the stairs to her apartment when a man asks to perform cunnilingus on her for money. The scene then cuts to a shot of the man with his back to the camera, as Marie obliges his request. During the course of the encounter the man turns Marie over and anal sex ensues, after which the man runs away, with Marie screaming after him that she is not ashamed, leaving suspended the knowledge of whether Marie consents to anal sex with the stranger.

In "'X' Marks the Spot: Classifying *Romance*," Adrian Martin examines differing opinions about this scene. In the report by the Australian Office of Film and Literature Classification, which initially imposed a ban on the film, the scene is described as one of "implied sexual violence" wherein "the man orders her to turn over. She objects, tries to scuffle away from him."[14] This description clearly implies that it is a rape that takes place. Martin states, "My problem with this account is that I did not see Marie try to 'scuffle away' during the scene, or be forced to turn over.... I do not believe that Breillat is presenting an act of sexual violence as currently defined."[15] I also view the scene as not presenting a clear-cut case of rape. Throughout the film, scenes of sadomasochism pervade Marie's sexual exploration, so it remains completely uncertain as to whether the scene is one of rape or one of rough sex with a stranger. What is clear within this scene is Marie's refusal to be seen as a victim, shown by her defiant exclamation as the man leaves, as well as the fact that the incident does not seem to affect Marie deeply. Rather, it is shown as just one of her many sexual experiences.

By taking sexuality as her subject, Breillat, as Sade did before her, examines the power dynamics that govern all human interactions. What defines a victim is the guilt and shame that he/she feels about what he/she has experienced. This is what separates Sade's Justine from her sister Juliette. While Justine views lust as a sin, Juliette embraces it, willingly participating in all manner of sexual activity and gladly becoming a prostitute. Yet there are similarities between the two girls' stories, as Maurice Blanchot explains:

> We see this virtuous girl [Justine] who is forever being raped, beaten, tortured, the victim of a fate bent on her destruction. And when we read *Juliette* we follow a depraved girl as she flies from pleasure to pleasure ... the two sisters' stories are basically identical, that everything that happens to Justine also happens to Juliette, that both go through the same gauntlet of experiences and are put to the same painful tests. Juliette is also cast into prison,

roundly flogged, sentenced to the rack, endlessly tortured. Hers is a hideous existence, but here is the rub: from these ills, these agonies, she derives pleasure; these tortures delight her.[16]

The two sisters in *For My Sister* can also be read as distinguished by the feeling of shame that separates Elena from Anaïs. After anal sex with Fernando, Elena says she feels "like crying" and that she is "ashamed." Anaïs, in contrast, tries to comfort Elena by saying, "It's sick that people think it's their business. It's sick being a virgin." This statement shows that Anaïs' thinking challenges the standard belief that it would be "sick" to suggest that young girls may have sexual thoughts and desires, and that, if this were the case, it would be wrong for them to act upon these desires. Anaïs, by contrast, thinks that her virginity is not something to cherish but rather to be discarded without regret.

Accordingly, Anaïs' moral attitude towards her loss of virginity through rape is presented with Breillat's trademark ambiguity. There is no doubt that Anaïs is raped; and there is no doubt that Anaïs secretly wanted it to happen. As Brian Price admits, "[T]here is no question that what we see is rape; the question is why this young girl would want to see it otherwise."[17] After Elena and her mother are murdered, Anaïs gets out of the car at the same time as the assailant does. Both stare at each other and wordlessly begin to walk toward the woods. There is a cut to a static wide shot as Anaïs is then pushed to the ground. The camera tracks up to Anaïs' face as the man pulls up her dress, and Anaïs says to the man, "You're not going to hurt me."

This statement recalls Marie's defiant scream that she is not ashamed — although physically the men are stronger, the women assert that they will not be overpowered. They refuse to be victims. As she is being raped, a close two-shot shows Anaïs' blank expression throughout the attack, and afterwards the two characters again stare at each other. That Anaïs remains stoic and is still able to look her attacker in the eye demonstrates her strength and lack of shame about what has happened to her. The film ends with Anaïs being led out of the woods by two policemen, one of whom remarks, "She was in the woods. She says he didn't rape her." Anais then replies, "Don't believe me if you don't want to," as she turns to look into the camera, which freeze-frames as the film ends. Anaïs' look straight into the camera is an expression of her defiance, her opposition to society's views of the sexuality of adolescent girls.

The societal repression of the adolescent body leads to it becoming a symbol of guilt, shame and forbidden sexuality. Breillat breaks the taboo

8. Adolescents

against adolescent sexuality by focusing on the two sisters' different attitudes toward their sexual feelings, just as Sade distinguishes between the sisters Justine and Juliette. What these stories of two sets of sisters reveal is that being ashamed of one's own natural sexual feelings is to become their victim. This demonstrates that the victim can find release and relief from victimization through transgression, for it is Juliette and Anaïs, the sisters who have cast off society's constraints, who find themselves in a stronger position. In the next section, in which I analyze Larry Clark's controversial film *Ken Park*, this struggle between the repression and expression of adolescent sexuality is again central to the narrative's exploration of victimization.

Good Boys and Girls: Ken Park

The social denial of the sexuality of the adolescent is continued in the restrictions on the sexuality of young people who have completed the process of puberty. Larry Clark's *Ken Park* focuses on older youth who are nevertheless still under the age of eighteen (an age that often represents the onset of adulthood) and therefore continue to be under the care of their parents and guardians. Although within the family scenario they remain as children — that is, as subject to the rule of the parents — the onset of sexual maturity inevitably causes friction within the family structure as the teenagers strive for independence.

Certainly the controversy that has surrounded the film demonstrates the extent to which sexuality of teenagers is denied by society, with the representation of their sexual feelings and desires constituting a taboo.[18] In contrast to societal norms, Clark suggests that redemption can come from sexual intimacy when it is carried out between consenting parties. Moreover, Clark's film shows that the shame usually associated with sexual desire leads only to the desire becoming perverted — that is, to its being used as a destructive rather than a healing force. In the same way, in Sade's writing, sexual desire, like all forces in nature, is understood as having both creative and destructive powers. In consequence, what I will argue in this analysis of *Ken Park* is that the taboo on teenage sexuality leads to the repression and perversion of these redemptive qualities. After being victimized and abused by adults, the teenagers participate in a transgressive sexual act, which is shown to have a positive and creative effect.

The crisis of the family constitutes one of the film's key themes. In fact, all the families in *Ken Park* are depicted as being in the process of breaking down. The four main characters, Claude, Peaches, Shawn and Tate, are caught in families where, as Larry Clark attests, "[T]he kids are getting none of their needs filled by their parents.... The adults are using the children in the most inappropriate way to try to fulfill their own emotional emptiness."[19] Clark shows that society's assumptions about the family are a fiction, that many children are abused, molested and exploited by the very people who are meant to protect them. Clark maintains that "the stories are true ... based on people I know," and that he is motivated to document "things that weren't talked about, that I knew were stories about real life, about things that I saw in my life that you really couldn't talk about."[20] In other words, as normative ideas about the family fail to reflect the real problems that people face, these impossible ideals often are the very cause of much of the trouble.

In contrast to normative family ideals, the family in Sade is a place of violence and sexual promiscuity. Many of his libertines commit incest with family members while also espousing that any notion of family ties is a fiction: "[W]e owe nothing to our parents ... the rights of birth establish nothing."[21] While society teaches that the family should be a structure based on care and nurturing, the families in Sade and *Ken Park* can be read as functioning within the natural hierarchy, where people think only of themselves and their own needs, and use others around them (namely, other family members) as a means to meet these selfish needs.

This hierarchy of power is represented in one of the film's opening scenes. Shawn is first seen on top of his little brother, holding his arms down, forcing him to say that he loves him and that Shawn is the "master," a typical torment by an older brother of a younger sibling. This game, however, shows the hierarchy that is at work in the film: the older control, and seek to dominate, the younger. The Sadean natural hierarchy is at play in this perfect suburban setting, and the two generations of characters, parents and children, are locked in a struggle for domination and control. Each person can be read as striving to become "master."

Due to these conflicts within the family unit, the teenagers fulfill their emotional needs by connecting with each other. The events in the film take place simultaneously, each character going through a significant event in the course of one day.[22] The four main characters are kept separate, with only three of them coming together in one of the film's final scenes. It is in this scene that the three characters experience an escape from their plight, finding comfort with each other. The only way for the young people

8. Adolescents

in *Ken Park* to escape the oppression and victimization that is forced upon them by adults is through transgression. Indeed, the scene reveals the connection between the teenagers through a prolonged sexual encounter between Shawn, Peaches and Claude, whose emotional intimacy is expressed sexually.

While most of the film follows a realist aesthetic, this sex scene is more stylized. This scene is shot in a bright, almost golden light, which contrasts with the previous scenes involving Tate, filmed using a cold blue filter (which I will discuss later). The golden light suggests that this is a scene of hope, which is supported by their talking about their hopes. A jazzy Van Morrison song plays in the background through the sequence (providing a contrast to the skater-punk music that has played previously in the film) as the characters are arranged in elaborate sexual tableaux. The transgressiveness of this scene is presented as positive and creative, as it is a way for the characters to overcome their torments.

The sex scene is intercut with shots of the three characters talking and playing games, such as a pillow fight and Twenty Questions. This game playing illustrates the fact that they are still childlike. In fact, while having sex they retain a certain degree of innocence, even though the adults have tried to take that innocence away, either by exploiting them or telling them that they are bad and unclean. Yet, not only are they open to each other sexually, they also talk openly about their dreams for the future. This is reminiscent of Sade's libertines, who also revert to a childlike state during their sexual encounters, in which the adult socialized world is rejected in favor of childish play and transgression. This rejection of the "adult" is a rejection of the social order as a whole.

In *Ken Park* this is also a rejection of the victimization that these characters have sustained, and an act of defiance against the adults who have abused them sexually and psychologically. The utopian nature of the scene is made clear when Claude tells the others about a book he has read called *Island of Paradise*, about an island where all that the inhabitants ever do is to have sex. Claude describes it as a place of peace and harmony, "some kind of utopian society or something." Certainly this scene itself is like an island within the harshness of the film: a sunny, happy place surrounded by dark waters. Here the characters create their own utopia, a society unlike the one in which they are marginalized because of their age.

This scene in particular highlights how Clark exposes all that is repressed in modern society. As Robin Wood writes in his influential article "American Nightmare," there is "basic repression," which "makes us distinctively human, capable of directing our own lives and co-existing with others," as well as "surplus repression," which "is specific to a particular culture and is the process whereby people are conditioned from earliest infancy to take on predetermined roles within that culture."[23] Wood identifies the four main themes of surplus repression in Western culture: sexual energy in general; female sexual power; bisexuality; and the sexuality of children. All four of these areas are explored within *Ken Park*, explicitly detailed in the threesome scene. For just as the monster is coded as Other, Wood remarks how this "Othering" can be extended "to other genres: substitute for 'Monster' the term 'Indians,' for example, and one has a formula for a large number of classic Westerns; substitute 'transgressive woman' and the formula encompasses numerous melodramas."[24]

Following from this, the protagonists in *Ken Park* can also be interpreted as representations of the Other because they embody all that is repressed in Western culture. The sexuality of children, something which, as Wood states, is repressed from infancy into adolescence, and encompasses any "expression of sexuality before marriage,"[25] is one of the Western culture's fundamental taboos (the anger which this film created certainly testifies to this fact). What makes *Ken Park* so controversial is that Clark directly opposes this taboo. The process of becoming Other, of taking part in an act that is rejected by society as completely transgressive, is shown as positive and creative.

The threesome scene is transgressive in every sense, but what is most interesting and different is that this transgression is not eradicated or vanquished — it is celebrated. Like Sade, Clark consciously transgresses sexual norms and explores taboos in a direct and confronting manner, in an attempt to overturn the social order. Both artists work on the edge of what is deemed acceptable, with Clark constantly being questioned about his apparent obsession with adolescent and teenage sexuality (see, for example, the title of an article on Clark from *The Guardian*: "King Leer").[26] Clark presents a direct affront to societal norms, a point proven by *Ken Park*'s reception, with its struggle to find a distributor in the USA, its banning in Australia, and numerous articles in the press linking the film to child pornography.[27] However, through the lens of Sade's work, its direct and detailed depiction of societal taboos can be read as an attempt to fully explore the power and possibility of sexual expression, and the positivity of transgression.

Yet, Clark also does not shy away from presenting the darker and more destructive aspects of sexuality and transgression. The sexual aspect

8. Adolescents

of violence is explored through the character of Tate, the only protagonist not involved in the threesome scene. This is because Tate is unable to connect physically or emotionally with anyone. He lives with his grandparents, his emotional distance from them represented by their vast age difference. While it is not explained why his parents are absent, it is apparent that Tate is full of rage, and that this is something that no one will acknowledge. When his grandmother enters his room, Tate calls her a "bitch" for invading his privacy. His grandmother responds by ignoring the abuse and asking Tate if he wants some cookies. While the other characters interact with people their own age, Tate is never seen with any of his peers. In contrast, he is always seen isolated.

This isolation and self-hatred is demonstrated in a scene where Tate practices autoerotic asphyxiation by masturbating with a cord tied around his neck. This scene shows actual masturbation, played out in real time. The camera tracks up and down Tate's body, showing in close-up Tate's face as his mouth froths at the moment of ejaculation, and tracks down to show the trail of semen. That the scene is both explicit and prolonged demonstrates the complete loneliness that Tate feels.

For Tate, sex and violence have become intertwined, the only expressions of feeling within his numb existence. As a result, Tate's rage culminates in the murder of his grandparents. After the murder, a close-up shows Tate's face bathed in blue light as he talks into a Dictaphone, narrating what he has done. The film then flashes back to the murders. Tate is seen walking from his room naked; just as Shawn, Claude and Peaches are nude during their moment of escape through sexual indulgence, so Tate too is naked when he commits an act of escape through murderous violence. However, Tate explains that he was naked "so I wouldn't get any blood on my clothes." Tate then proceeds to stab his grandparents, with his narration describing the event without emotion: "His skin was thick, like leather. And he twitched a little. Like a chicken." His moment of escape, through murder, also provides him with sexual relief: "When I saw them there like that, I started to get an erection."

Indeed, the murder is sexualized, with Tate standing nude as he penetrates his grandparents with a knife. Again, Clark unflinchingly portrays the violent and destructive side of sexuality. While the sex between Shawn, Claude and Peaches is an expression of love, the sexual violence of Tate is an expression of rage at not feeling loved. As Tate remarks in voiceover, while shown sitting in the back seat of a police car, "I never had one true girlfriend." Just as Sade wrote of a world propelled by the forces of sex,

Part Three: Victims

Clark can also be understood as presenting a world where sexual desire guides relationships. Both artists show this force to be both creative and destructive. Violence becomes a substitute for those who are denied sex, bringing with it feelings of power and pleasure. There is a direct divergence from Sade here: this scene of violence is shown as negative, as it is provoked by and produces suffering, with no positive or creative effects. In fact, the film's overt contrast between Tate and the other three teens seems to contain a moralizing message that in the end condemns the violence of the adult world — which makes the criticism against the film all the more hypocritical.

Yet, just as Sade's tale of the sexual initiation of an adolescent, *Philosophy in the Bedroom*, ends with the obliteration of the family unit (depicted as a key tool of societal oppression), so too does *Ken Park*. In *Philosophy in the Bedroom*, Eugénie's mother is raped by Eugénie, who dons a massive dildo for the occasion, and afterward she sews her mother's vagina shut with red thread. The sealing of the vagina symbolizes what the mother has been trying to impose on the daughter, as well as seeking to ensure that no more procreation will occur. As a result of this, the family is no longer.

Likewise, in *Ken Park* the opening credits show a young man skateboarding through suburbia on his way to the local skating park. As he glides through the streets he seems the epitome of carefree youth. Yet, when he arrives at the park he shoots himself in the head. Voiceover narration from Shawn explains that the boy was named Ken Park. The narrative then leaves the story of Ken behind, only returning to him at the very end of the film, when the voiceover explains that Ken had impregnated his young girlfriend. He is then shown working at a diner, a dead-end job that he visibly hates. The next shot shows him and his girlfriend sitting on a park bench, discussing what to do. Ken's girlfriend objects to abortion, stating that she doesn't want to be a "baby killer," and then adds, "Aren't you glad your mom didn't abort you?" Ken doesn't reply; he just leans forward in his seat as the film ends.

His subsequent suicide, like Eugénie's violation of her mother in Sade's story, can thus be read as an act that kills the family unit and stops it from continuing. While the two actions differ — one is self-inflicted, the other is an assault on another person — both are actions taken by adolescents in a gesture of independence from the family. In these works the family is represented as an oppressive institution from which one can break free only through sex or violence. With his girlfriend pregnant, hat-

8. Adolescents

ing a job that will probably go nowhere, Ken is on the road to becoming one of the fathers that the film depicted. The film, rather pessimistically, shows that the only way to end the cycle is death.

Sexuality in *Ken Park* is represented as a force of Sadean nature, containing both creative and destructive elements, encompassing the urges of both lust and aggression. Some of the characters experience their sexuality as a destructive force which leads to rape, murder and suicide. In contrast, in the group sex scene discussed above, the creative and redemptive aspects of sexuality are realized through the transgression of societal taboos. In this respect, the film presents transgression as a positive and creative force, and as a means of overcoming victimization.

PART FOUR

Sexual Transgressors

While Part One established transgression as a force derived from nature, Part Two demonstrated that this force is driven by the repetition of actions which violate social and cultural norms. Yet, as Part Three realized, it is possible that those who transgress may be punished for their behavior by the social authorities. However, as I will demonstrate, the attraction to transgression lies precisely in its status as dangerous and forbidden. This is expressed through representations of sex in which it is transgression itself that is shown to be the chief component of sexual pleasure. For the characters examined here, satisfaction can only be attained through sexual acts which are aberrant and taboo.

Thus, it must be understood that the transgressive body is a sexual body. Within this type of body, seemingly non-sexual elements and activities, especially those that are violent in nature, are incorporated into the whole body for the purposes of sexual pleasure. The application of Sadean philosophy to the analysis of films that present this process of sexualization — through acts of sadism and masochism — will reveal that the sexual and the violent instincts are not separate forces but are actually connected. In fact, Sade's philosophy makes clear that much of the pleasure gained through the combination of sex and violence directly depends on the activity being transgressive in some way: the forbidden nature of transgression adds to the pleasure felt while participating in it.

This idea is central to Sade's philosophy, all of his works entailing the search for sexual satisfaction through the violation of taboos, with violence being a vital part of sexuality. Societal norms and laws try to restrain the desire for sex and violence (as both separate and combined forces) by classifying them as expressions of an abnormal and aberrant mind and body, denying that the two are at all linked. The majority of modern societies express the need for temperance and moderation in the areas of sex and violence through laws that prohibit extreme behavior. Also, in the area of medicine and psychology, heightened sexual and violent behav-

Part Four: Sexual Transgressors

ior is pathologized into certain conditions and behaviors. Sadism and masochism, even when expressed within a loving relationship of equals, is still a popular subject for study in the field of psychology. Sade is significant in that he is one of the few thinkers who have confronted the violent nature of sexuality while not masking this by following it with a moral condemnation. Sade created works that examine and, most significantly, celebrate the affinity between sex and violence.

9

Sadists

It was in reference to the work of the Marquis de Sade that Richard von Krafft-Ebing first coined the term "sadism" in 1886 as a name for the sexual excitement that certain people feel when inflicting pain upon another. That his own name has come to mean the conflation of pain infliction and sexual pleasure bears witness to the overt and radical way in which Sade's writings explore the link that exists between sex and violence. For although tales of sex and violence have been around for as long as humans have told stories, Sade's uniqueness lies not only in his use of sex and violence as narrative devices, but mainly that he develops an original philosophy by having his characters explicitly debate the subject.

Within his stories one finds a conscious meditation on how and why the sexual and violent instincts are so attractive. When standard narratives depict scenes of violent sexuality they generally do so in order to illustrate that such behavior is morally wrong: languishing in the lurid and the criminal is excusable as long as bad behavior is ultimately eradicated and order restored. On the contrary, Sade's works celebrate the joy that is provoked by the exploitation of violence for purely selfish sexual pleasure.

According to Krafft-Ebing, sadism is "the association of lust and cruelty," and such is the power of this bond that sexual satisfaction is impossible without the use of physical or psychological violence.[1] As time has progressed, sadism has become a recognized psychological condition, with a definition in *The Diagnostic and Statistical Manual IV*:

> Over a period of at least six months, recurrent intense sexually arousing fantasies, sexual urges, or behaviors involving acts (real, not simulated) in which the psychological or physical suffering (including humiliation) of the victim is sexually exciting to the person.[2]

While an expression of sexualized violence may take place in the form of a consensual arrangement between adults in the context of masochistic play (which I will discuss in the next chapter), the sexual pathology described in this statement refers instead to individuals who can derive sexual pleasure only by provoking suffering upon others without their consent.

Although there are situations in Sade's writing in which his libertines indulge in consensual sexual play with each other, the main focus of his sexual scenes is the infliction of pain upon an unwilling victim. As Berner, et al. state: "The ideas of the Marquis de Sade are an excellent example of the unity of sadistic drives reaching from rather harmless acts of symbolic humiliation to the most vicious acts such as long protracted killing full of relish and gratifying in an inevitable instinctual sense."[3]

Sade's works explore the escalation of sadism, its trajectory toward ever-increasing acts of sexual violence. One film which details sadism's gradual intensification is Pier Paolo Pasolini's *Salò* (1975), an adaptation of Sade's *The 120 Days of Sodom*. Since its release in 1975 this film has been a scandalous work, as it unflinchingly represents Sade's sadistic fantasies.

Into the Inferno: Salò, or the 120 Days of Sodom

Of all the adaptations of Sade's works, Pasolini's *Salò* is the best known, as well as the most controversial. Although Jess Franco adapted several of Sade's works for the screen, these films were made as soft-core erotica, with sadomasochism used to create a titillating effect. In *Salò*, Sade's work is used as a means to explore the cruelest and darkest aspects of human nature. It depicts the abuse of power and how it can be used to exploit and degrade those with less power. What makes *Salò* so disturbing is that this abuse is perpetrated for the sole purpose of sexual arousal. Like the libertines in *The 120 Days of Sodom*, the four protagonists in the film find pleasure in the pain and suffering of their captives, with both sadism and suffering shown in great detail by Pasolini. Thus, while *Salò* constitutes a cinematic representation of the sexual sadism described in Sade's works, in this analysis I will argue that Pasolini's film goes further to realize a fully fledged exploration of the political content in the relationship between the sadist and the victim by focusing on the sexual and seductive aspects of political power.

In order to discuss the politics of sexual sadism explored in *Salò*, in this chapter sadistic and masochistic sexualities have been separated from each other. This distinction is based on Gilles Deleuze's argument that "sadomasochism" is a problematic option because, in principle, sadism

9. Sadists

and masochism are two distinct sexual practices. In *Salò*, four Masters kidnap a group of teenagers and subject them to sexual activity against their will, with the captives' anguish and lack of consent adding to the Masters' pleasure. For example, when Renata, one of the kidnapped teenagers, cries, the Duke announces that "this howling is the most exciting thing I've ever heard." As Deleuze states, "[A] genuine sadist could never tolerate a masochistic victim."[4] Part of the pleasure is to feel the power one has over another, to have the ability to make someone act against his or her will. This ensures that the victim caters to the sadist's pleasure instead of being concerned with his or her own satisfaction. Sade states this clearly in *Philosophy in the Bedroom*: "The idea of seeing another enjoy as he enjoys reduces him to a kind of equality with that other, which impairs the unspeakable charm *despotism* causes him to feel."[5] As this statement illustrates, the sadist feels that he or she is superior to the victim. Indeed, the sadist feels that he or she is a despot, an absolute ruler, similar to those who have full political power. As stated above, it is this political aspect of sexual sadism that mainly concerns *Salò*.

Prior to the making of *Salò*, *The 120 Days of Sodom* was thought to be an unfilmable text, for not only does it detail acts that could never be shown onscreen, but the book itself remains unfinished.[6] Beginning as a relatively coherent narrative, the book gradually degenerates into a list of atrocities. The book's main storyline entails the exploits of four libertines who kidnap sixteen adolescent girls and boys and use them to enact a variety of sexual activities while aided by the stories told to them by three middle-aged prostitutes. To combat Sade's book's narrative difficulties, Pasolini takes the central plot and relocates it from eighteenth-century France to 1944 Italy. The film is set, and takes its name, from the town of Salò, the site of a Fascist puppet government set up by the Nazis at the very end of World War II. As Jane Mills explains, it was at this place that "2000 villagers were massacred, the women and children were sexually tortured and many were killed."[7] Thus, in this film Pasolini superimposes Sade's darkest fantasies upon actual, deeply tragic, historical events.

Sade's writings, as I have mentioned on several occasions, have a history of trouble and controversy. It is not surprising, then, that one of Sade's books would be adapted to the screen by Pasolini, an artist who has also repeatedly had encounters with the law because of the nature of his work. By connecting these two artists, it becomes apparent that not only were they obsessed with the sexual aspects of crime, but that both were punished by society for dealing with taboo issues. For example, Pasolini's

Part Four: Sexual Transgressors

first novel, *Ragazzi di vita* (1955), was charged with "offences to public decency," and his film *La Ricotta* (1963) was criticized as "an outrage against the established religion."[8] His final film, *Salò*, was released in a storm of controversy just two weeks after Pasolini was found murdered; and the movie was later labeled obscene in Italy and banned in most countries.[9]

Pasolini did not mellow with age, and *Salò* is the most notorious and disturbing film in his oeuvre. Just as Sade consciously sought to write about all of his most depraved and taboo sexual fantasies without regard for law or decency, so Pasolini made a conscious effort to continuously challenge "decency" in his work. In his own words:

> If a maker of verses, of novels, of films, finds himself honored, accepted or understood in the society in which he works, he is not an author. An author can only be a stranger in a hostile land: he in fact cultivates death rather than accustoms himself to life, and the feelings he provokes in others are feelings more or less strong of racial hatred.[10]

This statement situates the artist, or the author, as completely outside of society. Indeed, Pasolini himself was a social outcast in many ways: he was an atheist and a homosexual in Italy, a still predominantly Catholic country. Known as a Marxist, it was his homosexuality which led to his expulsion from the Communist party. Certainly *Salò* expresses a sense of outsiderness, as it delivers a pessimistic view of humankind brought down to its most base level, and this negativity engendered extreme objections in many who saw it. Gary Indiana notes that after his murder, "One French reviewer urged that *Salò* be shown as a defense exhibit at the murderer Pelosi's trial, on the assumption that anyone capable of directing such a film was practically begging to be murdered."[11] The fact that the movie continues to be banned in so many countries bears witness to the transgressiveness of Pasolini's work, so much so that it had to be banished from sight.

However, the point that all this moralist polemic distracts us from is that there is an important statement that Pasolini makes in *Salò* through its superimposition with Sade's *The 120 Days of Sodom*. In reframing the narrative historically so that it takes place in Fascist Italy, Pasolini exacerbates the political potential of Sade's book. By 1975, the year in which *Salò* was made, Italy had largely chosen to ignore its Fascist past and its part in World War II, with many textbooks and historical accounts diluting, and in some cases removing entirely, references to the nation's conduct during the war.[12] With *Salò*, Pasolini sought to give his Italian audience a painful reminder of what life under Fascism was like. However, to achieve

9. Sadists

this aim, Pasolini did not need to link Italian history to a Sadean text. Why do so? It is my contention that, while exploring the atrocities that result from the gross misuse of power, Pasolini also seeks to explore its seductive aspects.

He achieves this by taking the power and domination wielded by those in political power and placing it within a sexual context, in the style of Sade's writings. Pasolini illustrates the allure of power by placing the four Masters in total control of the beautiful teenagers. The beginning of the film shows the young people being kidnapped and rounded up. Once captured, they are taken to the Masters for an audition, where their bodies are inspected. One girl with a crooked tooth is sent away for not living up to the Masters' meticulous standards. The teens stand silently as their clothes are pulled off or down in order to expose their "hidden charms." After two young boys are stripped, and their chests, genitals and legs are exposed, the camera tilts down their bodies so that their heads are no longer in the frame, as if to signify that they are no longer people but a collection of attractive body parts. In fact, they are there only to serve as victims. As a result, the film narrative does not develop them as characters, and, indeed, they are referred to by the names of the actors who play them. As Indiana asserts, "[T]hey lack the amplitude that would merit the second naming of fiction."[13] The total power of the Masters results in total objectification and depersonalization of the victim.

Furthermore, when not in matching clothes, the victims are most frequently nude. Their clothing, or lack thereof, is intended to show their compliance, not their individuality. As Marcel Henaff remarks:

> The body stripped bare is no longer anything but what it offers the eyes, nothing but that thing for which it is stripped bare: a system of sexualized functions at the disposal of sexual pleasure. The elimination of clothes says to the body: You are there only for my pleasure, and only in this respect do you exist.[14]

In this regard, Pasolini himself remarked, "[W]hat best characterizes power — any power — is its natural capacity to turn human bodies into objects. Nazi-Fascist repression excelled in this."[15] Baring the victims makes them simultaneously alluring and anonymous. As many of the scenes are filmed predominantly in wide shot, with the characters arranged in stylized tableaux, it becomes difficult to distinguish one victim from another. Rather, they work as a collective body specifically designed to serve the sexual appetites of the Masters.

This is illustrated most clearly in a scene in which the Masters

Part Four: Sexual Transgressors

organize a "Best Bottom" competition in which the victims are arranged crouched on the floor in a circle with their heads facing inwards. The lights are turned down and the Masters walk around the circle, shining a flashlight on the body part. The Masters remark that they cannot even recognize the gender of the person they are looking at.[16] The Masters have systematically destroyed the victims' identities, making them less than human. This allows them to use the victims for their own pleasure and to then discard them without remorse. Pasolini counters "the personal is political" with "the political is sexual"; everything returns to the body, for all ideas are expressed through and upon it.

As well as politics, *Salò* also incorporates religious imagery. Although both Sade and Pasolini were outspoken atheists, they were also radical iconoclasts, frequently invoking religious ritual and imagery in their works in order to invert it. In *Salò*, Pasolini deviates from Sade's story by dividing the narrative into Circles, a device taken from Dante's *Inferno*. The film begins with the "Ante-Inferno," which is an antechamber to Hell; this is followed by "The Circle of Manias," where the Masters explore perversions from sexual intercourse; "The Circle of Shit," which involves activities that are anal in nature; and "The Circle of Blood," where the Masters embrace torture and murder. In this way Pasolini constructs his representation as a vision of Hell, yet a Hell that is not part of a mythical afterlife but a real event from the recent past. Hell is, in fact, always within our reach: Sade shows that it is in our minds and our fantasies, while for Pasolini it is an ever-present reality. While the Masters in *Salò* think they have created a Paradise, they have, in fact, created a Hell on Earth, a place where the worst sins and perversions are committed: rape, abduction, pedophilia, coprophagy, mutilation, necrophilia, torture and murder.

Indeed, religious imagery permeates Pasolini's works, with one of his films being about the life of Christ: *The Gospel According to Matthew* (1964). For example, many of his movies evoke images of the crucifixion, such as *Accatone* (1961), *La Ricotta* (1963), and *The Gospel According to Matthew*. Furthermore, the Last Supper is depicted in *Accatone*, *Mamma Rosa* (1962), *La Ricotta*, *The Gospel According to Matthew* and *Salò*.[17] But, as Sam Rohdie observes, in Pasolini's depictions of the Last Suppers,

> [E]verything was reversed. The sacred was not found in a celestial heaven, but in terrestrial shit. Pasolini reversed the conventional order of the sacred and in so doing offered a criticism of the existing order, and of order itself, especially that of the authorities, of power. He countered power with shit and in a language often composed of it.[18]

9. Sadists

This is clearly demonstrated in *Salò*, where the Masters order all of the victims' feces to be saved and then served for dinner. This Banquet of Shit is a feast to celebrate the wedding of the Judge to Sergio, one of the kidnapped teenagers, who is attired in a white wedding dress. As one of the film's storytellers, Signora Maggi, pronounces, this feast is a "rite" which restores "the divine character of monstrosity." This statement illustrates the significance of the meal, which is a complete reversal of the Christian ideal of a celebratory feast: the food is made up of waste matter and, therefore, symbolizes death. Also, the representation of a boy as the bride serves to mock the ritual of marriage, especially since Sergio had already been married to Renata in a previous scene.

Interestingly, in this scene everyone takes part in the eating of excrement. While earlier in the film, coprophagy had been used as a punishment (for example, when Renata is made to eat the Duke's feces in response to her crying and praying over her dead mother), at the banquet both Masters and storytellers eat with the victims. While the victims are seen retching, the Masters take delight in the meal. As Gary Indiana observes:

The victims are forced to perform perverted wedding ceremonies in *Salò, or the 120 Days of Sodom* (1975).

Part Four: Sexual Transgressors

> The salient point of *Salò*'s banquet is not whether we believe the shit is real, but the fact that everyone has to eat it, regardless of his placement in the hierarchy; those at the top are obliged to demonstrate sophisticated connoisseurship of this most rarefied of meals, and to scoff at the disgust of those below them, like aristocrats amused by a peasant's aversion to caviar.[19]

This is illustrated by Signora Maggi's comment after Renata finishes her punishment: "That stupid girl's making a scene over such a delicacy!" As in the plight of Sade's Justine and Juliette, that which some people see as a painful ordeal can be seen by others as an opportunity for sexual pleasure. Yet the difference between the Masters and the victims is the former's complete control over the whole process. Before the banquet, the Masters impose a ban on all unauthorized defecation: since permission has to be sought, all the excrement can be collected and conserved. The Masters search the rooms and inspect everyone's chamber pots. The names of those who have defecated unlawfully are recorded in a book so that the individuals can be punished at a later date. Thus, the most natural and private of processes has in *Salò* become as regulated and public as all the sexual activity practiced in the villa.

Yet, the depiction of coprophagy in *Salò* constitutes a reference not limited to World War II Italy but applicable to contemporary Western societies. Indeed, Pasolini once stated that the use of coprophagy in the film is an analogy of the processed and fast food industries. In his words, "[T]he manufacturers force the consumer to eat excrement ... [a]ll these industrial foods are worthless refuse."[20] The Masters' command that the victims eat the excrement extracted from them is analogous to the way manufacturers use the labor of the people (although instead of the sweat of the laborer, it is excrement that the Masters require) in order to produce substandard food, which is then consumed by those who made it. In our society there is a constant stream of consumption and waste, repeated over and over in the form of a Sadean narrative. And, like all Sadean fantasies, this repetition leads not to satisfaction but rather to more emptiness.

The film also comments on the place of the body in neo-capitalist society, using the metaphor of the sadist to demonstrate the injustices of society at large. This affinity between capitalism and sadism is contained in Deleuze's statement that "[t]he sadist is in need of institutions," as both capitalism and sadism rely on strict hierarchies and organizations.[21] Although the Masters have set up a situation where they can fully explore their darker and more base desires, they have arranged themselves within

9. Sadists

a strict hierarchy. They have organized rules and regulations in order to ensure that each perversion and each victim is explored to its fullest potential. According to Pasolini, the power that the Masters wield is "a representation of what Marx called the commodification of man, a reduction of the body (through exploitation) to a thing. Therefore, sex is still called upon to play a horrible metaphorical role."[22] According to a Marxist view of society, in capitalism, resources are plundered until all moneymaking potential is wrung from them, this being true of the land as well as the people who work within the system. In *Salò*'s hierarchical economy of pleasure, the bodies of the victims are exploited for sexual gratification and, as a result, are reduced to the level of resources, with no regard given to the person to whom the body belongs.

Salò clearly represents the Sadean notion that in order to create a situation where the Masters can live out their wildest desires, they require strict rules and regulations. For example, when we first see the Masters they are sitting together at a table, each signing a contract on the rules that are to govern their activities. From then on, each sadist will conduct his or her sexual activities without emotion, as though these were organized, clinical experiments. In the works of Sade this is illustrated by the writing style, which is descriptive and repetitious. As MacKendrick observes, "[T]he Sadistic text often takes on the character of a mathematics textbook."[23]

Pasolini also casts a cold and intellectual eye over the proceedings. For example, in the opening credits there is a bibliography of texts about Sade, which cites Roland Barthes, Maurice Blanchot, Simone de Beauvoir, Pierre Klossowski and Phillipe Sollers. This reference list highlights the fact that the film is an intellectual exploration, not ordinary mainstream entertainment. Furthermore, the Masters indulge in intellectual debate and analysis in conjunction with their sexual experimentation, referring to authors such as Baudelaire, Nietzsche and Huysmans. Moreover, the mise-en-scène also reflects this intellectual quality, with the sets decorated with works of abstract and Futurist art. Finally, each shot is composed stylistically as though it were a painting (the prevalence of the wide shot highlighting this), and the emphasis is on where objects are placed within the frame rather than emotion. Given this lack of feeling, sexual and violent acts are no longer differentiated and instead become mere possibilities for pleasure.

Pasolini also incorporates repetition, with many shots and techniques being repeated throughout the film. For example, each of the Circles begins with a shot of the storyteller looking at herself in the mirror, and is followed by a wide shot that shows her walking downstairs into the Hall of Orgies. Even though each circle centers on a different perversion, these shots of the storyteller symbolize that each perversion will be explored in the same way. Each story is then followed by an activity directly inspired by the storyteller's narration. Furthermore, the final Circle, the Circle of Blood, is edited to follow a pattern according to which shots are repeated. In this Circle the Masters torture and murder their victims. While three Masters carry out the tortures, one watches through binoculars from inside the Villa. The Masters switch places so that each gets to torture and watch. As in Sade's works, this endless repetition leads to an excess without climax. The Masters' games have escalated in degrees of violence, yet this does not provide them with the ultimate orgasm. They instead sit and watch the atrocities silently and calmly. The film ends without any resolution.

Hence, there is a movement toward darker, nastier and more violent perversions as the film progresses. As Bataille writes about *The 120 Days of Sodom*, "The language of *The 120 Days of Sodom* is that of a universe which degrades gradually and systematically, which tortures and destroys the totality of the beings which it presents."[24] This is also true of Pasolini's *Salò*. The Circles offer a gradual system of degradation, culminating in the scenes of torture by the Masters. What is most disturbing about these scenes is that by showing the atrocities from the Masters' voyeuristic point-of-view (we see through their binoculars, we see what they see), Pasolini puts the audience in the sadist's position. In consequence, Pasolini makes clear how easy it is to comply with such behavior — that one may become an accomplice to atrocities just by watching and doing nothing. Perhaps, it is also suggested in this scene, there is not much of a leap between watching and doing nothing, to watching such behavior and finding pleasure in it. This, in fact, is the most unsettling aspect of the film, as it invites the viewer to go to places so dark that they are forced to confront who she or he really and truly is.

Thus it is for this reason that *Salò* remains so disturbing, as Sade's ideas become a real possibility — not just through the transposition of the story into a real historical context, but also through the film's visual style. As a result, the film becomes real for the viewer in the sense that he/she is implicated in the action, much in the same way that Sade continually refers to his "friend-reader."[25] Pasolini uses Sade's work in order to examine what he sees as the brutality and cruelty that lie in humanity's heart

9. Sadists

of darkness. Thus, Pasolini's greatest affinity with Sade is his depiction of the abuse and degradation of human beings as a sadist's pleasure and an entertainment (although it is for this very reason that the film is disturbingly and unmistakably un-pleasurable to view). This idea of sadism as entertainment is also examined in Takashi Miike's *Ichi the Killer*.

"100% Sadist": Ichi the Killer

Takashi Miike's cult film *Ichi the Killer* (2001) has become renowned for its audacious and extreme depiction of violence. A gangster film set in the world of the Japanese yakuza, it distinguishes itself by commenting directly on the genre's inherent sadism. Through an excessively graphic style, the film highlights not only that the act of violence is central to the genre, but also that violence can be a source of pleasure. These characteristics of the film invite comparisons with Sade's works because these also revel in sexual violence while consciously commenting on it. Miike's *Ichi the Killer*, not unlike Sade's texts, represents violence not only as a highly erotic activity, but as replacing sex as a means of bodily pleasure. Thus, a Sadean reading of this film foregrounds the transgressive elements contained in representations of sadism, which highlight a radical crossing of the boundaries of sexuality, as it becomes polymorphously perverse.

Ichi the Killer follows the exploits of a gangster, Kakihara, who indulges in masochistic games with his boss, Anjo. When his boss vanishes, it appears that he has been killed by Ichi, an unknown assassin who is notorious for the extreme fashion in which he eviscerates his victims. Kakihara then sets out to find Ichi, not only in order to find out what happened to his boss, but also in anticipation of the potential pleasures that may come from meeting someone who is "one hundred percent sadist." The narrative is driven by Kakihara's search for the ultimate sadist and for his own ultimate sexual climax.

The film's own inherent sadism is illustrated in its opening scene. After the bodyguard Kaneko asks where Boss Anjo is, the camera cuts to a freeze-frame of a man, unfreezing as his fist flies toward the camera. An edit then reveals a young prostitute, Sailor, falling back from the punch, with a close-up showing her bloody, beaten face. After punching the young girl, the man, who happens to be Sailor's pimp, proceeds to rape her. Intercut with this are shots of a young man who climbs to a window and watches the scene. He wears a black outfit reminiscent of a superhero costume, with the figure "1" emblazoned on the back ("Ichi" being Japanese for "one"). Yet, instead of saving the girl, he just continues to stare. When the Boss checks outside the window, the man flees, leaving behind a trail of semen dripping from a pot plant. From the pool of semen on the floor rises the film's title, *Ichi the Killer*. This image directly represents the film's intermingling of sex and violence, desire and death: semen will only be produced through the act of murder.

In the world depicted by the film, violence and sex are inseparable. Sexual acts always become violent, while scenes of violence are so extreme as to become almost pornographic. It is fitting then that the words *Ichi the Killer*— a reference to the title character's propensity for murder and violence — should rise up out of a puddle of sexual fluids. For Ichi, taking life in an extreme and brutal fashion is an expression of sexual desire. In fact, for most of the film's characters, violence has replaced sex, so much so that sadism becomes the primary form of sexuality represented. The characters can thus be understood as driven by the same kind of desire that compels Sade's libertines, for as Paglia observes: "[f]or Sade, sex is violence"[26] in which "[t]he orgasm is a burst of violence."[27] Therefore, it is only through the violation of another's body that these characters are able to feel pleasure in their own body.

The film's opening scene also demonstrates how generic expectations will be consistently frustrated. In this scene, Ichi arrives dressed like a superhero with a number one on his back, just as a girl is being molested. He frustrates expectations by not stepping in and rescuing the girl. He also fails to live up to his superhero image by fleeing from the scene, having masturbated like a pathetic Peeping Tom (although a later flashback will reveal that Ichi does return). As the film progresses, Ichi, whose name has become legend in yakuza circles due to the brutality of his work, is revealed in daily life to be shy, submissive and over-sensitive (this is similar to the representation of the sadist Asami in Miike's previous film *Audition* [2000], who is initially represented as the stereotype of the quiet, subservient Asian woman). It is also revealed that he is under the control of Jijii, an older man who uses hypnosis and false memories to get Ichi to carry out hits on yakuza in order to increase his own power and financial gain. Ichi's submissiveness is balanced out by the character of Kakihara, who seeks the ultimate masochistic pleasure, yet conducts his business with extreme sadism.

Playing with genre expectations and representing extreme violence are typical features of Miike's approach to storytelling. Many of his films

9. Sadists

are characterized by fast, frenetic editing, lots of flash and color, and extreme, even gratuitous violence. His style, simply put, is that of excess—even the sheer volume of Miike's output (over fifty films in just ten years) suggests an excessive nature. This propensity to excess is demonstrated by the scene in which Ichi murders Sailor's pimp. After the pimp rapes Sailor, who remains semi-conscious from the beating she received, he sees Ichi outside the window and drags him inside. At first Ichi stands submissively, cries, and says, "I'm sorry." Yet, as the pimp begins to slap him around, a blade in Ichi's shoe snaps out, and in a flash Ichi kicks up his leg and slices through him. A close-up of the stunned pimp shows his head beginning to split in half, and as it breaks apart the insides of his head are visible. A wider shot sees his body also split open, and then a cut to a mid-shot of Ichi through the pimp's legs sees his internal organs slide out of his body and fall to the floor in the foreground of the shot, with Ichi watching. A close-up shows Ichi grab his crotch, and the camera tilts up to show he is grinning, thus illustrating the sexual release that Ichi feels after the kill. The extremely graphic shot of the pimp splitting in half (a computer-generated effect) may be understood as pornographic in that it shows, overtly and in great detail, hidden parts of the body. Indeed, the "porno-graphic" character of this scene signifies the sexual and the violent as closely linked.

Scenes in *Ichi The Killer* such as the one described above are similar to the graphic descriptions provided by Sade in his novels, where not only is no detail left out, but the excessiveness of these details evokes a visceral response. Thus, both Sade and Miike rely on the repetition of violence to arouse an effect. On this relation between repetition and excess, Deleuze remarks:

> It has been said that an excess of stimulation is in a sense erotic. This eroticism is able to act as a mirror to the world by reflecting its excesses, drawing out its violence and even conferring a "spiritual" quality on these phenomena by the very fact that it puts them at the service of the senses.[28]

Therefore, according to Deleuze, excess itself is erotic. As a result, the violence in Sade and Miike can be understood as becoming erotic through its excessiveness because the characters gain pleasure from consistently and repetitively engaging in violent activity.

However, at the same time, excess may create the opposite effect of causing a numbing of sensation. Just as Sade's works almost drown in the repetitive nature of violent scenes—"Boredom seeps from the monstrosity

Part Four: Sexual Transgressors

of Sade's works," says Bataille[29] — Miike's films also run the same risk. In his study of Miike's cinema, Tom Mes explains that

> [F]or all the director's expert manipulation of the medium of cinema, the approach he takes runs one risk that can undo the effect he's trying to achieve: boredom. The violence in *Ichi the Killer* is omnipresent and therefore potentially repetitive. The repetition of violence is very much a part of the director's intentions, since it underlies its futility.[30]

Miike's excess, not unlike Sade's, leads only to negation and apathy, and, as Mes notes, this can be experienced both by the audience and the characters. This statement highlights how the Deleuzian separation of sadism and masochism can also apply to the audience's position in relation to a film's representation of sexual transgression. As *Ichi the Killer* illustrates, the sadist's predilection for repetitive excess is expressed in the film's structure, which relies on scene after scene of violence. This contrasts with the masochist's desire for suspense, which will be discussed further below in regards to *Secretary*. In contrast to *Secretary*, which keeps its audience in suspense over whether the two leading protagonists will get together and consummate their relationship, *Ichi the Killer* offers no such suspense and tension: everything is immediately displayed and taken to its absolute extreme. At several points during the film Kakihara expresses disappointment, as his experiences never quite live up to his excitement and anticipation. But, despite this, Kakihara remains locked in a cycle of repetition, never giving up his search for the ultimate sadist.

The character of Kakihara is a perfect representation of the excess found in Miike's films, a flamboyant counterpoint to the shy Ichi. While Ichi's black costume, which he wears when he commits murder, helps him to hide in the shadows, Kakihara's outlandish and colorful suits, by contrast, are complemented by his peroxided blond hair and body piercings. His face has deep, clean scars that have obviously been deliberately cut into his skin for aesthetic, and erotic, purposes. His body modifications express his fascination with pain and his penchant for excessive behavior. He has cut and scarred his own face in order to feel pleasure through pain. While Kakihara never participates in sexual intercourse over the course of the film, he constantly seeks sexual satisfaction, which can be satisfied only through violence.

Furthermore, like the Sadean libertine, Kakihara searches for sexual pleasure that can be felt throughout the whole surface of the body. And since this can only be achieved beyond a focus on the genitals, as Sade

9. Sadists

points out, it is pain which causes the greatest sensations. Sade explains this idea:

> [I]t is purely a question of exposing our nervous system to the most violent possible shock; now there is no doubt that we are much more keenly affected by pain than by pleasure: the reverberations that result in us when the sensation of pain is produced in others will essentially be of a more vigorous character.[31]

Consequently, for Sade's libertines, as for Kakihara, pleasure is to be found in an excess of sensation, and since pain exposes the body to such an excess, it then becomes a great source of pleasure. Sexual satisfaction may, as a result, be gained from activities that do not seem to be sexual in nature, such as being cut or beaten. While the Sadean libertine is principally a sadist, in the sadistic scene there is room for roles to be exchanged. According to Roland Barthes, "In the scene, all functions can be interchanged, everyone can and must be in turn agent and patient, whipper and whipped, coprophagist and coprophagee, etc."[32] Even Deleuze admits that there are elements of masochism within sadism, and vice versa.[33] Thus, in Miike's film, Kakihara professes to be a masochist, yet he demonstrates that the boundary separating sadism from masochism is very tenuous and can be transgressed. Just as the Sadean libertine is able to reverse its sadism and find pleasure in his/her own pain, Kakihara, a professed masochist, is seen participating primarily in sadistic torture.

However, despite this area of transgression there is still a clear distinction between sadism and masochism, as both are motivated by different wants and desires. Kakihara's sadistic actions, for instance, are solely motivated by his quest for the ultimate sadistic partner who will drive him to his own ecstatic levels of pain. After Boss Anjo goes missing, Kakihara, refusing to believe that he is dead, becomes obsessed with finding him. This obsession is fuelled not by loyalty to his gang boss, however, but by his fear that he has lost the one person who successfully satisfies his masochistic desires. It becomes apparent that Kakihara and Anjo have a sexual relationship: Anjo beats Kakihara in order for both to feel sexual pleasure. While both Anjo and Kakihara are represented as heterosexual, they nevertheless find the perfect sexual symbiosis in the violent encounters they shared with each other. As Kakihara searches for his boss, several characters remark that he had a "crush" on Anjo, with one of them adding that this is "[n]ot because you're queer or you admired his balls. It was because you relished the pain that he inflicted when he beat you up."[34]

This is illustrated by Kakihara's attempt to establish a relationship with Karen (who was previously Anjo's girlfriend before he was killed). Karen becomes Kakihara's woman after she gleefully joins in on his tormenting of a restaurant owner. Having been refused entry, Kakihara grabs the owner's cheek and begins to pull and stretch the skin. The owner pleads to Karen for help, but she instead joins in, moaning with pleasure as close-ups reveal the stretched skin. The next scene in which they are together is in a dungeon setting, with both in SM costumes. Kakihara is in chains as Karen punches him repeatedly. Kakihara coaches her, saying, "When you're hurting someone, don't think of the pain that he feels. Only concentrate on the pleasure of causing him pain. That's the only way to show true compassion for your partner."

Kakihara advocates a completely selfish sexuality in which all the focus is on one's own pleasure, a view shared by Sade, who stated that "Nature has endowed each of us with a capacity for kindly feelings: let us not squander them on others...."[35] Thus, Kakihara and the Sadean libertine are able to have partners of either gender because the partner is actually irrelevant — the only thing that matters is the sensations that the partner causes them to experience. As a result, although Karen is represented as strong, intelligent, beautiful and vicious, her inability to beat Kakihara with the level of ferocity that he desires leads him to tell her that "the boss was a lot better at this.... You let me down." His disappointment with Karen causes Kakihara to become fixated on finding Ichi, whose sadistic killings inspire amazement in him: "There's something inhuman to this carnage. Most people have a touch of both sadism and masochism inside them, but this Ichi is one hundred percent pure sadist. I can't wait to meet him."

Yet, Kakihara's statement is only partially true, as Miike portrays his characters as being capable of both sadism and masochism. In fact, although he seeks masochistic pleasure, Kakihara commits sadistic torture. After he is set up by Jijii into thinking that a rival gangster, Suzuki, is responsible for Anjo's disappearance, Kakihara has Suzuki kidnapped and enacts an elaborate and prolonged torture upon him. A close-up shows Suzuki coming to consciousness, and a high-angle long shot reveals that he is naked and suspended in mid air by metal hooks through his skin. As Suzuki screams, Kakihara comes over to him, holding a long, sharp skewer. As Suzuki pleads ignorance to the claims made against him, Kakihara rams the skewer through his cheek, and then pours boiling oil over his back and head.

All of this is shown in close-up, intercut with shots of Kakihara smil-

9. Sadists

Self-proclaimed masochist Kakihara (Tadanobu Asano) still delights in the sadistic torture of Suzuki (Susumu Terajima) in *Ichi the Killer* (2001).

ing madly at his work. In fact, throughout this torture scene almost every conceivable angle is used, with everything shown in great detail. In this scene we see the body of Suzuki transformed through torture. Close-ups and long shots show the hooks through Suzuki's back, the skin being punctured and stretched. In conjunction with the large yakuza tattoo that covers his back, the camera's focus on the tortured flesh makes it clear that Suzuki's body has been largely modified through pain. *Ichi the Killer* reveals that, like the Sadean libertine, the gangster plays with the body, testing and exploring its limits and possibilities. By definition, the gangster is a violent type, and this film confronts the sexual aspects of his violence, which he uses to attain power and, through this power, pleasure. Yet Kakihara turns this power and violence back onto himself, even though he relishes the violence he inflicts upon others, which is an essential part of his job. As he pours boiling oil on Suzuki, a close-up shows the scorched and tattooed skin as it begins to burn and blister, becoming almost unrecognizable as human flesh. The unrelenting sadism of Kakihara's behavior even shocks other members of the yakuza, who enter the room and demand an explanation, to which Kakihara replies, "Just a little torture." Several other scenes show that Kakihara, who claims to be seeking masochistic pleasure, is capable of, and seems to take as much pleasure in, extreme sadism.

The portrayal of sadism in this film diverges from Deleuze's idea that sadism and masochism are two different forms, as Ichi and Kakihara show tendencies toward both. Yet, Deleuze does note, as I have shown earlier, that "[t]here is a certain masochism in Sade's characters: in *The 120 Days of Sodom* we are told of the tortures and humiliations which the libertines deliberately undergo."[36] Indeed, one of Sade's libertines speaks hypothetically of the sadist's enjoyment of punishment:

> [H]ow are the punishments inflicted upon him you wish to reform ever to succeed, since ... the state of degradation which characterizes the situation in which you place him when you punish him, pleases him, amuses him, delights him, and inwardly he relishes the self that has gone as far as to merit being treated in this way?[37]

Kakihara's behavior certainly expresses this sentiment. For instance, after torturing Suzuki he is reprimanded by his yakuza superiors. As a result, Kakihara offers an "apology," which involves cutting off the tip of his tongue with a knife. An extreme close-up shows the knife cutting through the tongue, and then in mid-shot a blood-soaked Kakihara holds the piece of flesh toward the camera, offering it to his superiors (and the audience) as he groans incoherently. A deep-focus wide shot reveals that everyone at the meeting is staring at Kakihara in disbelief. In the foreground one of the yakuza sways back and forth as though he is about to faint. This episode illustrates that Kakihara does not see pain as punishment, and in fact relishes any opportunity to undergo painful treatment. He indulges in sadistic behavior in order to find the person who will kill him in the extreme fashion that he feels he deserves. But perhaps Kakihara is really looking for himself: in a perverse reversal of the Christian principle, he is looking for one to do to him exactly what he does to others.

Therefore, Kakihara's eventual meeting with Ichi is inevitably a disappointment. When it becomes apparent that they are both in the same apartment building, Kakihara giddily remarks, "I'm scared of myself. All this anticipation.... The few times I've felt this I've been let down." The action periodically goes into slow motion when both see each other on the roof and run after each other, a device used to increase suspense. They are joined by Kakihara's bodyguard Kaneko, who Ichi has been brainwashed into thinking is his long-lost brother. Ichi is therefore more pre-

9. Sadists

occupied with establishing a bond with Kaneko. After Kaneko shoots Ichi in the leg, Ichi, in self-defense, kills him by slashing his neck. When he realizes what he has done, Ichi falls to the floor and weeps uncontrollably. He is then kicked while he is down by Takeshi, Kaneko's son, who has witnessed the scene. Kakihara sees his "one hundred percent sadist" on the floor, crying and being kicked by a child. Kakihara pleads with Ichi to get up: "How can we have our challenge match if you keep acting this way?"

For Kakihara has imagined Ichi to be the provider of pain of such intensity that he will achieve the ultimate orgasm, one from which he will never recover. This scene reveals that Kakihara's masochism is actually a death wish: both his torturing of others and relishing of his own pain signal that he no longer fears death — in fact, he courts it. Kakihara's fascination with violence is thus in reality a fascination with death. Once he realizes that Ichi will not grant his death wish, he takes a skewer in each hand and raises them to his ears. In extreme close-up the skewer is shown as it passes through his ear canal; and in a close-up of his eyes, sound becomes silence. Suddenly the picture is over-exposed, as Kakihara fantasizes his own ultimate death. As Ichi runs toward him, he stops Ichi's foot-blade just as it is about to enter his head, which leaves a straight wound on his forehead. But Kakihara is pushed back against a stair rail and falls back over it. As he falls, he says, "This is amazing!" Like the Sadean libertine, his excesses have led to his own negation. Kakihara ultimately finds fulfillment in fantasy, for as Sade demonstrates, excessive behavior leads merely to apathy: it is only in the mind that one can find the ultimate pleasure.

In summary, the sadism inherent in the gangster film becomes the plot's driving force in *Ichi the Killer*. The politics within the yakuza gangs, of which both Ichi and Kakihara are a part, becomes secondary to Kakihara's quest for sexual and existential fulfillment. The sexualization of violence is also highlighted by the film's graphic visual style, with acts of sadism being depicted in almost pornographic detail. Through a Sadean reading, these acts of sadism can be understood as transgressive, in that they incorporate all parts of the body, demonstrating that the transgressive body sexualizes formerly non-sexual body parts and activities. This analysis of *Ichi the Killer* has also shown that sadistic desires can cross over into masochistic pleasure. The link between Sade and masochism will be explored further in the next chapter.

10

Masochists

We have understood that while the sadist revels in inflicting pain, the masochist takes pleasure in receiving it. This equation has traditionally led to the assumption of a pact between the sadist and the masochist. However, as Deleuze points out, a true sadist would not enjoy having a partner who liked the pain and torture that the sadist imposes, just as a true masochist would not want a sadist.[1] Therefore, the main issue where sadism and masochism diverge is in the area of consent. The masochist chooses a torturer. What will take place is carefully negotiated; in many cases a formal contract is drawn up. In other words, a genuine masochist is not the helpless, subdued victim of a sadist but someone who remains in control of the pain inflicted upon them and who chooses their position at every stage.

As discussed above, the incorporation of pain sees sexual pleasure experienced in all parts of the body, and tests the limits and endurance of those involved. All aspects of the scene contrive to heighten tension and create suspense by avoiding release through sexual intercourse and orgasm. In many cases the sex play of masochism actually replaces sexual intercourse, as both sadism and masochism involve the transgression of normative sexual practices, and the aim of heterosexual intercourse and reproduction. Due to this fundamental similarity between sadism and masochism, Sade's discourse on pain and violence and its place in the search for sexual fulfillment is useful when examining films that incorporate masochistic sexual scenes. Through the Sadean analysis of *Secretary* (Steven Shainberg, 2002) and *In the Realm of the Senses* (Nagisa Oshima, 1976), the transgressive body will be revealed as a highly sexualized, polymorphous body that incorporates violence and other previously non-sexual practices into its sexual play.

Love Hurts: Secretary

Steven Shainberg's *Secretary* subverts the romantic comedy genre by presenting a masochistic love story in which the latter acts as a metaphor

10. Masochists

for the joy and the pain that one experiences when falling in love. The narrative presents a young woman, Lee, who takes a job as a secretary and finds herself falling in love with her boss, E. Edward Grey. What makes this film different from others in the genre is that their relationship develops through Grey's initiation of Lee into masochistic sex play. Progressively we see that from these experiences Lee blossoms into an independent and confident young woman who embraces her masochistic tendencies and is empowered by them. The relationship between Lee and Grey is not an exploitative one, but rather a meeting of two people who complement each other perfectly.

Needless to say, in consequence, the relationship in *Secretary* is completely different from the sexual relationships detailed in Sade's works. However, as I have discussed earlier, sadistic and masochistic sexualities can be viewed as involving common elements that demarcate them as transgressions of normal reproductive practice. This includes the use of pain and violence, the theatrical staging of sexual scenarios, and polymorphous pleasure. The incorporation of these elements thus enables us to understand *Secretary* through Sadean philosophy, as a text that presents transgressive sexuality as a source of power and pleasure.

Whereas sex became a form of extreme violence in the other films discussed earlier in the previous chapter, *Secretary* seeks a more realistic portrayal of alternative sexual relationships. In keeping with Deleuze's separation of sadism from masochism, the set of real sexual practices referred to as "sadomasochism" (as well as by the abbreviations S&M, SM and BDSM),[2] can be understood as fitting in with Deleuze's conception of masochism. In the masochist scenario, the one who inflicts the pain is not a sadist but an essential element of masochism. Consistent with this distinction from sadism, *Secretary* clearly differs from the sexual violence found in Sade's novels, where the protagonist searches for sexual fulfillment alone and without regard for others. Conversely, although both violence and pain are inflicted in the sex scenes of *Secretary*, these are mild and, above all, consensual.

Nevertheless, while the sexual exploration detailed in this film deviates from the Sadean scenario of victim and victimizer, it is important when discussing sadism and masochism to incorporate representations of these practices in the context of a safe and stable relationship because violent sexuality does not only exist within the dichotomy of non-consenting victim and violent perpetrator. As Tanya Krzywinska notes, in reference to *Secretary* and other films which focus on consensual SM relationships:

Part Four: Sexual Transgressors

> Although these films work with the increasing legitimation and acceptance of BDSM in contemporary culture, as part of a general trend in which sexual identity is regarded and aired through the media more diversely, they nonetheless trade on images and topics charged with transgressive kudos that hitherto were the preserve of outlying and marginal cinemas.[3]

As Krzywinska's comment suggests, films such as *Secretary*, which present SM relationships as consensual and loving, still foreground the transgressive, violent and polymorphous perversity of such sexual activity, thereby suggestively invoking Sade.

Inviting comparisons with Sade's *Philosophy in the Bedroom*, *Secretary* tells the story of a young girl's initiation into a sexual world where the aim is not sexual intercourse but rather the exploration of all bodily possibilities. Lee is initially the embodiment of childlike innocence, someone who has to be looked after by others. At the beginning of the film she is seen leaving a mental health institution in which she has stayed after a failed suicide attempt. She is being returned to the care of her parents. One of the first shots focuses on Lee's feet as she lifts a sagging sock, and subsequent scenes show her in clothes that are baggy or ill-fitting, as though she has yet to grow into them. Her posture is stooped, her limbs gangly and awkward. She looks as though she is in her early twenties, but her behavior suggests that she is still trapped in an early adolescent stage. Her family treats her like a child, and her bedroom is decorated in pink and purple, as though a little girl inhabited it.

Even her rituals of self-mutilation are carried out in a childish manner. Whenever something distresses her, such as seeing her father get drunk or her parents fight, Lee is unable to cope and runs away to administer tiny cuts or burns into her skin. A flashback to her attempted suicide shows that it was the result of a knife slipping, Lee commenting in voiceover: "I'm not sure how I could've misjudged — I'd been doing it since seventh grade." This remark reveals that this pattern of behavior began in late childhood, the phase in which she seems to be stuck. The instruments that she uses to cut herself are kept in a box decorated with butterflies, and she cuts herself with a ballerina figurine whose foot has been sharpened to a point. These tools that inflict pain look like children's toys, and, just like children's toys, they are used to create feelings of security and to alleviate fear and loneliness.

When Lee goes to the interview for the secretary job, she is dropped off by her mother, wearing a purple plastic cloak reminiscent of the one worn by Little Red Riding Hood. As I argued earlier in the discussion of

10. Masochists

The Company of Wolves, this fairy-tale, in which a young girl journeys alone and meets the Big Bad Wolf, serves as a metaphor for burgeoning female sexuality. And, as in the fairy-tale, Lee also ventures out alone and meets a Big Bad Wolf, one who promises her both pain and pleasure. This childishness makes Lee both open to learning and ripe for a sexual education. Thus, as mentioned earlier, Lee's story invokes Sade's *Philosophy in the Bedroom*, which also unfolds a narrative of the sexual education, in all its forms and aberrations, of a young woman (in fact, the book's second edition was released with the subtitle "The Immoral Teachers").[4]

However, the libertines, even when adopting the role of teacher, also retain their infantile erotic polymorphousness, with many of their sexual activities being played as games or performances, even though always within a strict framework and hierarchy. This focus on the educational aspects of sexual experimentation is also evident in Lee and Grey's relationship, which can be read as one of pupil and teacher. While Lee learns and flourishes under Grey's tutelage, Grey, in turn, embraces Lee's childlike personality and teaches her through the use of games and role-playing. At the same time, as the disciplinarian, Grey also enforces strict rules and guidelines.

One of these rules is that none of their encounters will culminate in sexual intercourse. For example, when Grey orders Lee to lift her skirt, she looks hesitant about the request, to which Grey replies, "You're not worried that I'm going to fuck you, are you? I'm not interested in that. Not in the least." In a similar vein, in the stories of both Sade and Masoch, the sexual scenes often fail to include sexual intercourse, because in both sadism and masochism it is pain and violence which provides sexual fulfillment. In *Secretary*, fulfillment comes from the creation of a scene in which both participants play designated roles. The roles that Lee and Grey take on are exaggerations of the roles that they have at work. Grey is the boss and Lee is the secretary, someone who assists Grey and follows his orders. When Lee makes a mistake, Grey proceeds to devise an elaborate "punishment" for her. For instance, when Lee first begins to work at Grey's office, he becomes exasperated by her bad habits and sloppy appearance: "You're tapping your toe all the time and playing with your hair. You're either going to have to wear a hairnet or stop playing with your hair.... Do you realize that you're always sniffling?" After being chastized, Lee immediately tries to correct her faults, making it apparent that she is willing to obey his commands.

After discovering a typo, Grey admonishes Lee, and as he walks away,

Part Four: Sexual Transgressors

she sniffles. Grey then calls Lee into his office. As she walks down the corridor, the camera is placed above her, looking down, signaling that a change is about to occur in their relationship. When she enters, Grey commands her to "put your elbows on the desk, bend over, get your face close to the letter and read it aloud." She does as he says, and in close-up she reads the letter. Suddenly out of frame, Grey smacks Lee on the bottom; she stops in shock but then continues to read. There are intercuts between close shots of both of them, and when Grey asks her to read it again, she smiles. As she reads again, the camera no longer shows close-ups of them separately, but wider shots that include both of them in the frame, the presence of both in the shot signifying a shared pleasurable experience. Incidentally, this scene is similar to a sex scene, as it gains in momentum and climaxes with both characters falling against the desk in exhaustion.

This scene, in which work activities are sexualized into forms of pleasure, demonstrates that the theatricalized situations found in both sadism and masochism carry within them a symbolic value. For just as the sadistic sexual practices in *Salò* and *Ichi the Killer* comment on fascism and the gangster lifestyle respectively, in *Secretary* the masochistic scenario is an exaggeration of the roles that Lee and Grey play in the corporate world. Similarly, Sade's works comment on his social place within the aristocracy. Indeed, the four Masters in *The 120 Days of Sodom* use their positions as pillars of society, exploiting their superior social power for sexual gain. All situations, although widely different, illustrate how transgressive desires are expressed in daily life, even in symbolic form. In *Secretary* this takes the form of punishments that Grey, the boss, inflicts on Lee, his subordinate, whenever she commits an error in her work. For example, if Lee makes a typo she gets a spanking. Soon Lee is making spelling mistakes on purpose so that her "punishments" continue—in fact, a typo soon becomes an indication from Lee to Grey that she is keen to participate in another session.

As the narrative progresses, and the sessions between Lee and Grey become more regular, we see a montage that shows the various sexual activities in which they participate. Like many sadistic and masochistic practices, the activities presented in this montage are polymorphous—that is, they do not center on genital stimulation. While two of the shots have Lee on all fours in a subordinate position, we see her facing the camera and looking into the lens with defiance. She, in fact, dominates the screen, while Grey becomes secondary. Thus, this sequence demonstrates that Lee has grown and changed through the exploration of her sexuality. In con-

10. Masochists

Another day in the office for Lee (Maggie Gyllenhaal) in *Secretary* (2002).

trast to the awkward young woman with messy hair and baggy clothes seen at the beginning of the film, she is now a stylish and confident businesswoman.

Another important moment in this montage has Grey tell Lee what she is allowed to have for dinner. Lee's family looks on in disbelief as Lee follows Grey's orders, with four peas arranged delicately on her plate. This demonstrates a trait that is inherent, as well as transgressive, in both sadism and masochism. This trait is the sexualization of activities that are not innately sexual, such as the amount of food that one eats for dinner. But what is sexual about these activities? It is the control over the body and its urges, as well as the incorporation of new urges that are themselves sexualized. This is represented in masochism in the form of the ritual, a theatrical process played out in order to cause a rise in tension. In the masochistic ritual, events are heightened and prolonged so that tension is increased and then finally released.

A variation of this theme is found in sadism, where events are ordered and analyzed before being played out. In *The 120 Days of Sodom*, as in *Salò*, a rulebook is drawn up in which it is stated that even though sexual activity will take place, the Masters must refrain from taking the virginity of the victims until after a certain amount of time has passed. However, it is important to note that the order imposed upon the sadistic scene differs from the tension created in the masochistic scene. As Deleuze states:

> The aesthetic and dramatic suspense of Masoch contrasts with the mechanical, cumulative repetition of Sade. We should note here that the art of suspense always places us on the side of the victims and forces us to identify with him, whereas the gathering momentum of repetition tends to force us onto the side of the torturer and make us identify with the sadistic hero.[5]

While the escalation of violence in Sade's fiction creates a numbing effect, in *Salò* it is not suspense but disgust that is increased; in fact, there is no intensity over whether the victims may escape or be rescued, and the narrative instead gradually descends further into hell. In this sense, atrocity is heaped upon atrocity, with no hope of relief.

Secretary, in contrast, uses masochism to heighten the tension within the sexual scenes, as well as within the narrative itself. Because the film is a romance, there is suspense over whether the two leads will get together and how this will happen. Deleuze observes, in relation to the use of suspense in the work of Masoch:

10. Masochists

Masoch was the first novelist to make use of suspense as an essential ingredient of romantic fiction. This is partly because the masochistic rites of torture and suffering imply actual physical suspension (the hero is hung up, crucified or suspended), but also because the woman torturer freezes into postures that identify her with a statue, a painting or a photograph. She suspends her gestures in the act of bringing down the whip or removing her furs; her movement is arrested as she turns to look at herself in a mirror.[6]

In *Secretary*, the creation of suspense through physical suspension and the delaying of movement is illustrated by Lee's last desperate attempt to win Grey's heart. While trying on a wedding dress for her impending marriage to another man (after her romantic and working relationship with Grey has failed), Lee runs away to Grey's office to tell him she loves him. Grey says, in reference to their masochism, "We can't do this twenty-four hours a day, seven days a week," to which Lee replies, "Why not?" Grey then commands Lee to sit at his desk, with her palms facing down, and orders her not to move until he returns. He then leaves the office and watches her through the window. Lee doesn't move a muscle. The camera tilts down under her chair to show that Lee urinates on herself rather than disobey orders. Peter, Lee's fiancé, arrives, trying to convince her to come back to him. He notices that Lee is sitting still, refusing to move. They have the following exchange:

PETER: Are you doing something sexual, right now?
LEE: Does this look sexual to you?
PETER: I don't know, Lee!

That Peter does not understand Lee's sexual desire shows their incompatibility. In fact, earlier in the film Lee and Peter kiss, and Lee stops and lies across him, her bottom poised for a smack. Peter, of course, has no idea what she wants; and when they have sex, a close-up of Lee reveals that she is clearly bored as she moans unconvincingly. When Peter then asks, "I didn't hurt you, did I?" Lee forlornly answers, "No." For Lee, pain is an integral part of pleasure.

As Lee sits at the desk and refuses to leave, a procession of people arrive to talk to her, each presenting a different view of her situation. This sequence, where each person talks straight to the camera (which represents Lee's point-of-view), could either be reality or Lee's own internal argument over whether she should stay and wait for Grey (who by now has gone home). One man says she should express her love in "more conventional ways," while a feminist offers Lee a pile of books and asks that she learn about "women's struggle."

Part Four: Sexual Transgressors

These viewpoints are common arguments against sadomasochism: that it is weird and perverted, and that a woman who puts herself in the masochistic position is conforming to patriarchal stereotypes of passive femininity. But, as discussed earlier, rather than conforming to societal norms, sadism and masochism play with and transgress gender stereotypes. As MacKendrick asserts:

> This playfulness with gender, here as elsewhere, is unsettling to more traditional feminisms, which require a firm sense of gender boundaries if they are to be supportive of women. Thus s/m takes its place among the practices of the postmodern, in which the identity of the subject becomes a performance, sometimes fluid, sometimes an open question.[7]

In masochism, gender is not fixed but, rather, open for deconstruction and change. In this context the female's status as submissive victim is particularly explored and subverted. Sade's Justine and Juliette provide an instructive and suggestive illustration of this idea. While Justine suffers in her passive role, Juliette always dominates; even though both women undergo similar treatment, Juliette turns these situations into opportunities for her own pleasure. Commenting on the difference between victim and libertine, Barthes states, "[S]he makes herself a victim because she chooses to scream; if, under the same circumstance, she were to ejaculate, she would cease to be a victim, would be transformed into a libertine."[8] This statement makes it clear that the scenario in which a boss smacks his secretary would have very different meaning if Lee did not also find this activity a source of pleasure.

In this same scene in which Lee refuses to move, she is also visited by her doctor, who mentions that "there's a long history of this in Catholicism," in reference to traditions in which pain is used as a form of repentance and transcendence. He even adds, "Who's to say that love needs to be soft and gentle?" This statement is central to the film, in which masochism represents a playing out of the pain and pleasure that is an integral part of love. After Grey fires her and their relationship ends, Lee continues to explore her masochistic tendencies, and is shown at one point listening to a tape titled "How to Come Out as a Dominant/Submissive," which says:

> Most people think that the best way to live is to run from pain. But a more joyful life embraces the entire spectrum of human feeling. If we can fully experience pain as well as pleasure, we can live a much deeper and more meaningful life.

10. Masochists

This point of view supports the idea that the forces of sex and violence are connected in the human capacity to feel both pleasure and pain. While these forces are repressed in modern society (in order to prevent complete chaos), they nevertheless can find a controlled release in masochism. Grey is seen writing a letter to Lee in which he explains, "This is disgusting. I'm sorry. I don't know why I'm like this." Although he doesn't give her the letter, he fires her, telling her, "You have to go or I won't stop." But in stopping the affair, Grey is miserable. He tries to deny who he is, while Lee embraces her newfound sexuality. Therefore, Lee's refusal to move from Grey's desk proves to him that not only does she love him, but also that she is willing to push herself to the limit for him. They really can do this "twenty-four hours a day, seven days a week." When Grey realizes what Lee has done for him, he goes to her and carries her out of the office and into his home. He rests her naked on what appears to be an elevated patch of grass. In voiceover, Lee intones: "I finally felt beautiful, finally part of the earth. I touched the soil and he loved me back."

This statement, along with the image of Lee resting on grass, incorporates imagery of the natural world ("part of the earth ... touched the soil"). Moreover, throughout the film transgressive sexual encounters only take place in settings that are decorated with elements from nature. The proliferation of nature into the sexual scene can be understood through Sade's assertion that all sexual urges are natural. This notion is expressed through the film's mise-en-scène. Grey's office is different in design from all of the other sets used in the film. While most of Lee's world seems plastic and artificial, Grey's office is furnished with wood and contains a small garden filled with exotic plants. It is the one place where the natural world flourishes. The mise-en-scène reflects the view that the sexual relationship that develops in this setting is natural. That it takes place in the brightness of day illustrates that it is not a dark, shameful secret that must be kept hidden from sight. In Sade's words:

> [A]ll are a part of Nature; when she created men, she was pleased to vary their tastes as she made different their countenances, and we ought no more be astonished at the diversity she has put in our features than at that she has placed in our affections.[9]

Therefore, the sexuality exhibited by Lee and Grey, although classified as "aberrant" (a point illustrated by the different opinions that Lee hears as she sits in Grey's office), is validated from a Sadean point-of-view as natural, and just as valid as so-called "normal" heterosexual practice.

Part Four: Sexual Transgressors

Secretary can thus be read as depicting a sexual relationship that represents Sade's view of nature. Masochism's status as different, as a variation of the norm, illustrates its naturalness. In this sense, masochistic sexuality shares similarities with the sexuality in Sade's works. Both involve the incorporation of pain and violence into the sexual scenario, and demonstrate the proposition that transgressive pleasure is experienced through activities that seem distinctly unpleasurable and non-sexual. These sexualities, both transgressing normal reproductive practice and violating many societal taboos by the introduction of violence into the sexual scene, also represent a potential break with society itself. I will address the latter idea through a discussion of Nagisa Oshima's *In the Realm of the Senses*.

Going All the Way: In the Realm of the Senses

In the Realm of the Senses depicts a sexual relationship that is so intense that the lovers must seclude themselves from the outside world in a space where there are neither rules nor boundaries. As a result, the couple's sexual experimentation escalates to include violence, as they search for ever-increasing pleasure. However, the lovers soon discover that the inevitable climax of their affair must result in the death of one or both of them. Thus, the affair represented in this film can be understood as following a Sadean narrative trajectory: those seeking pleasure hide themselves away from society and, in that context, sex games gradually culminate in violence and murder. The masochistic relationship in *In the Realm of the Senses* follows this trajectory toward the ultimate orgasm, which is death itself. Therefore, in this discussion of *In the Realm of the Senses*, I will argue that the violent, masochistic relationship between the lovers represents the intimate link that exists between sex and death. This demonstrates that the transgressive body sexualizes seemingly non-sexual experiences, for in this film the experience of death, an event that is usually surrounded by taboo, becomes a vital element within the sexual scene.

Nagisa Oshima's *In the Realm of the Senses* is based on true events, centering on an obsessive and highly sexual relationship between a servant, the (aptly named) Sada, and her employer, Kichi. The two lovers leave their home and travel to various inns, where they gradually begin to incorporate pain, mostly via strangulation, into their sex play. This culminates

10. Masochists

in Sada strangling Kichi to death while they have sex. Sada then castrates Kichi and lies next to his corpse.

Made in 1976, the film transgresses the boundary separating the art film from pornography, as the sex scenes are not simulated. They present real sexual acts and contain shots that show in detail the sexual organs. Due to the mainstream success of the pornographic film *Deep Throat* (1972), there was a time in the 1970s when there was a slight relaxation of laws and regulations when it came to the filming of sexual activity (at least within the United States and Europe). Films such as *Last Tango in Paris* (Bernando Bertolucci, 1972), *Behind the Green Door* (Artie and Jim Mitchell, 1972), *Pink Flamingos* (John Waters, 1972), *Emmanuelle* (Just Jaeckin, 1974), *The Beast* (Walerian Borowczyk, 1975) and *The Realm* all utilized real, or very real-looking simulations, of sex. Also common to these films is the exploration of sexuality away from the idea of straight, genital-centered heterosexual intercourse.

Oshima wanted to make a film about sex that was free of social and cultural constraints. In order to combat Japan's strict laws against nudity and pornography, Oshima's film was financed by a French company, and its rushes were shipped to France for editing. While Japanese law allowed the presentation of graphic violence and rape, the showing of pubic hair and sexual organs was forbidden. However, Oshima believed that "[s]exual expression carried to its logical conclusion would result in the direct filming of sexual intercourse."[10] By collaborating with a company from another country, he was able to circumvent Japan's laws and create a piece of art that was free from government intervention, as well as from the prevailing moral restrictions of the time. The approach that Oshima takes toward sex in *The Realm* is encapsulated in a story from one of his essays:

> I have a friend who was ordered by his company to make a porno film as his first film. He made the film based on a crucial decision — that he had to shoot the anomalous. I think he was right. If you intend to pursue sex directly, you have no choice but to make some sort of anomaly your theme.[11]

Oshima seems to imply that just showing genital sex within a happy marriage is boring, as well as idealistic, and that it is people's kinks and perversions that both make and reveal them for who they actually are.

Sade also has sex as his main theme and explores it through the description of all sexual possibilities, regardless of prevailing social norms. By rejecting the social morals of the day, Sade's works have become timeless, in that they represent unfiltered and uncensored sexual desires in

Part Four: Sexual Transgressors

which sex and violence, and sex and death, are no longer separated by outside taboos. While bisexuality or any other form of "alternative" sexual practice was seen as morally wrong in Sade's time, even outlawed, he chose not to follow the morality of the time and, as a result, is still relevant today. As Sade remarks, "[T]here is no act really considered criminal everywhere upon the earth, none which, vicious or criminal here, is not praiseworthy and virtuous a few miles hence, that it is all a matter of opinion and of geography."[12] Focusing on the anomalous, and not complying with the morals of the day, ensures that works that deal with sex are more than just a mere artifact of the time and place in which they were made. As stated throughout this book, Sade identifies sex and aggression as base instincts—that is, as part of the primal self that civilization seeks to repress. For him, as these desires are a fundamental part of humanity, they transcend the morals of any time, as morality is always historically and culturally contingent.

In order to create this timeless feel, many stories and films which focus on sexual exploration isolate its characters away from outside interference. The setting of *The Realm* is similar to the use of space in other films that feature obsessive love relationships with masochistic tendencies, such as *Last Tango in Paris*, *The Night Porter* (Liliana Cavani, 1973) and *Blue Velvet* (David Lynch, 1986). Sade's libertines also require an isolated place away from prying eyes, as Barthes attests: "the Sadian [sic] site is unique: one travels only to shut oneself away."[13] Sada and Kichi travel from inn to inn, but this is only in order to limit interference from others. As mentioned earlier in regards to *Secretary*, these settings often incorporate natural elements, which represent how the base natural desires of sex, violence and death are expressed within the room.

The rooms in these films thus signify both the womb and the tomb (as previously discussed in the section on *Crash* in regard to representations of the interior of the car). They are spaces where sex takes place (sex being the act that creates life); yet the incorporation of violence and masochism also signifies death. The rooms where sex takes place are small, insular places, comforting like a womb, yet also isolating like a tomb. That the lovers in these rooms are completely separate from the outside world is, for example, demonstrated by a scene in *The Realm* when Kichi actually ventures into the outside world. As he walks down a street, he is off to the side as troops of soldiers march by him in the opposite direction. People surround them, waving Japanese flags. Oshima comments on the militarism of Japan at that time (1936), something to which Sada and Kichi

10. Masochists

are completely oblivious. The world marches on without them, and they are too caught up in each other to realize. In this scene Kichi hardly acknowledges the presence of others as they walk by him. He and Sada have become completely isolated from society and its events.

When Kichi returns, Sada scolds him because while he left the room unoccupied it has been cleaned. Earlier in the film a servant complains to Sada and Kichi that their room has a "funny smell." In reference to the film's title, all of the senses are stimulated in this space, as not only is the touch of sex enjoyed by the lovers, but also the tastes, smells, sights and sounds. The room now smells of sex, as neither their bodies nor the room have been cleaned. It is a smell created by their love, and Sada cries when the room is cleaned and the smell is removed. On one of the few occasions when they stop having sex in order to eat, Sada dips the food into her vagina before feeding it to Kichi. Throughout the film Kichi tastes many of Sada's fluids, such as her menstrual blood and tears. When he drinks sake he kisses Sada so that the drink drips from both their mouths, and a close-up shows Sada fellating Kichi, with semen dripping from her lips.

By applying Sadean philosophy to the analysis of this scene, it becomes tangible that what usually is regarded as a source of disgust (the body's fluids) can become a sensual delight. Sade's libertines also indulge all of the five senses in their sexual exploits. In *The 120 Days of Sodom* the orgies take place in a great hall so that all activity can be seen by the other participants. These orgies are preceded by stories and discussion. For example, in one scene a libertine proclaims: "It is commonly accepted amongst authentic libertines that the sensations communicated by the organs of hearing are the most flattering and those whose impressions are the liveliest."[14] Many of the stories and activities are devoted to the smelling and tasting of the body and its fluids, while the latter part of the book explores the power of touch through the infliction of pain and violence. Similarly, by consuming each other's fluids, Sada and Kichi also transgress the boundaries that separate them. They become one through the mutual consumption of their body fluids, and their constant physical connection through sexual intercourse. This incorporation of all the senses highlights how sexual desire involves the whole body and is not just a means of reproduction. It is an activity that encompasses all facets of existence: the sensual, the emotional, and the violent.

In Oshima's film, this radically sensual notion of sexuality is expressed through the representation of sex as performance. Many of Sada and Kichi's sexual encounters are observed by servants and geishas, with the geishas often singing and playing the samisen in accompaniment. When Sada and Kichi first leave their house they take part in a mock marriage ritual attended by geishas. After the ceremony they retire to their room, and the geishas watch as they consummate their "marriage." A shot begins with a man dancing, and as the camera tracks out we see that he is performing in front of Sada, Kichi and the geishas as they participate in an orgy. The marriage ceremony has transformed into a group sex ritual. The wide shot displays them all arranged together, a sea of naked flesh. That the shot begins with the man performing, and then tracks out to show the orgy, illustrates that sexual activity is part of a performance.

The theatricality of sex is, indeed, an important aspect of sadism and masochism. In both practices the participants take on roles and act them out. Often they involve props and costumes. Care is taken in how space is used and how people are positioned. In Sade's depiction of the sadistic scene, this allows for all possibilities to be explored and displayed to others. In Masoch's representation of the masochistic scene, the theatricality derives from creating suspense and prolonging the climax. Sexual pleasure is inseparable from the aesthetics of the scene. In Masoch's writing, sexual scenes incorporate florid descriptions of how rooms are decorated, as well as details of the clothes worn. For Masoch, it is not just the sexual act that creates pleasure, but all of the elements that make up the scene.

It is thus the masochistic scene that is represented in *The Realm*. In contrast to pornography, in which the camera focuses directly on the sexual act, *The Realm*'s sexual scenes, although actual, are staged in a way that complements the scenery. The film is a triumph of color and composition, unlike most pornography (which is a genre not known for its technical achievements). As a period piece, the camera revels in the details of costume and setting, with the characters wearing richly colored kimonos in luxurious fabrics. As Maureen Turim notes, the kimono acts as a stage curtain that is parted to reveal the body beneath it, showing the sexual organs forbidden by Japanese law.[15] For example, at one point the red material of Sada's kimono fills the whole screen. As it is rearranged, a flash of Sada's thighs and vagina are glimpsed.

Sada is frequently seen in the color red, a color that connotes passion. Red is also the color of blood, and of engorged and aroused sexual organs: it symbolizes both sex and violence. Sada thus follows in the tradition of cinema's "scarlet women." And, in fact, it is with a red cord, reminiscent of the red thread used by Eugénie in *Philosophy in the Bedroom* to sew up her mother's vagina, that Sada strangles Kichi. Both the red cord and the

10. Masochists

red thread are thus used in acts of violence committed in order to produce sexual pleasure. Sada is also often associated with blood, such as in the scene in which Kichi licks her menstrual blood, or the final scene in which she castrates Kichi's corpse and writes "SADA KICHI THE TWO OF US FOREVER" across his chest in blood. Her association with the color red therefore represents her as both sexual and violent.

This mixing of the sexual and the violent is expressed in the narrative arc of *In the Realm*. The film follows a Sadean trajectory as sex games become increasingly more violent. Like the libertines who search for the ultimate pleasure, Sada and Kichi also seek ever more heightened gratification. Rather than waning over time, the ardor increases to the point where Sada wishes Kichi would always be inside her, so that she can experience an eternal orgasm. When Sada expresses the desire to cut off Kichi's penis so he will no longer sleep with his wife, she also says, "If I cut him off, I can keep him inside me." While Sada finds happiness with Kichi, she also becomes obsessed with finding a way for them to always be together, to be permanently connected in mutual orgasm. In this respect, Bataille writes: "[O]nly the beloved can in this world bring about what our human limitations deny, a total blending of two beings, a continuity between two discontinuous creatures. Hence love spells suffering for us insofar as it is a quest for the impossible."[16]

In his book *Eroticism*, Bataille argues that the union of two people through sex is an attempt to transcend death by joining together and creating a new being — "a continuity between two discontinuous creatures."[17] However, two people cannot be connected together continuously, as the "little death" of the orgasm brings the connection to an end. Sada's quest, alas, is an impossible one. This idea is demonstrated in Sade through the excess of sexual activity and orgasm, which has a numbing effect, contributing to the complete apathy of the libertine. By feeling everything, they end up feeling nothing. Thus, the libertine must participate in increasingly more violent and atrocious activity in order to feel the slightest sensation. In *The Realm*, the same logic is expressed through the culminating of excessive sexual activity, resulting in the death of Kichi. All experience eventually ends in death. Excess leads to oblivion.

For Sade, death is present in all activities. Indeed, Sade sees no distinction between the states of life and death: "The principle of life in all beings is no other than that of death: at the same time we receive the one we receive the other, we nourish both within us, side by side."[18] This is because, in nature, all is in a state of constant motion, regardless of

Part Four: Sexual Transgressors

whether these forms are alive or dead. Even in death, matter still continues to move and change:

> Matter, deprived of the other portion of matter which communicated movement to it, is not destroyed for that; it merely abandons its form, it decays—and in decaying proves that it is not inert; it enriches the soil, fertilizes it, and serves in the regeneration of the other kingdoms as well as of its own. There is, in the final analysis, no essential difference between the first life we receive and this second, which is the one we call death.[19]

Here Sade argues that for nature to continue to thrive there must be creation and destruction. Both contribute to nature's constant flux. In this sense, the activities of his libertines, in which a new order is created through the destruction of the body, follows nature's principles. The sexual exploits of his libertines embrace the forces of both life and death.

For Sada and Kichi, death becomes a part of their sexual pleasure rather than the reason it will end. This is reminiscent of Sade's statement that life and death are the same, and that death is with us all the time. Necessarily, death is a part of sexual life. The sexual scenes between them gradually start involving elements of masochism, with Kichi in the submissive role, while Sada is shown wielding a knife and using a red cord for strangulation. But despite her name, Sada is not a sadist but a central element of masochism, which is an active one. Just as in *Secretary*, the two lovers are also employer and employee, the male being in the superior position of boss. But unlike *Secretary*, where the characters' sexual roles are exaggerations of the roles they have in the workplace, in *The Realm* it is the subordinate female who is the aggressor and switches to the dominant position.

At the beginning of the film Sada conforms to her role, with Kichi leering at her and making lecherous remarks about her body. It is Kichi who contrives situations so they can be alone, and while they have sex he makes her play the samisen so as to disguise what they are doing and avoid interruption. She must do what he says. However, when they leave the household they are no longer master and servant but two lovers. Free from the world around them, Sada now demands constant sexual satisfaction. Even while Kichi sleeps, she continues to hold and lick his penis. She also becomes the financial provider (she visits an old client), which is traditionally a male role. Sada is shown to have aggressive tendencies, seen early in the film when she gets into a fight with another servant and pulls out a knife. When she walks into a room and sees Kichi having sex with his wife, Sada fantasizes about slashing Kichi's wife with a razor. At several

10. Masochists

points in the film she threatens to cut off Kichi's penis. Thus, it is Sada who assumes the dominant role in their masochism. When they first begin to experiment with strangulation, Kichi tries to strangle Sada, but says he is unable to see her suffer. Sada, however, finds strangulation highly stimulating.

Kichi becomes more passive, willingly going along with whatever Sada wants, trying mercilessly to satisfy her voracious desire. He makes several remarks to the effect that he is now her possession, saying, "My body is yours. Do as you like." He wants only to make her happy — even if it means giving up his life. Toward the end of the film Kichi lies in bed, completely exhausted from the constant sex. He refuses to surrender to his fatigue and says to Sada, "I don't think I'll be able ... but come." In a long shot Sada mounts Kichi's frail body, and close-ups show his head beginning to loll to one side as he passes out. In another close-up Sada's hand grabs his penis and he then regains consciousness. The following exchange takes place:

KICHI: If I fall asleep, will you strangle me again?
SADA (nods): Do you want me to pull hard?
KICHI: If you start, don't stop in the middle. It hurts too much afterwards.

With this last statement, Kichi reveals his wish to die. His body is weak, and he can no longer satisfy Sada in the way that she needs. The only way he can make her reach orgasm is through his death. The next shot shows he has fallen asleep. In a long shot Sada grabs the red cord and mounts Kichi. In a long take she begins to pull the cord around his neck, cutting to a close-up of Kichi's face as he struggles to breathe. Once he is dead, Sada castrates Kichi.

Sada is now a woman who possesses a phallus, a symbol of her voracious sexual appetite and lust for violence. Sada is a "phallic woman," a type of female frequently found throughout Sade's works. Several of his female characters, because they possess obstructed vaginas and enlarged clitorises, embody the idea of the phallic woman — for example, Durand in *Juliette*. These women are therefore able to penetrate their partners as though they had a penis. Other women in Sade own dildos or, in the case of Clairwil from *Juliette*, a mummified penis. As Carter explains:

> When Clairwil in *Juliette* masturbates with a mummified penis, the penis becomes an object, disassociated from any human context. It is no longer a symbol of manhood. It is "the scepter of Venus," "the primary agent of love's pleasure," and may be wielded by whomsoever chooses to do so, regardless of the bearer's gender.[20]

Part Four: Sexual Transgressors

Sex games turn deadly for Sada (Eiko Matsuda) and Kichi (Tatsuya Fuji) *In the Realm of the Senses* (1976).

Gender in Sade's works is subverted from cultural, or even biological, norms. It is possible for a woman to possess a phallic sexuality, just as it is possible for many of his male characters to possess feminine traits (for instance, Durcet in *The 120 Days of Sodom* or Bressac in *Justine*). Searching for the ultimate pleasure, Sade's female libertines cast off gender constraints so that all possibilities become open to them. Sada, too, quests after the ultimate and never-ending orgasm. Throughout the film she is tireless in her lovemaking. The inevitable climax of the affair, the death of her partner, makes it possible for her to reach her goal of keeping Kichi's penis inside her at all times. At that moment Sada possesses the phallus and believes that her pleasure will never end.

Sada and Kichi's transgressions, which culminate in murder and castration, thus follow a Sadean trajectory. Sex becomes violence and then murder. The characters' sexual exploration incorporates the entire body and all of its senses, thus illustrating that the transgressive body is a highly sexual being, open to all possibilities for pleasure. In isolating themselves from society and the outside world, Sada and Kichi contrive the vanishing

10. Masochists

of all rules and boundaries. Instead, the couple becomes obsessed with finding the greatest pleasure and the ultimate orgasm, which in *In the Realm of the Senses* is shown to be death itself. The sexualization of pain culminates in death itself being experienced as a sexual act. And it is with this final transgression, in which death becomes the ultimate sexual act, that the analysis of the transgressive body comes to a close.

Conclusion

While the body has always been at the center of Western culture, there has been a shift in thought in regards to the body's place in the formation of the human subject. Whereas the earlier focus was on the configuration of the body as a symbol of dominant, hegemonic forces (for example, in early Marxist theory), more recent work has concentrated on bodies that have been previously rejected and marginalized (such as studies on the representations of women and ethnic minorities). What this shift reveals is that what was formerly marginalized is not the "Other" but a representation of parts of ourselves that are otherwise hidden or repressed.

This idea, that the human subject can be comprised of many different traits, is true for Sade since, for him, everything comes from nature. Nature is a force continually changing and transforming, with transgression being its one immutable trait. Nothing is unnatural because in nature everything is possible. Yet, for every new creation of nature there is also destruction, a continuous cycle of birth and death. These two elements, creation and destruction, are felt and expressed by the human subject through the sexual and the violent instincts. However, these instincts are then repressed by external influences in an attempt to impose order upon nature's constant and chaotic flux.

This then sets nature in opposition to the forces of culture and society, which seek to restrain nature and its primal urges. This is achieved through the production of cultural norms and standards in which the body is constructed as an exterior representation of the internal life of the subject. The body thus becomes a determining factor in whether the subject is defined as being a part of society or as one of its outcasts. This notion, that the external body symbolizes internal processes, serves as the foundation of dominant discourses on the subject in Western systems of knowledge — for example, philosophy, politics, sociology and science — leading to the marginalization of those discourses which do not conform to dominant theorizations. For instance, Sade's philosophy was rejected by societal

Conclusion

forces because what he advocated was a concept of the human subject as primarily biological, sexual and natural. This, of course, clashed with the prevailing idea that the subject was clean, self-contained, and dedicated to maintaining order.

However, when looking across other artistic mediums, this dominant concept of the subject is not always sustained. As the medium of cinema began to assume its place as the most popular form of mass entertainment, attitudes toward prevailing ideas of the human subject began to change. For while Sade was being rediscovered and re-evaluated in the mid-twentieth century as a source for understanding the body as transgressive, in the cinema this obsession with the body and its transgressions was being played out and presented to the public. There was a desire to see the body as a transgressive force, which pushes boundaries and explores new possibilities. This is proven by the fact that the bodies on display in cinema are most often presented in states of distress, desire or transformation: these bodies go against the norm in an attempt to attain even greater heights of power or pleasure. For in most film narratives the goal is not to achieve the norm but to transcend it, to go beyond it to something more spectacular.

This goal of the cinematic body can be traced back to aims of the libertine in Sade's fiction. While critical reflection on Sade's ideas has mainly taken place within the area of literary studies, it has only been explored within the area of film analysis in a few isolated cases. This is so despite the wide range of studies devoted to the examination of non-normative body imagery in the cinema, undertaken within the methodological fields of psychoanalysis, semiotics, and poststructuralism. Hopefully my analysis will open the possibility of more Sade-based film theory.

Certainly a Sadean approach to film analysis can be applied to many recent trends in cinema. The phenomenon of "torture porn" horror films, typified by the *Saw* and *Hostel* franchises, thrives on graphic portrayals of sadism and violation of the body in a way that seems ripe for Sadean interpretation. Furthermore, other recent films such as *Martyrs* (Pascal Laugier, 2008), *Antichrist* (Lars von Trier, 2009), *The Human Centipede (First Sequence)* (Tom Six, 2009), *A Serbian Film* (Srdjan Spasojevic, 2010), and *The Woman* (Lucky McKee, 2011) clearly seek to probe and test the same boundaries as Sade did, by pushing depictions of sexuality, violence and bodily transgression into areas not previously explored. A Sadean reading of these contemporary films will uncover how norms of the body and sexuality can be challenged in a way that also comments on contemporary

Conclusion

cultural and political concerns by focusing on transgression as a method of producing new, radical ideas and pleasures.

Bringing cinematic representations of the body together with Sade's notion of the body as a transgressive force of nature has been the function of this book. Through the textual analysis of representations of the transgressive body in cinema, these representations, just like the bodies represented in Sade's works, are found to carry with them significant social meanings. By investigating these meanings, the transgressive body in cinema can help us better understand who we are as human subjects, as these representations are not constructed as unnatural aberrations but as humans who are subject to the same feelings and urges as us all — with the only difference being how these urges are expressed. By seeking to understand these subjects, we learn something about ourselves and our own fascination with transgression.

Filmography

A.I. Artificial Intelligence (Steven Spielberg, 2001)
Accatone (Pier Paolo Pasolini, 1961)
The Addiction (Abel Ferrara, 1995)
American Pie (Chris and Paul Weitz, 1999)
American Psycho (Mary Harron, 2001)
An American Werewolf in London (John Landis, 1981)
The Anatomy of Hell (Catherine Breillat, 2004)
Antichrist (Lars von Trier, 2009)
Arabian Nights (Pier Paolo Pasolini, 1974)
Audition (Takashi Miike, 2000)
Baise-Moi (Virginie Despentes and Coralie Trinh Thi, 2001)
Beast, The (Walerian Borowczyk, 1975)
Beau Travail (Claire Denis, 1999)
Behind the Green Door (Artie and Jim Mitchell, 1972)
The Beyond (Lucio Fulci, 1981)
Blade (Stephen Norrington, 1998)
Blade Runner (Ridley Scott, 1982)
The Blair Witch Project (Daniel Myrick and Eduardo Sanchez, 1999)
Blood and Black Lace (Mario Bava, 1964)
Blue Velvet (David Lynch, 1986)
Bluebeard (Catherine Breillat, 2009)
Bram Stoker's Dracula (Francis Ford Coppola, 1992)
Breaking the Waves (Lars Von Trier, 1996)
Bullet Ballet (Shinya Tsukamoto, 1998)
Cannibal Apocalypse (Antonio Margheretti, 1980)
Cannibal Ferox (Umberto Lenzi, 1981)
Cannibal Holocaust (Ruggero Deodato, 1981)
The Canterbury Tales (Pier Paolo Pasolini, 1972)
City of the Living Dead (Lucio Fulci, 1980)
Chocolat (Claire Denis, 1988)
The Company of Wolves (Neil Jordan, 1985)
Copycat (Jon Amiel, 1995)
Crash (David Cronenberg, 1996)
Dahmer (David Jacobson, 2002)
Dancer in the Dark (Lars von Trier, 2001)
Dawn of the Dead (George A. Romero, 1979)
Day of the Dead (George A. Romero, 1985)
The Decameron (Pier Paolo Pasolini, 1971)
Deep Red (Dario Argento, 1975)
Deep Throat (Gerard Damiano, 1972)
Def by Temptation (James Bond III, 1990)
Deliverance (John Boorman, 1972)
Diary of the Dead (George A. Romero, 2007)
Dogville (Lars von Trier, 2003)
Double Indemnity (Billy Wilder, 1944)
Ed Gein (Chuck Parello, 2000)
88 Minutes (Jon Avnet, 2007)
The Element of Crime (Lars von Trier, 1984)
Emmanuelle (Just Jaeckin, 1974)
Epidemic (Lars von Trier, 1987)
Eugenie ... The Story of Her Journey Into Perversion (Jess Franco, 1969)
Eugenie de Sade (Jess Franco, 1970)

Filmography

eXistenZ (David Cronenberg, 1999)
Fascination (Jean Rollin, 1979)
Female Vampire (Jess Franco, 1973)
The Fly (David Cronenberg, 1986)
For My Sister (Catherine Breillat, 2001)
Friday the 13th (Sean S. Cunningham, 1980)
From Dusk 'Til Dawn (Robert Rodriguez, 1996)
Gacy (Clive Saunders, 2003)
Ginger Snaps (John Fawcett, 2000)
The Gospel According to Matthew (Pier Paolo Pasolini, 1964)
Hannibal (Ridley Scott, 2001)
Henry: Portrait of a Serial Killer (John McNaughton, 1990)
The Hills Have Eyes (Wes Craven, 1977)
The Hills Have Eyes (Alexandre Aja, 2006)
The House by the Cemetery (Lucio Fulci, 1981)
The Human Centipede (First Sequence) (Tom Six, 2009)
The Hunger (Tony Scott, 1983)
I Can't Sleep (Claire Denis, 1994)
I Spit on Your Grave (Meir Zarchi, 1977)
I Was Teenage Werewolf (Herbert L. Strock, 1957
Ichi the Killer (Takashi Miike, 2001)
The Idiots (Lars von Trier, 1998)
In the Realm of the Senses (Nagisa Oshima, 1976)
Interview with the Vampire (Neil Jordan, 1994)
Juliette (Jess Franco, 1975)
Ken Park (Larry Clark and Ed Lachman, 2002)
The Kingdom (Lars von Trier, 1994)
Kiss the Girls (Gary Fleder, 1997)
La Ricotta (Pier Paolo Pasolini, 1963)
Land of the Dead (George A. Romero, 2005)
Last Cannibal World (Ruggero Deodato, 1977)
The Last Seduction (John Dahl, 1993)
Last Tango in Paris (Bernardo Bertolucci, 1972)
Let the Right One In (Tomas Alfredson, 2008)
Let Me In (Matt Reeves, 2010)
Lips of Blood (Jean Rollin, 1976)
The Living Dead Girl (Jean Rollin, 1983)
Lolita (Adrian Lyne, 1997)
Mamma Rosa (Pier Paolo Pasolini, 1962)
Marquis de Sade's Justine (Jess Franco, 1968)
Martyrs (Pascal Laugier, 2008)
Medea (Lars von Trier, 1988)
Monster (Patty Jenkins, 2004)
Motel Hell (Kevin Connor, 1980)
Mysterious Skin (Gregg Araki, 2005)
The Night of the Living Dead (George A. Romero, 1968)
The Night Porter (Liliana Cavani, 1973)
Nightmare Detective (Shinya Tsukamoto, 2006)
Nine Songs (Michael Winterbottom, 2004)
The Nude Vampire (Jean Rollin, 1969)
The Ordeal (Fabrice du Welz, 2004)
Out of the Past (Jacques Torneur, 1947)
Peeping Tom (Michael Powell, 1960)
Psycho (Alfred Hitchcock, 1960)
Rabid (David Cronenberg, 1976)
The Rape of the Vampire (Jean Rollin, 1968)
A Real Young Lady (Catherine Breillat, 1975)
Rebel Without a Cause (Nicholas Ray, 1955)
Red Dragon (Brett Ratner, 2002)
Requiem for a Vampire (Jean Rollin, 1972)
Robocop (Paul Verhoeven, 1987)
Romance (Catherine Breillat, 1999)
Salò, or The 120 Days of Sodom (Pier Paolo Pasolini, 1975)
The Satanic Rites of Dracula (Alan Gibson, 1973)
Secretary (Steven Shainberg, 2002)
A Serbian Film (Srdjan Spasojevic, 2010)
Seven (David Fincher, 1995)
Sex and the Vampire (Jean Rollin, 1970)
Shivers (David Cronenberg, 1975)
The Silence of the Lambs (Jonathan Demme, 1990)
A Snake of June (Shinya Tsukamoto, 2002)

Filmography

Survival of the Dead (George A. Romero, 2009)
Taking Lives (D.J. Caruso, 2004)
Ted Bundy (Matthew Bright, 2002)
Teen Wolf (Rod Daniel, 1985)
Tenebrae (Dario Argento, 1982)
Terminator (James Cameron, 1984)
Tetsuo: The Iron Man (Shinya Tsukamoto, 1988)
Tetsuo 2: Body Hammer (Shinya Tsukamoto, 1991)
Tetsuo: The Bullet Man (Shinya Tsukamoto, 2009)
The Texas Chainsaw Massacre (Tobe Hooper, 1974)
There's Something About Mary (Bobby and Peter Farrelly, 1998)
Thirst (Park Chan-Wook, 2009)
35 Shots of Rum (Claire Denis, 2008)
36 Fillete (Catherine Breillat, 1988)
Tokyo Fist (Shinya Tsukamoto, 1995)
Trouble Every Day (Claire Denis, 2001)
Twilight (Catherine Hardwicke, 2008)
Two Orphan Vampires (Jean Rollin, 1995)
Underworld (Len Wiseman, 2003)
Vampyres (Jose Larraz, 1974)
Vampyros Lesbos (Jess Franco, 1971)
Videodrome (David Cronenberg, 1982)
Vital (Shinya Tsukamoto, 2004)
White Material (Claire Denis, 2010)
The Wicker Man (Robin Hardy, 1973)
Wolf (Mike Nichols, 1994)
The Woman (Lucky McKee, 2011)
Zentropa (Lars von Trier, 1992)
Zodiac (David Fincher, 2007)
Zombie Flesh Eaters (Lucio Fulci, 1979)
Zombie Flesh Eaters 2 (Lucio Fulci, 1988)

Chapter Notes

Introduction

1. Jacques Lacan, "The *Jouissance* of Transgression," in Jacques Lacan, *The Ethics of Psychoanalysis, 1959–60: The Seminars of Jacques Lacan* (London: Routledge, 1992), 191–203; Janine Chasseguet-Smirgel, *Creativity and Perversion* (London: Free Association Books, 1992); Michel Foucault, "Preface to Transgression," in Michel Foucault, *Language, Counter-Memory, Practice: Selected Essays and Interviews* (Oxford: Blackwell, 1977), 29–52; Michel Foucault, *The History of Sexuality* (New York: Vintage, 1990); Gilles Deleuze, *Coldness and Cruelty* (New York: Zone, 1989).

2. Sade was imprisoned for seven months in 1768 after picking up a beggar woman, Rose Keller, and promising her work as a housekeeper. Once at Sade's home, the woman was held captive, ordered to undress, beaten with a cat-o'-nine-tails, her flesh cut with a knife and hot wax poured on her wounds. Maurice Lever, *Marquis de Sade* (London: Flamingo, 1995), 150–166. Several other incidents led to an imprisonment of more than ten years in 1778. Ibid., 190–299. It was during his long detention, from 1778 to 1790, that Sade began to focus his energy on writing. Having been imprisoned for his debaucheries, Sade decided to write about them instead. In this writing, all of the elements from his life converged: isolated châteaus where debaucherous deeds take place; lascivious monks, nuns and clergymen; libertine aristocrats (both male and female); beautiful victims; and, most importantly, sexual experimentation and exploration involving blasphemy, sodomy, pain, violence and the transgression of all taboos. Ibid., 63.

3. In 1801, Sade was arrested after a raid on his publisher's office, in which copies of *Justine* and *Juliette* were seized. Ibid., 501–505.

4. Marquis de Sade, *Juliette* (New York: Grove Press, 1968); Marquis de Sade, *Justine* (New York: Grove Press, 1965).

5. Sade, *Juliette*, 418.

6. Marquis de Sade, *Philosophy in the Bedroom* (New York: Grove Press, 1965), 232–233.

7. Marquis de Sade, *The 120 Days of Sodom* (New York: Grove Press, 1987), 364.

8. Sade, *Juliette*, 43.

9. Ibid., 230.

10. Sade, *Juliette*, 69–70. Italics in original text.

11. Sade, *Philosophy in the Bedroom*, 240.

12. Sade, *Juliette*, 475.

13. Camille Paglia, *Sexual Personae: Art and Decadence from Nefertiti to Emily Dickinson* (New York: Vintage, 1991), 237.

14. Sade, *Juliette*, 60.

15. For example, the character of Eugénie proclaims, "Here I am: at one stroke incestuous, adulterous, sodomite, and all that in a girl who only lost her maidenhead today!" Sade, *Philosophy in the Bedroom*, 359.

16. Leo Bersani, "Is the Rectum a Grave?" in *AIDS: Cultural Analysis, Cultural Activism*, ed. Douglas Crimp (MA: MIT Press, 1988), 212.

17. Sade, *Philosophy in the Bedroom*, 238.

18. Sigmund Freud, "Character and Anal Erotism," in *The Freud Reader*, ed. Peter Gay (London: Vintage Books, 1995), 294.

19. Coprophilia is sexual play with feces, while coprophagy involves the eating of feces.

Notes — Part One and Chapter 1

20. Sade, *Juliette*, p. 79.
21. In his biography of Sade, Lever even states that Sade had "a negative Oedipus complex. Rather than kill the father the son forges an alliance with him and turns his powerful hostility against his mother. Later, when Donatien was forced to confront the redoubtable maternity of his mother-in-law, *la presidente* de Montreuil, his murderous and profanatory impulses would rise to the level of consciousness. He then developed an all-consuming hatred of all matriarchal values—compassion, tenderness, consolation, sacrifice, fidelity." Maurice Lever, *Marquis de Sade* (London, Flamingo, 1995), 14. See also Laurence Bongie, *Sade: A Biographical Essay* (Chicago: University of Chicago Press, 1998), 174; Francine du Plessix Gray, *At Home with the Marquis de Sade* (New York: Simon & Schuster, 1998), 11.
22. Sade, *The 120 Days of Sodom*, 293.

Part One

1. Sade, *Juliette*, 171.

Chapter 1

1. Marcel Henaff, *Sade: The Invention of the Libertine Body* (Minneapolis, University of Minnesota Press, 1999), 5.
2. Ibid.
3. Ibid.
4. Sade, *The 120 Days of Sodom*, 248.
5. This transference of bodily fluids within the sexual scene, in which death is the result, is a clear reference to the HIV/AIDS panic that was occurring at the time of *Bram Stoker's Dracula*'s release. Many other films, such as *The Satanic Rites of Dracula* (Alan Gibson, 1973), *The Hunger* (Tony Scott, 1983), *Def by Temptation* (James Bond III, 1990), *Interview with the Vampire* (Neil Jordan, 1994), *The Addiction* (Abel Ferrara, 1995), *Blade* (Stephen Norrington, 1998), *Underworld* (Len Wiseman, 2003) and *Thirst* (Park Chan-Wook, 2009), also present vampirism as a viral force.
6. Sade, *The 120 Days of Sodom*, 199.
7. Cynthia Freeland, *The Naked and the Undead: Evil and the Appeal of Horror* (Boulder: Westview Press, 2000), 137–8.
8. Sade, *The 120 Days of Sodom*, 304.
9. David Pirie, cited in Franco Moretti, "Dialectic of Fear," in *The Horror Reader*, ed. Ken Gelder (London: Routledge, 2000), 153.
10. Compare also the mythic figure of the Lamia from ancient Greece. The Lamia was a succubus that drank blood and fed on corpses. She was also linked to snakes. Alain Silver and James Ursini, *The Vampire Film: From Nosferatu to Interview with the Vampire* (New York: Limelight Editions, 1997), 18.
11. Freeland, 125.
12. Ibid.
13. Paglia, 237.
14. Sade, *The 120 Days of Sodom*, 506.
15. Joan Hawkins, *Cutting Edge: Art-Horror and the Horrific Avant-Garde* (Minneapolis: University of Minnesota Press, 2000), 16.
16. Rollin in particular has repeatedly taken the female vampire as his subject. The lesbian vampire is a recurrent character in his soft-core erotica genre films. His vampire films include *The Rape of the Vampire* (1968), *The Nude Vampire* (1969), *Sex and the Vampire* (1970), *Requiem for a Vampire* (1972), *Lips of Blood* (1976), *Fascination* (1979), *The Living Dead Girl* (1983), and *Two Orphan Vampires* (1995). This again demonstrates the female vampire as a figure that is both threatening and highly attractive. Indeed, her dangerousness is the main part of her allure.
17. Hawkins, 6.
18. Franco Moretti, "Dialectic of Fear," in *The Horror Reader*, ed. Ken Gelder, 148–160 (London: Routledge, 2000), 157.
19. Ibid.
20. Xavier Mendik, "Perverse Bodies, Profane Texts: Processes of Sadeian 'Mixture' in the Films of Jesus Franco," in *Necronomicon Book Two*, ed. Andy Black (London: Creation Books, 1998), 7–29. It should be noted that although Franco's Christian name is Jesus, in his films he is credited as Jess Franco.
21. Hawkins, 112.
22. Ibid.
23. Ibid., 6.
24. Ibid., 112.

25. Xavier Mendik, "The Sadeian Speaks: An Interview with Jesus Franco," in *Necronomicon: Book Two*, ed. Andy Black (London: Creation, 1998), 23.
26. Ibid.
27. Cathal Tohill and Pete Tombs, *Immoral Tales: European Sex and Horror Movies 1956–1984* (New York: St. Martin's Griffin, 1995), 113.
28. Sade, *Philosophy in the Bedroom*, 253.
29. Mendik, "The Sadeian Speaks: An Interview with Jesus Franco," 23.
30. Angela Carter, *The Sadeian Woman: An Exercise in Cultural History* (London: Virago, 1979), 27.
31. Sade, *Philosophy in the Bedroom*, 321.
32. Paglia, 12.
33. Ibid., 5.
34. Ibid., 30. In contrast, Paglia also defines the Apollonian: it "gives form and shape, marking off one being from another. All artefacts are Apollonian." Ibid.
35. The exceptions here are gross-out comedy films such as *There's Something About Mary* (Bobby and Peter Farrelly, 1998) and *American Pie* (Chris and Paul Weitz, 1999). However, in these films the bodily fluids are depicted as disgusting and therefore conform to the cultural taboos against them.

heavily cut when first released in the U.S. and was not available in its complete form until 1998. In Australia the uncut version was refused classification until 2004.
10. Georges Bataille, *Literature and Evil* (London: Marion Boyars, 1997), 115–116.
11. Michael Grant, "Fulci's Waste Land: Cinema, Horror and the Dreams of Modernism," in *Unruly Pleasures: The Cult Film and its Critics*, ed. Xavier Mendik and Graeme Harper (Godalming: FAB Press, 2000), 61.
12. Gilles Deleuze, *Coldness and Cruelty* (New York: Zone Books, 1989), 31.
13. Ibid., 27.
14. Ibid., 31.
15. Phillipe Roger, "A Political Minimalist," in *Sade and the Narrative of Transgression*, ed. David S. Allison, Mark S. Roberts and Allen S. Weiss (Cambridge: Cambridge University Press, 1995), 88.
16. Sade, *Juliette*, 178.
17. Carter, 140.
18. Steven Shaviro, *The Cinematic Body: Theory Out of Bounds, Volume 2* (Minneapolis: University of Minnesota Press, 1993), 85.
19. Kim Newman, "Bite of the Living Dead," *Sight and Sound* 18, no. 3 (March 2008): 49.
20. G. D'Agnolo-Vallan, "Let Them Eat Flesh," *Film Comment* 41, no. 4 (July/August 2005): 23.

Chapter 2

1. Julia Kristeva, *Powers of Horror: An Essay on Abjection* (New York: Columbia University Press, 1982), 4.
2. Ibid.
3. Leo Bersani, *The Freudian Body: Psychoanalysis and Art* (New York: Columbia University Press, 1986), 51.
4. Ibid.
5. Sade, *Juliette*, 55.
6. Noël Carroll, *Philosophy of Horror, or Paradoxes of the Heart* (New York: Routledge, 1990), 51.
7. Sade, *The 120 Days of Sodom*, 195.
8. Ibid., 652.
9. Like many of Sade's works, *The Beyond* has had its own battle with censorship to contend with. The film was

Chapter 3

1. W. Herz, cited in Adam Parfrey, "Latter Day Lycanthropy: Battling for the Soul of Feral Man," in *Apocalypse Culture*, ed. Adam Parfrey (Los Angeles: Feral House, 1990), 17.
2. Jonathan Ross, *The Incredibly Strange Film Book: An Alternative History of Cinema* (London: Simon and Schuster, 1993), 134.
3. While most werewolf films focus on a male's transformation into a wolf, *Ginger Snaps* has the process happening to a young girl. The wolf's attack on Ginger is an incident that highlights how both menstruation and lycanthropy (representing the sexual and the violent instincts) go through lunar cycles. As both happen simultaneously, there is a conflict over

whether Ginger's changes are due to the wolf's bite or are just "hormonal."

4. John Landis interview from the *An American Werewolf in London* DVD, released in 2001 through Universal Pictures, Region 4.

5. Sade, *The 120 Days of Sodom*, 201. Italics added for emphasis.

6. Carter, 117.

7. Sade, *Philosophy in the Bedroom*, 359.

8. Carter, 118.

9. Certainly the scatological meaning of this phrase is relevant here, given Sade's own obsession with bodily fluids. Later in *The Company of Wolves* one character, before his transformation into a werewolf, announces his intention to exit his house in order to answer "the call of nature"—a reference to urination that also foreshadows his eventual fate.

10. Sade, *Juliette*, 143.

11. Sigmund Freud, "Civilization and Its Discontents," in *The Freud Reader*, ed. Peter Gay (London: Vintage, 1995), 742.

12. Sade, *Juliette*, 10.

13. Mike Nichols, cited in Linda S. Kauffman, *Bad Girls and Sick Boys: Fantasies in Contemporary Art and Culture* (Berkeley: University of California Press, 1998), 118.

14. Freud, "Civilization and Its Discontents," 749.

15. Sade, *Juliette*, 119.

Chapter 4

1. In *The 120 Days of Sodom* the four protagonists who perpetrate violence and torture on a group of adolescents are a judge, a bishop, a duke and a financier, each a representative of the four main power centers of society: the law, the church, the aristocracy and business, respectively.

2. Mark Seltzer, "The Serial Killer as a Type of Person," in *The Horror Reader*, ed. Ken Gelder (London: Routledge, 2000), 97–8.

3. Ibid.

4. Maurice Blanchot, "Sade," in *Justine, Philosophy in the Bedroom and Other Writings*, ed. Austryn Wainhouse and Richard Seaver (New York: Grove Press, 1965), 41.

5. Georges Bataille, *Eroticism* (London: Penguin, 2001), 173.

6. Sade, *The 120 Days of Sodom*, 28.

7. Ibid., 442.

8. Deleuze, *Coldness and Cruelty*, 31.

9. Credits at the beginning of the movie state: "This film is a fictional dramatization of certain events. *Henry* is not intended to be an accurate portrayal of a true story. The film is based partly on confessions of a person named Henry, many of which he later recanted. As to Otis and Becky, the film is fictional."

10. What these films offer is a hero-cop's perspective, which is in direct contrast to that of the villain-serial killer. Audiences for these movies do not see the events from the killer's point-of-view, with the identity of the killer not revealed until the end of the film (or else they are characters constructed not as "real" people but rather as an embodiment of the notion of "evil"). And even though the character of Hannibal Lecter is popular, as well as appealing, he is always set in opposition to either the equally appealing Clarice Starling, a character who stands for all that is good and true, or Will Graham, who, despite his ability to put himself in the killer's place, nevertheless resists these urges and fights to stop the killing. In other words, these narratives are constructed in terms of a moral binary opposition—that of good versus evil—whereby the narrative's aim is to displace the latter through celebration of the former.

11. Phillip L. Simpson, *Psycho Paths: Tracking the Serial Killer Through Contemporary American Film and Fiction* (Carbondale and Edwardsville: Southern Illinois University Press, 2000), 139.

12. Marquis de Sade, "Reflections on the Novel," in *The 120 Days of Sodom and Other Writings*, ed. Austryn Wainhouse and Richard Seaver (New York: Grove Press, 1987), 112.

13. Sade, *The 120 Days of Sodom*, 671-2.

14. James McDonough, cited in Phillip L. Simpson, 140–141. For the censors, the film's failure to offer a moral judgment of Henry in itself constitutes a threat, one no

less shocking than the open celebration of the serial killer.

Chapter 5

1. Sade, *Philosophy in the Bedroom*, 230.
2. Sade, *Juliette*, 43–4.
3. Mikita Brottman, "Eating Italian," in *The Bad Mirror: A Creation Cinema Collection Reader*, ed. Jack Hunter (London: Creation Books, 2002), 111.
4. Sade, *The 120 Days of Sodom*, 250–251.
5. Neil Smith, "Claire Denis: *Trouble Every Day*," BBC, 2002, retrieved 3 June 2005, http://www.bbc.co.uk/films/2002/12/24/claire_denis_trouble_every_day.html.
6. Todd McGowan, "Resisting the Lure of Ultimate Enjoyment: Claire Denis' *J'ai pas sommeil* (*I Can't Sleep*, 1994)," *Kinoeye* 3, no. 7, retrieved 15 June 2005, http://www.kinoeye.org/printer.php?path=03/07/mcgowan07.php.
7. Paglia, 97.
8. Ibid., 94.
9. Ibid., 30.
10. Ibid., 239.
11. Havelock Ellis, cited in Moira Martingale, *Cannibal Killers* (New York: St. Martin's Paperbacks, 1995), 209.
12. "...Dalle as the Mesmerisingly Feral Coré..." Phillipe Met, "Looking for Trouble: The Dialectics of Lack and Excess," *Kinoeye* 3, no. 7, retrieved 8 January 2004, http://www.kinoeye.org/printer.php?path=03/07/met07.php.
13. Sade, *Philosophy in the Bedroom*, 253.
14. Lucienne Frappier-Mazur, *Writing the Orgy: Power and Parody in Sade* (Philadelphia: University of Pennsylvania Press, 1996), 114.
15. Paglia, 241.

Chapter 6

1. "What Is a Posthuman?" *World Transhumanist Association*, retrieved 26 September 2005, http://www.transhumanism.org/index.php/WTA/faq21/56/.
2. In this section I have chosen to focus on the work of Cronenberg and Tsukamoto rather than on other films where the future of the human body is shown in the form of the synthetically made human or other robot/human hybrids. Films such as *A.I. Artificial Intelligence* (Steven Spielberg, 2001), *Terminator* (James Cameron, 1984), *Blade Runner* (Ridley Scott, 1982), and *Robocop* (Paul Verhoeven, 1987) contain characters that fit into the idea of the "posthuman," in which humans have been synthetically created or modified completely by technology; whereas Cronenberg's and Tsukamoto's characters more adequately exemplify the idea of the "transhuman." What is explored here is the transitional, and transgressive, stage where flesh and technology first come into contact and begin to affect each other.
3. Chris Rodley (ed.), *Cronenberg on Cronenberg* (London: Faber and Faber, 1997), 65.
4. Ibid.
5. Sade, *Juliette*, 60.
6. Linda S. Kauffman, 162.
7. Iain Sinclair, *Crash: David Cronenberg's Post-Mortem on J.G. Ballard's "Trajectory of Fate"* (London: BFI Publishing, 1999), 62.
8. Rodley (ed.), 199.
9. Ibid., 199.
10. Sade, *120 Days of Sodom*, 496.
11. Kauffman, 183.
12. Marcel Henaff, *Sade: The Invention of the Libertine Body* (Minneapolis: University of Minnesota Press, 1999), 204.
13. Mikita Brottman and Christopher Sharrett, "End of the Road: Cronenberg's *Crash* and the Fading of the West," in *Lost Highways: An Illustrated History of Road Movies*, ed. Jack Sargeant and Stephanie Watson (London: Creation, 1999), 280.
14. From *Juliette*: "[R]emember well that by presenting only your ass for a target you infinitely lessen the risks you run, both as touches your honour and your health: no offspring, virtually never any illnesses, and pleasures a thousand-fold sweeter" (59); from *The 120 Days of Sodom*: "At the first of these gatherings, the one exclusively given over to the pleasures of sodomy, only men were present; there would always be at hand 16 young men, ranging in age from 20–30, whose immense faculties permitted our 4

heroes, in feminine guise, to taste the most agreeable delights" (194); from *Justine*: "[A]lthough this is the most sacred temple it is howbeit the most voluptuous; what is necessary to happiness is found nowhere else" (488).

15. Carter, 104.
16. Ibid., 105.
17. Sade, *Juliette*, 60.
18. Rodley (ed.), 198.
19. Sade, *Philosophy in the Bedroom*, 344.
20. Rodley (ed.), 82.
21. Sinclair, 62.
22. Blake, "Brief Interview with Shinya Tsukamoto on *Nightmare Detective*," *Twitch* (2007), retrieved 15 March 2010, http://twitchfilm.net/interviews/2007/09/brief-interview-with-shinya-tsukamoto-on-nightmare-detective.php.
23. Donna Haraway, "A Cyborg Manifesto: Science, Technology, and Socialist-Feminism in the Late Twentieth Century," in *Simians, Cyborgs and Women: The Reinvention of Nature*, ed. Donna Haraway (New York: Routledge, 1991), 149.
24. It must be noted that Haraway is working from a strictly feminist standpoint.
25. Roland Barthes, *Sade, Fourier, Loyola* (Berkeley: University of California Press, 1989), 125–126; Marcel Henaff, 24; Annie LeBrun, *Sade: A Sudden Abyss* (San Francisco: City Light Books, 1990), 153–157.
26. Paglia, 236.
27. Sade, *Juliette*, 172–173.
28. Blanchot, 52–53.

Part Three

1. Sade, *Juliette*, 173.
2. Paglia, 3.
3. The libertine cannot be punished, for even if he/she is caught by the authorities his/her subsequent punishment is viewed simply as another possibility for pleasure. For example, after Justine finds herself kidnapped by a counterfeiter, Roland, he initiates her into a sexual game in which a rope is put around his neck and he is asphyxiated. This game is played in anticipation of what Roland believes will be his eventual fate: to be hung at the gallows for his crimes. As he states, "I am as firmly persuaded as I can possibly be that this death is infinitely sweeter than it is cruel." Sade, *Justine*, 686.

Chapter 7

1. Laura Mulvey, "Visual Pleasure and Narrative Cinema," in *Popular Television and Film: A Reader*, ed. Tony Bennett (London: Open University Press, 1981), 206.
2. Barbara Creed and Mandy Merck, "General Introduction," in *The Sexual Subject: A Screen Reader in Sexuality*, ed. Barbara Creed and Mandy Merck (London: Routledge, 1992), 4.
3. Victims in the films of von Trier can be understood as direct descendents of Sade's Justine. Nevertheless, the figure of the victim appears in all genres, and in horror films in particular. In fact, in horror sub–genres such as the slasher (examples being the *Halloween* and *Friday the 13th* cycles of films) and the Italian *giallo* (such as *Blood and Black Lace* [Mario Bava, 1964], *Deep Red* [Dario Argento, 1975] and *Tenebrae* [Dario Argento, 1982]), most characters are ultimately victims. In addition, while this section focuses on the victim as female, the figure of the male victim is also an important subject of analysis. While the victim is traditionally thought of as female, there are many movies that feature a male victim, for example: *Deliverance* (John Boorman, 1972), *The Wicker Man* (Robin Hardy, 1973) and *The Ordeal* (Fabrice du Welz, 2004). Genres such as the Western and action film foreground countless male deaths and murders, and many *films noir*, such as *Double Indemnity* (Billy Wilder, 1944), *Out of the Past* (Jacques Torneur, 1947), and *The Last Seduction* (John Dahl, 1993), represent the male as a pawn and a patsy—helpless victims of a *femme fatale*.
4. In his article "Our Town," J. Hoberman examines *Dogville*'s depiction of America: "Abused by the 'good' Americans of Dogville, our long-suffering Grace pays them back with some exceedingly rough 'American' justice. Exploitation is

Notes—Chapter 8

all-American and violent overkill too!" J. Hoberman, "Our Town," *Sight and Sound* 14, no. 2 (2004): 27.

5. Sade, *The 120 Days of Sodom*, 252.
6. Sade, *Juliette*, 96.
7. This trait is found in all of von Trier's films, as Beltzer remarks: "He demonstrates, from *[The] Element [of Crime]* to *Dancer [in the Dark]*, that being an idealist does not mean imparting a rosy, unrealistic view of things. In *Element, Epidemic, Zentropa, Medea* and *The Kingdom*, the protagonists are idealists who are so helpless in living out their ideals that they actually end up being a catalyst for evil rather than an ameliorative factor." Thomas Beltzer, "Lars von Trier," *Senses of Cinema* (2002), retrieved 3 December 2003, http://www.sensesofcinema.com/contents/directors/02/vontrier.html.
8. Sade, *Justine*, 503.
9. The trilogy is named after a children's book that von Trier read as a child. As von Trier explains, the book, entitled *Guld Hjerte* (*Golden Heart*), is the story of "a little girl who goes out into the woods with some breadcrumbs in her apron and on her way she gives away both her food and her clothes. And when the rabbit or the squirrel tells her that now she doesn't have a skirt on, her answer is every time: 'I'll be alright.'" Adam Atkinson, "On the Nature of Dogs, the Right of Grace, Forgiveness and Hospitality: Derrida, Kant, and Lars Von Trier's *Dogville*," *Senses of Cinema* (2005), retrieved 26 July 2005, http://www.sensesofcinema.com/contents/05/36/dogville.html.
10. Beltzer.
11. Sade, *Justine*, 556.
12. However, von Trier closes his film with the suggestion that Bess has, in fact, been welcomed into Heaven. Early in the movie Bess tells Jan of her love for church bells, which are forbidden by the Calvinist Church. In the film's final scene, Jan, back at work on the oil rig, is roused out of bed and taken to the ship's deck, where the sound of bells can be heard. Having been "consigned to Hell" by the church after her death, this closing shot instead suggests that Bess is calling to Jan from Heaven.
13. Carter, 70.
14. Sade, *Justine*, 503.
15. Beltzer.
16. *The Idiots*, in contrast, maintains its rough and gritty style throughout. As the second film of the Dogma movement, *The Idiots* had to follow the aesthetic rules laid out in the Dogme '95 Manifesto, which states that only a handheld camera and natural lighting must be used.

Chapter 8

1. Sade, *Philosophy in the Bedroom*, 185.
2. Brian Price, "Catherine Breillat," *Senses of Cinema* (2002), retrieved 31 December 2002, http://www.sensesofcinema.com/contents/directors/02/breillat.html.
3. Ibid.
4. Sade, *Philosophy in the Bedroom*, 340.
5. Sade, *Juliette*, 151.
6. Libby Brooks, "The Joy of Sex," *The Guardian* (2002), retrieved 31 December 2002, http://www.film.guardian.co.uk/censorship/news/0.11729,660428,00.html.
7. Ibid.
8. Price.
9. Ibid.
10. Brooks.
11. As Breillat explains, "The problem is that censors create the concept of obscenity. By supposedly trying to protect us they form an absurd concept of what is obscene. She's got a body that is acceptable and normal for a young girl, yet it shouldn't be shown by a film director." Ibid.
12. Ibid.
13. Annie LeBrun, *Sade: A Sudden Abyss* (San Francisco: City Light Books, 1990), 16.
14. Adrian Martin, "'X' Marks the Spot: Classifying *Romance*," *Senses of Cinema* (2000), retrieved 31 December 2002, http://www.sensesofcinema.com/contents/00/4/romance.html.
15. Ibid.
16. Blanchot, "Sade," 49.
17. Price observes further: "[B]y refusing codes of distress, Breillat, it seems to me at least, asks us to see this rape from Anaïs' perspective. That is, Anaïs does not

want to view it as rape, but as a sexual experience, especially as her age, body and attractive older sister have previously stood in the way of her sexual desires. But this is not to excuse the rape. At all. Rather, by courting ambiguity, Breillat presents us with a complicated, if very controversial, portrait of the psychology of a young girl. We can judge the scene any way we choose." Price.

18. In Australia, Canada, and the United Kingdom the law states that one can legally have sexual relations, an adult practice, from the age of sixteen (in the U.S. this age of consent can vary between sixteen and eighteen within each state), yet one is still regarded by the law as a child until the age of eighteen. The confusion surrounding this period of life is demonstrated by the fact that even though people of sixteen years of age can legally have sex, the representation of these acts (which Clark insists are simulated and not real, with the exception of a scene of masturbation) has led *Ken Park* to accusations of child pornography.

19. "Censorship Forum at the Sydney Film Festival," *Senses of Cinema* (2003), retrieved 9 September 2003, http://www.sensesofcinema.com/contents/03/27/censorship_forum.html.

20. Ibid.

21. Sade, *Philosophy in the Bedroom*, 284.

22. The taboo theme of incest dominates *Ken Park*, with three of the teenagers experiencing a sexually dysfunctional relationship with an older adult: Claude's father attempts to sexually molest him; Peaches' father catches her having sadomasochistic sex with a fellow teenager, and so forces her to participate in a religious ritual of purification — which turns out to be a ceremony that weds Peaches to her father; and Shawn enters into a sexual affair with his girlfriend's mother. Tate, meanwhile, lives with his grandparents and, due to his inability to emotionally connect with anyone, acts out violently, killing his grandparents while they sleep.

23. Robin Wood, *Hollywood from Vietnam to Reagan* (New York: Columbia University Press, 1986), 72–73.

24. Ibid., 79.

25. Ibid., 72.

26. Stuart Jeffries, "King Leer," *The Guardian* (2002), retrieved 1 December 2005, http://film.guardian.co.uk/interview/interviewpages/0,,659674,00.html.

27. Nick Ferret, "*Ken Park* Is Dangerous to Those Most Vulnerable to Sexual Exploitation," *On Line Opinion* (2003), retrieved 1 December 2005, http://www.onlineopinion.com.au/print.asp?article=563.

Chapter 9

1. Richard von Krafft-Ebing, *Psychopathia Sexualis: The Case Histories* (London: Creation, 2001), 20.

2. Wolfgang Berner, et al., "Sexual Sadism," *International Journal of Offender Therapy and Comparative Criminology* 47, no. 4 (2003), 384.

3. Ibid., 394.

4. Gilles Deleuze, *Coldness and Cruelty* (New York: Zone, 1989), 40.

5. Sade, *Philosophy in the Bedroom*, 344.

6. The book ends with detailed description of how each of the victims shall be tortured and killed. Surely no film will ever be able to depict the extreme cruelty that Sade describes. For example: "The Duc thrusts his hand into her cunt and cuts through the partition dividing the anus from the vagina; he throws aside the scalpel, reintroduces his hand, and rummaging about in her entrails, forces her to shit through her cunt ... then, availing himself of the same entrance, he reaches up and tears open her stomach. Next they concentrate upon the visage: cut away her ears, burn her nasal passages, blind her eyes with molten sealing wax..." Sade, *The 120 Days of Sodom*, 658–659.

7. Jane Mills, *The Money Shot: Cinema, Sin and Censorship* (Annandale: Pluto Press, 2001), 127.

8. Gino Moliterno, "Pier Paolo Pasolini," *Senses of Cinema* (2002), retrieved 30 December 2002, http://www.sensesofcinema.com/contents/directors/02/pasolini.html.

9. Gary Indiana, *Salò, or the 120 Days of Sodom* (London: BFI Publishing, 2000).

Notes—Chapter 10

10. Pasolini, cited in Sam Rohdie, *The Passion of Pier Paolo Pasolini* (London: BFI Publishing, 1995), 70.
11. Indiana, 13.
12. Mills, 128.
13. Indiana, 79.
14. Henaff, 49.
15. Pier Paolo Pasolini, "A Mad Dream," *British Film Institute* (2000), retrieved 28 February 2002, http://www.bfi.org.uk/features/salo/foreword.html.
16. An analogy can be drawn between this scene and the ways that the enemy is dehumanized in wartime. Pasolini has transposed into the sexual realm the tactics used in combat. Indeed, this scene came directly to mind when I first saw the photos taken by American soldiers at Abu Ghraib, where prisoners were forced to pose naked in a human pyramid. What is most ironic is that this photo of an actual atrocity was shown on the evening news, while the fictional representation in *Salò* has been repeatedly banned and censored.
17. Rohdie, 122.
18. Ibid.
19. Indiana, 79.
20. Pasolini, cited in Adam Young, "Pasolini, Salò, Sade," in *Flesh and Blood Compendium*, ed. Harvey Fenton (Godalming: FAB Press, 2003), 45.
21. Deleuze, 20.
22. Pasolini, cited in Adam Young, 46.
23. Karmen MacKendrick, *Counterpleasures* (Albany: State University of New York Press, 1999), 42.
24. Georges Bataille, *Literature and Evil* (London: Marion Boyars, 1997), 121–122.
25. Sade, *The 120 Days of Sodom*, 253.
26. Paglia, 234.
27. Ibid., 236.
28. Deleuze, 37.
29. Bataille, *Literature and Evil*, 116.
30. Tom Mes, *Agitator: The Cinema of Takashi Miike* (Surrey: FAB Press, 2003), 243.
31. Sade, *Philosophy in the Bedroom*, 252.
32. Barthes, 30.
33. Deleuze, 31.
34. Research on masochistic practice shows that it is not always the gender of the partner that is important or that turns a person on, it is more about the experience itself, the pleasure and the pain that is felt. Therefore, it is possible that the person who most ably satisfies someone in a sadomasochistic relationship need not be of the gender to which the latter is traditionally attracted. As MacKendrick writes, "S/m is not a set of practices or experiences distinguished primarily by gender. Indeed, recent theory suggests that gender may be another of the boundaries with which it delights in playing." MacKendrick, 100.
35. Sade, *Philosophy in the Bedroom*, 217.
36. Ibid., 38.
37. Sade, *The 120 Days of Sodom*, 496.

Chapter 10

1. Deleuze, 40.
2. S&M is an abbreviation of sadism and masochism, while SM stands for sadomasochism, a term which blends the two practices into one form. BDSM is an acronym for the four elements that make up this form of sexual play: Bondage, Domination, Submission, Masochism. Taylor and Ussher, in their essay "Making Sense of S&M: A Discourse Analytic Account," define this form of sexual play as "best understood as comprising those behaviors which are characterized by a contrived, often symbolic, unequable distribution of power involving the giving and/or receiving of physical and/or psychological stimulation. It often involves acts which would generally be considered as 'painful' and/or humiliating or subjugating, but which are consensual and for the purpose of sexual arousal, and are understood by the participant to be SM." Gary W. Taylor and Jane M. Ussher, "Making Sense of S&M: A Discourse Analytic Account," *Sexualities* 4, no. 3 (2001), 301.
3. Tanya Krzywinska, *Sex and the Cinema* (London: Wallflower Press, 2006), 216.
4. Sade, *Philosophy in the Bedroom*, 179.
5. Deleuze, 34.
6. Ibid., 33.
7. MacKendrick, 100.

Notes — Chapter 10

8. Barthes, 143.
9. Sade, *Philosophy in the Bedroom*, 227.
10. Nagisa Oshima, *Cinema, Censorship, and the State: The Writings of Nagisa Oshima 1956–1978* (Cambridge: MIT Press, 1992), 257.
11. Ibid., 249.
12. Sade, *Justine* (New York: Grove Press, 1965), 696.
13. Barthes, 15.
14. Sade, *The 120 Days of Sodom*, 218.
15. Maureen Turim, *The Films of Nagisa Oshima: Images of a Japanese Iconoclast* (Berkeley: University of California Press, 1998), 130–131.
16. Georges Bataille, *Eroticism* (London: Penguin Books, 2001), 20.
17. Ibid.
18. Sade, *Juliette*, 769.
19. Ibid., 769–770.
20. Carter, 126.

Bibliography

Atkinson, Adam. "On the Nature of Dogs, the Right of Grace, Forgiveness and Hospitality: Derrida, Kant, and Lars Von Trier's *Dogville*." *Senses of Cinema*, 2005, retrieved 26 July 2005, http://www.sensesofcinema.com/contents/05/36/dogville.html.

Barthes, Roland. *Sade, Fourier, Loyola*. Berkeley: University of California Press, 1989.

Bataille, Georges. *Eroticism*. London: Penguin, 2001.

———. *Literature and Evil*. London: Marion Boyars, 2001.

Beltzer, Thomas. "Lars Von Trier." *Senses of Cinema*, 2002, retrieved 3 December 2003, http://www.sensesofcinema.com/contents/directors/02/vontrier.html.

Bennett, Tony (ed.). *Popular Television and Film: A Reader*. London: Open University Press, 1981.

Berner, Wolfgang, Peter Berger and Andreas Hill. "Sexual Sadism." *International Journal of Offender Therapy and Comparative Criminology* 47, no. 4 (2003): 383–395.

Bersani, Leo. *The Freudian Body: Psychoanalysis and Art*. New York: Columbia University Press, 1986.

———. "Is the Rectum a Grave?" In *AIDS: Cultural Analysis, Cultural Activism*, edited by Douglas Crimp, 197–222. Massachusetts: MIT Press, 1988.

"The Beyond." *Refused Classification: Film Censorship in Australia*, n.d., retrieved 4 December 2007, http://www.refused-classification.com/Films_B.htm.

Blanchot, Maurice. "Sade." In *Justine, Philosophy in the Bedroom, and Other Writings*, edited by Austryn Wainhouse and Richard Seaver, 37–72. New York: Grove Press, 1965.

Bongie, Laurence. *Sade: A Biographical Essay*. Chicago: University of Chicago Press, 1998.

Brooks, Libby. "The Joy of Sex." *The Guardian*, 2002, retrieved 31 December 2002, http://www.film.guardian.co.uk/censorship/news/0.11729,660428,00.html.

Brottman, Mikita. "Eating Italian." In *The Bad Mirror: A Creation Cinema Collection Reader*, edited by Jack Hunter, 109–124. London: Creation Books, 2002.

———, and Christopher Sharrett. "End of the Road: Cronenberg's *Crash* and the Fading of the West." In *Lost Highways: An Illustrated History of Road Movies*, edited by Jack Sargeant an Stephanie Watson, 275–286. London: Creation, 1999.

Carroll, Noël. *Philosophy of Horror, or Paradoxes of the Heart*. New York: Routledge, 1990.

Carter, Angela. *The Sadeian Woman: An Exercise in Cultural History*. London: Virago, 1979.

"Censorship Forum at the Sydney Film Festival." *Senses of Cinema*, 2003, retrieved 9 September 2003, http://www.sensesofcinema.com/contents/03/27/censorship_forum.html.

Bibliography

Chasseguet-Smirgel, Janine. *Creativity and Perversion*. London: Free Association Books, 1992.

Creed, Barbara, and Mandy Merck. "General Introduction." In *The Sexual Subject: A Screen Reader in Sexuality*, 1–12. London: Routledge, 1992.

_____, and _____. *The Sexual Subject: A Screen Reader in Sexuality*. London: Routledge, 1992.

Crimp, Douglas (ed.). *AIDS: Cultural Analysis, Cultural Activism*. Massachusetts: MIT Press, 1988.

D'Agnollo-Vallan, Giulia. "Let Them Eat Flesh." *Film Comment* 41, no. 4 (July/August 2005): 23–24.

Deleuze, Gilles. *Coldness and Cruelty*. New York: Zone, 1989.

Du Plessix Gray, Francine. *At Home with the Marquis de Sade*. New York: Simon and Schuster, 1998.

Fenton, Harvey (ed.). *Flesh and Blood Compendium*. Surrey: FAB Press, 2003.

Ferrett, Nick. "*Ken Park* Is Dangerous to Those Most Vulnerable to Sexual Exploitation." *On Line Opinion*, 2003, retrieved 1 December 2005, http://www.onlineopinion.com.au/print.asp?article=563.

Foucault, Michel. *The History of Sexuality*. New York: Vintage, 1990.

_____. *Language, Counter-Memory, Practice*. Edited by Donald F. Bouchard. Oxford: Blackwell, 1977.

Frappier-Mazur, Lucienne. *Writing the Orgy: Power and Parody in Sade*. Philadelphia: University of Pennsylvania Press, 1996.

Freeland, Cynthia. *The Naked and the Undead: Evil and the Appeal of Horror*. Boulder, CO: Westview Press, 2000.

Freud, Sigmund. "Civilization and Its Discontents." *The Freud Reader*, edited by Peter Gay, 722–771. London: Vintage, 1995.

_____. *The Freud Reader*. Edited by Peter Gay. London: Vintage, 1995.

Fuery, Patrick. *New Discourses in Film Theory*. London: MacMillan Press, 2000.

Gelder, Ken (ed.). *The Horror Reader*. London: Routledge, 2000.

Grant, Michael. "Fulci's Waste Land: Cinema, Horror and the Dreams of Modernism." In *Unruly Pleasures: The Cult Film and Its Critics*, edited by Xavier Mendik and Graeme Harper, 61–72. Godalming: FAB Press, 2000.

Haraway, Donna. "A Cyborg Manifesto: Science, Technology, and Socialist-Feminism in the Late Twentieth Century." In *Simians, Cyborgs and Women: The Reinvention of Nature*, 149–181. New York: Routledge, 1991.

_____. *Simians, Cyborgs and Women: The Reinvention of Nature*. New York: Routledge, 1991.

Hawkins, Joan. *Cutting Edge: Art-Horror and the Horrific Avant-Garde*. Minneapolis: University of Minnesota Press, 2000.

Henaff, Marcel. *Sade: The Invention of the Libertine Body*. Minneapolis: University of Minnesota Press, 1999.

Hoberman, J. "Our Town." *Sight and Sound* 14, no. 2 (February 2004): pp. 24–27.

Hunter, Jack (ed.). *The Bad Mirror: A Creation Cinema Collection Reader*. London: Creation, 2002.

Indiana, Gary. *Salò, or the 120 Days of Sodom*. London: British Film Institute, 2000.

Jeffries, Stuart. "King Leer." *The Guardian*, 2002, retrieved 1 December 2005, http://film.guardian.co.uk/interview/interviewpages/0,,659674,00.html.

Kauffman, Linda S. *Bad Girls and Sick Boys: Fantasies in Contemporary Art and Culture*. Berkeley: University of California Press, 1998.

Krafft-Ebing, Richard von. *Psychopathia Sexualis: The Case Histories*. London: Creation, 2001.

Kristeva, Julia. *Powers of Horror: An*

Bibliography

Essay on Abjection. New York: Columbia University Press, 1982.

Krzywinska, Tanya. *Sex and the Cinema*. London: Wallflower Press, 2006.

Le Brun, Annie. *Sade: A Sudden Abyss*. San Francisco: City Light Books, 1990.

Lever, Maurice. *Marquis de Sade*. London: Flamingo, 1995.

MacKendrick, Karmen. *Counterpleasures*. Albany: State University of New York Press, 1999.

Martin, Adrian. "'X' Marks the Spot: Classifying *Romance*." *Senses of Cinema*, 2000, retrieved 31 December 2002, http://www.sensesofcinema.com/contents/00/4/romance.html.

Martingale, Moira. *Cannibal Killers*. New York: St. Martin's Paperbacks, 1995.

McGowan, Todd. "Resisting the Lure of Ultimate Enjoyment: Claire Denis' *J'ai pas sommeil* (*I Can't Sleep*, 1994)." *Kinoeye* 3, no. 7, retrieved 15 June 2005, http://www.kinoeye.org/printer.php?path=03/07/mcgowan07.php.

Mendik, Xavier. "Perverse Bodies, Profane Texts: Processes of Sadeian 'Mixture' in the Films of Jesus Franco." In *Necronomicon, Book Two*, edited by Andy Black, 7–17. London: Creation, 1998.

———. "The Sadeian Speaks: Interview with Jesus Franco." In *Necronomicon, Book Two*, edited by Andy Black, 18–29. London: Creation, 1998.

Mendik, Xavier, and Graeme Harper (eds.). *Unruly Pleasures: The Cult Film and Its Critics*. Surrey: FAB Press, 2000.

Mes, Tom. *Agitator: The Cinema of Takashi Miike*. Surrey: FAB Press, 2003.

Met, Phillipe. "Looking for Trouble: The Dialectics of Lack and Excess." *Kinoeye* 3, no. 7, retrieved 8 January 2004, http://www.kinoeye.org/printer.php?path=03/07/met07.php.

Mills, Jane. *The Money Shot: Cinema, Sin and Censorship*. Annandale: Pluto Press Australia, 2001.

Moliterno, Gino. "Pier Paolo Pasolini." *Senses of Cinema*, 2002, retrieved 30 December 2002, http://www.sensesofcinema.com/contents/directors/02/pasolini.html.

Moretti, Franco. "Dialectic of Fear." In *The Horror Reader*, edited by Ken Gelder, 148–160. London: Routledge, 2000.

Mulvey, Laura. *Visual and Other Pleasures*. Bloomington: Indiana University Press, 1989.

———. "Visual Pleasure and Narrative Cinema." In *Popular Television and Film: A Reader*, edited by Tony Bennett, 206–215. London: Open University Press, 1981.

Newman, Kim. "Bite of the Living Dead." *Sight and Sound* 18, no. 3 (March 2008): 48–49.

Oshima, Nagisa. *Cinema, Censorship, and the State: The Writings of Nagisa Oshima, 1956–1978*. Edited by Annette Michelson. Cambridge: MIT Press, 1992.

Paglia, Camille. *Sexual Personae: Art and Decadence from Nefertiti to Emily Dickinson*. New York: Vintage, 1991.

Parfrey, Adam (ed.). *Apocalypse Culture*. Los Angeles: Feral House, 1990.

Parfrey, Adam. "Latter Day Lycanthropy: Battling for the Soul of Feral Man." In *Apocalypse Culture*, edited by Adam Parfrey, 16–27. Los Angeles: Feral House, 1990.

Pasolini, Pier Paolo. "A Mad Dream." *British Film Institute*, 2000, retrieved 28 February 2002, http://www.bfi.org.uk/features/salo/foreword.html.

Price, Brian. "Catherine Breillat." *Senses of Cinema*, 2002, retrieved 30 December 2002, http://www.sensesofcinema.com/contents/directors/02/breillat.html.

Rodley, Chris (ed.). *Cronenberg on Cronenberg*. London: Faber and Faber, 1997.

Roger, Phillipe. "A Political Minimalist."

Bibliography

In *Sade and the Narrative of Transgression*, edited by David S. Allison, Mark S. Roberts and Allen S. Weiss, 76–99. Cambridge: Cambridge University Press, 1995.

Rohdie, Sam. *The Passion of Pier Paolo Pasolini*. London: British Film Institute, 1995.

Ross, Jonathan. *The Incredibly Strange Film Book: An Alternative History of Cinema*. London: Simon and Schuster, 1993.

Sade, Marquis de. *Juliette*. New York: Grove Press, 1968.

———. *Justine, Philosophy in the Bedroom, and Other Writings*. Edited by Austryn Wainhouse and Richard Seaver. New York: Grove Press, 1965.

———. *The 120 Days of Sodom and Other Writings*. Edited by Austryn Wainhouse and Richard Seaver. New York: Grove Press, 1987.

———. "Reflections on the Novel." In *The 120 Days of Sodom and Other Writings*, edited by Austryn Wainhouse and Richard Seaver, 91–116. New York: Grove Press, 1987.

Sargeant, Jack. "The Baying of Pigs: Reflections on the New American Horror Movie." *Senses of Cinema*, 2001, retrieved 29 March 2004, http://www.sensesofcinema.com/contents/festivals/01/15/biff_nightmare.html.

Sargeant, Jack, and Stephanie Watson (eds.). *Lost Highways: An Illustrated History of Road Movies*. London: Creation, 1999.

Seltzer, Mark. "The Serial Killer as a Type of Person." In *The Horror Reader*, edited by Ken Gelder, 97–110. London: Routledge, 2000.

Shaviro, Steven. *The Cinematic Body: Theory Out of Bounds, Volume 2*. Minneapolis: University of Minnesota Press, 1993.

Silver, Alain, and James Ursini. *The Vampire Film: From Nosferatu to Interview with the Vampire*. New York: Limelight Editions, 1997.

Simpson, Philip L. *Psycho Paths: Tracking the Serial Killer Through Contemporary American Film and Fiction*. Carbondale and Edwardsville: Southern Illinois University Press, 2000.

Sinclair, Iain. *Crash: David Cronenberg's Post-Mortem on J.G. Ballard's "Trajectory of Fate."* London: BFI Publishing, 1999.

Smith, Neil. "Claire Denis: *Trouble Every Day*." BBC, 2002, retrieved 3 June 2005, http://www.bbc.co.uk/films/2002/12/24/claire_denis_trouble_every_day.html.

Taylor, Gary W., and Jane M. Ussher. "Making Sense of S&M: A Discourse Analytic Account." *Sexualities* 4, no. 3 (2001): 293–314.

Tohill, Cathal, and Pete Tombs. *Immoral Tales: European Sex and Horror Movies 1956–1984*. New York: St. Martin's Griffin, 1995.

Turim, Maureen. *The Films of Nagisa Oshima: Images of a Japanese Iconoclast*. Berkeley: University of California Press, 1998.

Wood, Robin. *Hollywood from Vietnam to Reagan*. New York: Columbia University Press, 1986.

Young, Adam. "Pasolini, Salò, Sade." In *Flesh and Blood Compendium*, edited by Harvey Fenton, 44–46. Godalming: FAB Press, 2003.

Index

Accatone 154
The Addiction 196
A.I. Artificial Intelligence 199
Alighieri, Dante 154
American Pie 135, 197
American Psycho 64–71, 74, 102
An American Werewolf in London 52
The Anatomy of Hell 134
Andersen, Hans Christian 126
Antichrist 189
Araki, Gregg 128
Audition 160

Ballard, J.G. 95–96, 103–104
Barthes, Roland 157, 163, 176
Bataille, George 42, 65, 158, 161–162, 183
Baudelaire, Charles 30, 157
Bava, Mario 29
The Beast 179
Beau Travail 83
Behind the Green Door 179
Beltzer, Thomas 201
Bersani, Leo 11, 39
The Beyond 38–44, 197
Blade 196
Blade Runner 199
The Blair Witch Project 48
Blanchot, Maurice 65, 109, 157
Blood and Black Lace 200
Blue Velvet 180
Bluebeard 134
Bram Stoker's Dracula 20–26, 27, 31, 34, 196
Breaking the Waves 122–127
Breillat, Catherine 128–139, 201–201
The Brood 104
Brottman, Mikita 80–81, 100
Bullet Ballet 93
Buñuel, Luis 29

Cannibal Apocalypse 78
Cannibal Ferox 78
Cannibal Holocaust 78
Carmilla 34
Carter, Angela 35, 54, 56, 101, 124, 185
Chasseguet-Smirgel, Janine 1

Chocolat 83
The City of the Living Dead 38, 40
Civilization and Its Discontents 61
Clark, Larry 128, 139–145, 202
Coleridge, Samuel Taylor 30
The Company of Wolves 51–57, 171, 198
Coppola, Francis Ford 20–26, 31
Copycat 72
Crash 93–104, 180
Cronenberg, David 92–104, 199
The Cutting Edge: Art-Horror and the Horrific Avant-Garde 29, 32

Dahmer 72
Dancer in the Dark 122–123, 126, 201
Dawn of the Dead 44–49, 72
Day of the Dead 47, 49
de Beauvoir, Simone 157
Deep Red 200
Deep Throat 179
Def by Temptation 196
Deleuze, Gilles 1, 43, 70, 150–151, 156, 161, 162, 163, 166, 169, 174
Deliverance 200
Denis, Claire 83–91
Deodato, Ruggero 77–83
Diary of the Dead 48–49
Dogville 115–123, 200–201
Double Indemnity 200
Dracula (book) 30

Ed Gein 72
88 Minutes 72
The Element of Crime 201
Emmanuelle 179
Epidemic 201
Eroticism 183
Eugenie de Franval 31
Eugenie de Sade 31
Eugenie... the Story of Her Journey into Perversion 31
eXistenZ 93, 95

Fascination 196
Female Vampire 19, 31–36

Index

The Fly 93
For My Sister 128–139, 201–202
Foucault, Michel 1
Franco, Jess 29, 30, 31–36, 150, 196
Frappier-Mazur, Lucienne 89, 90
Freeland, Cynthia 23, 27
Freud, Sigmund 12–13, 58–59, 61, 134
Friday the 13th 64, 200
From Dusk Til Dawn 27
Fulci, Lucio 29, 37–44

Gacy 72
Ginger Snaps 52, 197–198
Golden Heart 122, 201
The Gospel According to Matthew 154
Greenaway, Peter 29

Halloween 200
Haneke, Michael 29
Hannibal 72, 77–78
Haraway, Donna 106, 108, 200
Hawkins, Joan 29, 32
Henaff, Marcel 12, 19–20, 100, 153
Henry: Portrait of a Serial Killer 64, 71–76, 102, 198–199
Herz, W. 50–51
The Hills Have Eyes 77
Hitchcock, Alfred 64, 67
Hoberman, J. 200–201
Hoffman, E.T.A. 30
L'Homme Facile 129
Hostel 189
The House by the Cemetery 38, 40
The Human Centipede (First Sequence) 189
The Hunger 196
Huysmans, Joris-Karl 157

I Can't Sleep 84
I Was a Teenage Werewolf 51–52
Ichi the Killer 159–167, 172
The Idiots 122–123, 126, 201
In the Realm of the Senses 168, 178–187
Indiana, Gary 152, 153, 155–156
Inferno 154
Interview with the Vampire 27, 28, 33–34, 196
isolism 44–49, 72

Jarman, Derek 29
Juliette (book) 6–7, 14, 15, 23, 40, 61, 79, 119, 137–139, 176, 185, 199
Juliette (film) 31
Justine 6, 10, 40, 111, 112, 115–117, 122–125, 127, 137–139, 176, 186, 200

Kauffman, Linda S. 99
Ken Park 128, 139–145, 202

The Kingdom 201
Klossowski, Pierre 157
Krafft-Ebing, Richard von 134, 149
Kristeva, Julia 37
Krzywinska, Tanya 169–170

Lacan, Jacques 1
Land of the Dead 48
Landis, John 52, 59
Larraz, Jose 27, 29, 30, 87
Last Cannibal World 77–83, 87, 90
The Last Seduction 200
Last Tango in Paris 179, 180
LeBrun, Annie 136
Le Fanu, Sheridan 34
Let Me In 27
Lever, Maurice 195–196
Lips of Blood 196
The Living Dead Girl 196
Lolita 128
Lucas, Tim 32
Lyne, Adrian 128

MacKendrick, Karmen 157, 176, 203
Mamma Rosa 154
Manderlay 115
Marquis de Sade's Justine 31
Martin, Adrian 137
Martyrs 189
McDonough, John 75
McGowan, Todd 84
McNaughton, John 71–76
Medea 201
Mes, Tom 162
Met, Phillipe 87
Miike, Takashi 159–167
Mills, Jane 151
Monster 72
Moretti, Franco 30
Motel Hell 77
Mulvey, Laura 114–115
Mysterious Skin 128

The Naked and the Undead: Evil and the Appeal of Horror 27
negation 43, 70–71, 100
Newman, Kim 48
Nichols, Mike 56–61
Nietzsche, Friedrich 157
Night of the Living Dead 47
The Night Porter 180
The Nude Vampire 196

The 120 Days of Sodom 6, 10, 12, 13, 14, 15, 21, 23, 24, 40, 42, 53, 55, 69, 74, 75, 82, 119, 134, 136, 150–159, 166, 172, 174, 181, 186, 198, 199–200, 202
The Ordeal 200

Index

Oshima, Nagisa 178–187
Out of the Past 200

Paglia, Camille 10, 28, 35, 84–85, 90, 112, 160, 197
Pasolini, Pier Paolo 3, 150–159, 203
Peeping Tom 64
Philosophy in the Bedroom 6, 11, 14, 52, 54, 56, 128, 130, 144, 151, 170–171, 182–183, 195
Pink Flamingos 179
Pirie, David 24
Poe, Edgar Allan 30
Powell, Michael 64
Price, Brian 133, 138, 201–202
Psycho 64, 67
psychoanalysis 1, 3, 12–13, 30, 37, 51, 59, 61, 114–115, 189

Queen of the Damned 27

Rabid 104
Ragazza di Vita 152
The Rape of the Vampire 196
A Real Young Lady 134
Rebel Without a Cause 52
Red Dragon 72
"Reflections on the Novel" 74
Requiem for a Vampire 196
La Ricotta 152, 154
Robocop 199
Rohdie, Sam 154
Rollin, Jean 29, 30, 196
Romance 129, 134, 136–138
Romero, George 37, 44–49
Ross, Jonathan 52

Sacher-Masoch, Leopold von 174–175, 182
The Sadeian Woman: An Exercise in Cultural History 54, 101, 124
Saló, or the 120 Days of Sodom 3, 100, 150–159, 172, 174
The Satanic Rites of Dracula 196
Saw 189
Secretary 162, 168–178, 180, 184
Seltzer, Mark 64
A Serbian Film 189
Seven 72
Sex and the Vampire 196
Sharrett, Christopher 100
Shaviro, Steven 46,

Shivers 102–103, 104
The Silence of the Lambs 72, 198
Simpson, Philip L. 73
A Snake of June 93, 105
The Snow Queen 126
Sollers, Phillipe 157
Stevenson, Robert Louis 86
Stoker, Bram 23, 30
The Strange Case of Dr. Jekyll and Mr. Hyde 86

Taking Lives 72
Taylor, Gary W. 203
Teen Wolf 52
Tenebrae 200
Terminator 199
Tetsuo: The Bullet Man 93
Tetsuo: The Iron Man 93, 104–110
Tetsuo 2: Body Hammer 93, 104, 107, 108–110
The Texas Chainsaw Massacre 64
There's Something About Mary 197
Thirst 196
35 Shots of Rum 83
36 Fillete 134
Tohill, Cathal 32
Tokyo Fist 93, 105
Tombs, Pete 32
Trier, Lars von 113, 115–127, 200–201
Trouble Every Day 83–91
Tsukamoto, Shinya 92–93, 104–110, 199
Turim, Maureen 182
Twilight 28
Two Orphan Vampires 196

Underworld 196
Ussher, Jane M. 203

Vampyres 27, 87
Videodrome 93, 95, 104
Vital 93, 105

White Material 83
The Wicker Man 200
Wolf 56–61
The Woman 189
Wood, Robin 141–142

Zentropa 201
Zodiac 72
Zombie Flesh Eaters 38